The Blunt End of the Grid

The Blunt End of the Grid

A memoir of motor racing

and other automotive escapades

Dave Roberts

The Book Guild Ltd

First published in Great Britain in 2019 by
The Book Guild Ltd
9 Priory Business Park
Wistow Road, Kibworth
Leicestershire, LE8 0RX
Freephone: 0800 999 2982
www.bookguild.co.uk
Email: info@bookguild.co.uk
Twitter: @bookguild

Typeset in Aldine401 BT

Printed and bound in Great Britain by CPI Group (UK) Ltd, Croydon, CR0 4YY

ISBN 978 1912575 640

British Library Cataloguing in Publication Data.
A catalogue record for this book is available from the British Library.

In memory of
Denise Hyde
and
Mel Thompson
Two unique and fearless characters
Gone far too soon
Their chuckling souls remain.

And to my wife Janet, without whom life over the last ten years would have been much more peaceful…
But not half as much fun.

Contents

1

Round and Round

120 mph round Thruxton. Thereabouts.
Getting it wrong.
Bouncing across the dewy grass.
That low splitter will get destroyed if you hit a divot.
Never mind the splitter, what about the car?
Where will it end up? In what state?
The driver? In what state…

Maybe my imagination is too good for a racing driver. Lying awake in the early hours. If? What? But…

Then I jump out of bed and open the van door. The thoughts disappear as I blink and look out at the campsite. It's an absolutely beautiful day. Bright blue sky and a sunny morning in the Conwy valley. Sun in Wales. You can't beat it.

I feel on top of the world as we drive home. The disappointing time round Anglesey on Sunday almost forgotten.

The pain almost buried.

When I had the engine rebuilt and collected the car, the lad who helped me load it said they had been to Anglesey and struggled. Then they changed some settings, and with nothing to lose changed to a set-up they had not tried before, and found a second a lap.

It clearly meant a lot to him and he probably wanted to chew the fat a bit longer, but I had to get back to do a couple of jobs on the car, and he was off to the rolling road with Tom, the engine builder, as soon as I left, so we just cracked on with our own preparations and preoccupations.

A second found.

I've just come back from Anglesey. I could've done with finding about seven seconds.

Just to beat my previous best in 2014.

When I had a lower-powered engine.

An old gearbox from the scrapyard.

A bit less care.

A bit less fear?

The worst thing is not knowing where it all went.

A bit on this corner.

A bit on the back straight which is really a curve.

Where you don't press the accelerator as hard as you should.

Flat out.

"Flat."

Is it flat?

The old adage.

The perennial topic.

Lovely trip back. Van doesn't miss a beat.

Mrs R collects the cats from the 'Cat Hotel.' They get better accommodation than us.

They cheer me up with their innocence and mad ways. If humans were like cats they would go out for a birthday gathering in the pub and one or two would crawl across the table and eat everybody else's food. Mrs R tries to discourage our two from bringing back birds, mice and the odd baby bunny to the back door. Mrs R is a formidable organising force but thousands of years of evolution are stronger. I wonder how sturdy the veneer of civilisation is in humans. Is it a rigid carbon-fibre shell born of accumulated knowledge and cleverness, or a piece of soggy plasterboard swept away on tides of war and intolerance?

I ring Thruxton. It's possible to go around there with an instructor for an hour or two. Mrs R thinks cycling round will be enough but she doesn't quite know the full reality, even though she endured a few passenger laps with me when I had the MR2.

Mr Ferrari thought his drivers lost a couple of seconds after they got married. Mrs R keeps telling me to be careful. You can't blame her.

I keep telling myself not to be too careful. To enjoy it, what's left. I will be a long time retired from it.

I watch a few videos on YouTube. The beauty of the modern world. You can watch others who have gone before you. I feel better for it.

The fear recedes…

The dread. The fear.

In fact I decide to stop writing in the style of *The Damned United*[1] and just go back to my usual verbal amble.

It's clear that I'm no tormented soul at the lonely pinnacle of professional sport. For me the word sport implies a pastime, a recreation. I've not even been diligent about my exercise walks this year. Yet. At all.

In fact the power from the new engine spec would allow for an extra pie before each outing. Otherwise I'd have to fit some ballast.

1 *The Damned United*. David Peace. 2006. Faber and Faber.
A novel said to be a fiction based on a fact, told from the imagined point of view of Brian Clough, the football manager, during his ill-fated tenure at Leeds United.

It's Wimbledon fortnight in the outside world. Mr Murray is knocked out, hobbled by his injury. Despite the thorough predictability of this, we are assumed to be amongst the legions of disappointed Brit followers. He drones on in the corner of the room. The televised press conference. I think it's actually national news, not just the Wimbledon coverage, as I look up from my book.

Sir Andy Murray. Provider of employment to countless physios, coaches and dieticians. Droning on. Provider of inspiration to all with his tireless work ethic. Hitting a ball to and fro. To and fro.

Nobody should be knighted until they are at least fifty. It's bread and circuses from cynical rulers. Or with the current government, more of a stale mouldy crust.

Nothing wrong with hitting a ball to and fro if that's what you like doing. Nothing wrong with going round in circles trying to go faster. If that's what you like.

I even meet people who clearly have less than even a passing interest in motor racing. And part of me thinks how strange that is. How strange not to be obsessed with it.

Before I got married, my prospective mother-in-law asked me what my motor racing activity consisted of. After I had explained what I could, inserting names of the more famous circuits such as Silverstone and Brands Hatch, she delivered the verdict.

"So you just go round and round."

"Yes. That's about it, Audrey. I just go round and round."

2

Not Moving On

I like a succinct summary, and Audrey's was impeccable both in its brevity and its precision. But I had spent many years waiting for the opportunity to go round and round, and it meant a lot to me.

There is an old black and white photo of me on an empty floor in my parents' brand new house in the Birmingham suburbs. No furniture at all. Just me and an extensive collection of Dinky toys, enjoying their motoring *tabula rasa*[2] as they were sent coasting across the endless linoleum landscape. Many years later, as we closed in on the turn of the century, my good friend Bob, no doubt thinking of the seven vehicles in various states of repair in my back garden, remarked that it was normal for small boys to have a collection of toy cars. And that in my case, I just hadn't moved on.

The small child in the picture is looking out into the black and white world of the mid 1950s, when marketing consisted of choosing a snazzy font for the manufacturer's name and most of today's supermarkets were fields. At the age of four, I was apparently able to name the maker of every car on the road. Not

2 Blank slate.

too remarkable a feat though, for they all had their corporate family resemblances, from Austins with their various sizes all looking like bulbous teapots, to the later Vauxhalls exhibiting their tragically mutated Detroit DNA, and every flavour of styling influence in between.

As I grew, I gained a smidgen more of automotive knowledge. On holiday trips I would half sit, half stand, behind my father's left shoulder in the family's Austin Cambridge. I would ask about each different car that approached, how many cylinders did it have? He would patiently divert the conversation towards more detailed explanations of the workings of the internal combustion engine. Although a keen and competent driver, he had no interest in the world of motorsport, as far as I knew. As an electronics engineer at Lucas, he worked at the centre of the British motor industry of the day, and would relate the occasional yarn, such as the tendency of Jaguar's test driver, probably the now legendary Norman Dewis, to calmly ask his passenger, "How are the brakes on your side?", as they pelted around the MIRA[3] banking at 120 mph. These were the days when the average family saloon was pushed to achieve 75 mph.

So I knew the theoretical principles of oversteer and understeer several years before I was old enough to drive. I remember the headlines about Hawthorn's fatal accident, and of course Stirling Moss was by then a household name. But none of these things exactly amounted to a childhood steeped in motorsport. I did however prevail upon my aunt, who lived in Leicester, to investigate the possibility of taking us to Mallory Park on one of our visits. My brother and I would sometimes be shipped down to stay with her during the holidays for a week or so, and on one such sojourn, in between us devouring every new Tintin book from the local library, she noticed a meeting

3 Motor Industry Research Association.

was taking place at Mallory, and took us along. It featured various sports cars of the day, and a single-seater field of more meagre numbers. I don't think the single-seaters were driven by anyone other than well-heeled amateurs, and I formed the impression, perhaps from the standard of presentation of the cars, that those at the front were the ones who had spent the most money. I overheard one driver in the paddock telling someone how he had outbraked someone, and how this was the most satisfying way of overtaking a competitor. I thought he sounded quite pompous.

One of the cars which the little boy in the photo was pushing across the floor was a Ferrari, of the type Ascari used to dominate the world championship in 1952 and 1953. For some reason it was painted navy blue with a yellow nosecone, rather than Italian red. I recalled it as I stood in Jeremy Phillips' small factory unit, Sylva Autokits, somewhere near Mablethorpe in deepest Lincolnshire.

It had been something over forty-five years since that photo had been taken, and my aunt, a spinster, had passed away a year or two earlier. Now I was about to sign a cheque for, and choose the colour of, a motorcar called a Sylva Striker.

I suppose it was the one and only time in my life that I would purchase a brand new car. The brand new bits, though, were a spaceframe chassis of box section steel, aluminium panelwork, moulded fibreglass bodywork sections, and various suspension parts, seats, and lighting. The rest you had to find; engine, gearbox, rear axle, wiring loom, radiator; plus a myriad of odds and ends that you had never thought about until you began to join up the various sub-systems of this automotive construction puzzle.

Not that I was complaining. The excitement was far too great. Spaceframe construction is the concept used by the racing cars of the early 1960s, with the strength and rigidity coming from clever triangulation. I liked the rocker arm suspension and inboard springs at the front, which harked back to the Lotus Grand Prix cars of the Jim Clark era.

I had seen a Sylva Striker once before, sometime I think in the late 1980s. It was parked at a scrapyard I was visiting, Winter's of Hessle. The driver had popped in for something, and I just had time to quickly admire the car and ask what it was, before he zoomed off. I suppose any carefully built sports car would look good compared to the machinery nearby, even if this was one of the more upmarket scrapyards of the era, with a concrete storage yard and cars stacked only two high.

The more common type of establishment at that time was exemplified by Jackson's of nearby Beverley, where one wandered through meandering aisles between haphazardly dumped wrecks, on and on as if through an overgrown and neglected mechanical garden, tendrils of broken bumpers and exhaust pipes protruding to threaten the unwary around every corner. Eventually the more intrepid explorers would penetrate far enough to encounter a solid wall of crushed cars, hundreds of yards across and extending upwards to about the height of a double-decker bus, more in places.

In the middle of this wall of unglued steel lay a gateway; the door, if you dared negotiate it, to a hidden realm. This entrance was formed by two scrap cars placed vertically, that is to say resting on their rear bumpers with what was left of the nose of the car uppermost. Picture them as two Saturn rockets, their tails the thrust nozzles, the driver looking straight up at the heavens, in case you are in any doubt as to the configuration.

Atop these two mighty pillars, completing the archway, sat a horizontal hulk, proudly perched. This itself was knitted into the towering structure by means of the gravity which pressed two more wrecks onto its ends. On from here, outwards, the structure extended, interlocking carcasses married in their afterlife, according to bricklaying principles. No vaunted temple or viaduct of ancient Greece or Rome, no imperious structure of Brunel or Telford, could match the vision of Jacko's wall of scrap, nor inspire such awe.

Through the thin arch, no wider than the width of a small car, parts hunters would briskly trot, hoping they had not forgotten any vital tools, the better to minimise the need of extra forays through this fearsome bulwark of jagged and uncemented steel. They would be rewarded with access to the treasures of another domain, where time moved more slowly amid the Austin Cambridges, Ford Populars and ancient mystic Rovers.

Jacko would inspect their booty at the exit, making it up as he went along.

"What you got, what you got? Eh? Ford, you say? Ford. Eh? Eh? Tenner. Eh? Tenner for that. Yeh. Yeh. Tenner OK? Eh?"

He was of a race apart, with his aquiline nose, and alert eyes always peering, peering. One of those men, probably in their late forties, who looks about fifty-five when you first meet them, and still looks exactly the same when you see them 15 years later. Legend had it that he had bought his house from an auction, paying in full with cash money that he tipped out of a plastic carrier bag from a supermarket. When regulations began to bite harder with the new century, it became essential to telephone before you visited, as he battened the hatches of his timeless kingdom, against the relentless minions of City Hall.

So. Yes. Ah, the Sylva Striker. It put me in mind of the Lotus/Caterham 7, very similar to the untrained eye, with its front cycle wings and minimalist two-seater shape. It managed to set itself apart though, with its more rounded tail and slightly more pointed snout. Its owner, before he set off, mentioned that he was going to drive down to Cadwell Park to see some kit car racing the following day. This intrigued me, so I went along on the Sunday, to witness an interesting meeting. I remember little detail other than that someone called Chris won one if not two kit car races in a Westfield. I motored back to Hull, where several years of trying to scratch a living at the bottom of the food chain awaited.

Eventually, with a file of about 500 rejection letters for graduate level positions, I gave up and trained to be a driving instructor. This gave me access to a normal world where people were ready and willing to pay for a simple straightforward service. No more bullshit and a relatively steady living.

It wasn't without its ups and downs, though. One day, after a lad I thought to be an excellent, safe driver had suffered a particularly unaccountable test failure at the hands of one of the 'difficult' examiners, I motored home on the backroads past an establishment I had noticed a few weeks earlier, which displayed a selection of prefabricated concrete garage designs. Ordering one in a size that maximised the use of my thin but fairly long back garden, I went home happier. I believe it's called 'shopping therapy'.

And, after going on holiday to Greece, buying a kit car magazine at the airport, planning on return to visit a kit car show at Doncaster, to compare the products of various manufacturers, calling there on my way from Manchester to Hull and finding the show cancelled... here I now stood at Sylva Autokits ready to part with money for the only kit car with which I had gained close acquaintance.

I was opting for a Striker on the grounds that if I went on track it might help to see where the front wheels were placed. I had test-driven Jeremy's attractive British Racing Green Phoenix, a car with full-width bodywork which shared the same underpinnings as the Striker, and had been suitably impressed. With the lightness and the sharpness of response, it was a type of vehicle unlike anything I had previously experienced.

Just before we finalised the order, Jeremy tried his Phoenix sales pitch.

"Just imagine that on your drive."

It was a good sales pitch. The Phoenix is a very pretty car.

Inwardly, I was thinking, I'd better not disillusion him.

Drive? What drive?

3

More Pleasure than Pain?

The meeting at Jeremy's works involved a bit of chit chat about my background. He seemed pleased to hear that I had messed about with old MGs, an activity which automatically imbues a degree of doggedness in dealing with mechanical matters, and, perhaps by osmosis, even a small degree of aptitude. I think he wanted to make sure that the customer would not return, ranting, if the jigsaw puzzle of parts proved too awkward for said customer's level of skill and determination.

I was about to enter a world where the range of possible outcomes could vary from 'unfinished project' to immaculately assembled and meticulously engineered work of mechanical art. Builders also seemed to range from those who enjoyed the process so much that they would quickly sell a completed kit car in order to finance a new project, to those who built the vehicle motivated mainly by the desire to enjoy driving it. I belonged to the latter end of this spectrum, I confess.

There was little point in owning a bare bones lightweight sports car, I reasoned, if it was not to be exploited in some sort of competitive environment. And I would later discover, given that Jeremy's designs of the time didn't give a lot of priority to weather protection, that going to work in one's kit car usually involved a pleasant day or two enjoying the wind in the hair feeling, followed by getting caught in a substantial shower on the next commute home, followed by a month or two using the everyday tin top. Or getting togged up like a motorcyclist before setting out, which I rarely had time for on working days.

It would be some time before reaching that stage of kit car ownership, though. A confident plan of being out on track in about six months was eventually adjusted to a somewhat disconsolate and disgruntled eighteen months. The early euphoria at having a rolling chassis in the garage, to the extent of being able to sit in it making engine noises (should I wish) and fantasising about pelting up Charlies Bend at Cadwell Park, gradually subsided under the weight of parts catalogues from the likes of Rally Design, Burton Power and Demon Tweeks. My Yorkshire conditioning had me agonising as I realised that yet another specialised mechanical trinket would be needed from, say, Rally Design in Kent. But I had just had some stuff from them a week earlier. Two lots of postage!!

Why couldn't my planning be more meticulous? Because I was learning as I went along, of course. And if the process of learning is enjoyed, that's hardly a problem. Most of the frustration could be traced to those two pillars of industry, Time and Money. Given that the project was a 'hobby', my grumbles were self-imposed. And from the perspective of the distant future in which I now find myself, the hiccups and glitches of this first project were an inevitable teething at the start of a long road of enjoyment in motorsport, an arena which many are never in a position to experience.

But in life, memories of the sticky bits lodge more firmly in the psyche, while the smooth passages become blurred. The 20% of the build which takes up 80% of the time. The learning by mistakes which you should never have made in the first place. The gnashing of teeth on the way to eventual success in building my own car, legal and driveable. All of it taught me a vital lesson, to be applied to any undertaking at the outset.

Will this project bring more pleasure than pain?

It has served me well since, at many of life's crossroads.

One might think, crikey, if that's what building a kit car is like, why do people even bother? The biggest hurdle is the realisation that it's nothing like repairing a production car. Every piece of a production car has a part number, and is, theoretically anyway, obtainable in a fairly straightforward manner, if you can afford it.

Most kit cars are nothing like that. The industry has changed over the years I have seen it, and in recent times component cars seem to feature more bespoke parts, whereas when I started with the Striker, there was more usage of production car parts, from things like Fords and Vauxhalls. The newer, fairly predictable, favourite is the Mazda MX5, with its rear-wheel drive underpinnings finding their way into a number of recent designs.

People used to ask, when seeing the car or hearing of its build, "What's it based on?". However, the types of kit more common in the 1970s or 1980s, which gave Joe DIY Public the chance to resurrect his rust-riddled Escort or Cortina with a chassis and body panels, plus maybe the odd flat window, were long gone by the dawn of the twenty-first century.

Nevertheless, I bought and dismembered a Ford Escort and a 2.8-litre V6 Ford Capri, to provide some of the bits for the Striker. Such actions, not very many years later, would be viewed with horror by many, so inflated have the prices for 'classic' cars become. I plead, Your Honour, that each vehicle cost me a mere fifty quid. I further plead in mitigation that the Escort was a 4-door, not a 2-door bodyshell Holy Grail jewel-encrusted model with the rarity value of a Fabergé egg.

The kit required the rear axle and the front stub axles from the Escort, which I took to Jeremy's for modification. Handy to live reasonably near your manufacturer when it comes to that sort of errand. Quite why I bought the Capri, I don't now recall. Perhaps it was because it was only fifty quid and I fancied the pepperpot alloys. Almost as an afterthought, as we unloaded the Escort running gear, I wondered aloud, "Would the V6 go into the Striker?"

"It would be cheap power," said Jeremy, seeing fit to humour my madness. In fairness to him, he did then try to gently implant the notion of a 2-litre Ford Pinto engine as a choice, but my blinkers had become firmly locked on in the short seconds between his two statements.

I failed to consider a couple of pertinent issues. The first was that the Ford V6 of the Capri era, though powerful for its day, was the weight of a sizeable asteroid.

The second was that 'its day' was by now some twenty years earlier. The owner of a taxi company I worked for back then had, creatively, replaced some Saabs he leased, with older Ford Granadas, cheaply bought, before selling the concern on. Thus I got to enjoy some overpowered gas-guzzling machinery without worry of ownership or fuel bills, on almost a daily basis, before the inevitable descent into unbalanced bookery began to cook the new owner's less than golden goose.

So I knew the potency of the Ford V6; even in a heavy saloon the rear end would break traction relatively easily, particularly in the wet. The Granada handled well though, a trait for which I was grateful one wet evening when negotiating a 90-degree turn on a small deserted housing estate, in rather too much of a rush, and getting caught by some leaves in the corner. The subsequent recovery included use of someone's small grass lawn, but fortunately there was no appreciable kerb and nobody was at home.

The most memorable incident involved the negotiation of a humpbacked railway bridge, again on a quiet weekday evening. The bridge had a very long, straight run-up, with small pavements and brick walls either side. The far side mirrored the layout, with another very long, straight run downwards. So there was no reason for anyone to have stopped there, but nevertheless I was reckless. *You should always drive at a speed such that you are able to stop within the distance you can see to be clear.*

It is also a fact that brakes are of no help once you have left the ground.

As the car took off at the crest, I had time for three thoughts.

1. I don't really need to be in such a rush, that fare at the hotel can wait a few minutes longer.
2. Keep the wheels straight on landing.
3. Glad this isn't my car.

When it landed, after what felt like a hundred feet further but was in truth probably more like thirty, there was such a thump that thought '3' immediately reiterated itself, after which I motored on in a somewhat more sedate manner.

Perhaps I was lucky. The chap responsible for routine checks on the cars was, in his day job, a vehicle examiner at the local HGV test station, universally loathed and feared, known as Vindictive Jack. His habitual grimace was less evident when collecting his retainer from the taxi company, though. It became evident that he was perhaps more interested in the monetary reward than in the diligence required to justify it, when the propshaft of one of the Granadas parted company with one of its anchorages.

The driver radioed in.

"You know that propshaft that's been knocking on the red car?"

"Yes, what's up?"

"I've just pole-vaulted into the Ravenoak car park."

There would be another 'pertinent issue' to consider later, regarding the potency or otherwise, of the Ford V6. Namely that

I had absolutely no idea about the condition of the particular engine in the Capri which now sat in the garage.

Ignoring this small detail, I hoicked the motor and gearbox out and made another trip to Sylva to collect the adapted Escort parts and leave Jeremy to make up some suitable engine mounts for the V6 installation, using the engine itself to get the measurements right. At a much later date, another trip to Lincolnshire was made, with the more complete car on the trailer, to leave it with Mike, an exhaust fabricator Jeremy recommended. His works was in a former aircraft hangar in the depths of the county, which he reckoned had been used as a secret storage facility during the Cold War. I wouldn't be able to find it again now, so perhaps the Russians wouldn't have been able to either.

I took Denise, my partner, along for the ride out. Stopping at a pay phone on the outskirts of Market Rasen to ask for final directions (very le Carré), I popped in to a nearby garage to purchase a snack, and spied some Maltesers, something I'd not sampled for many years. So ultimately the trip resulted in the acquisition of a tidy exhaust system, bespoke to the car, and a semi-addiction to Maltesers which lasted for several years afterwards.

Another unique and potty idea was to fit the Capri instrument binnacle to the Striker. It did go in, without any pretensions to being svelte. I spent a pleasant day or two sitting on the concrete outside the garage paring down the Capri wiring loom which I had laid out on the floor. My neighbour, chatting over the fence, praised my ingenuity. I saw it more as the exercise of patience. Zen with wire-snips.

I was not always known for patience. Around that time I was 'transitioning' (good twenty-first century word) in the sense of moving away from repairing assorted weather-beaten vehicles in the backyard, to becoming more of a mainstream respectable citizen, courtesy of my driving instructor qualification.

Working on cheap older vehicles without ramps and lifts can be more of a trial than being a professional mechanic with the use of proper facilities, though I'm not saying the design of modern vehicles makes their task a straightforward one. I developed well-honed neck muscles, crawling under various projects and acquaintances' vehicles with the gas torch, imbuing tired mechanical servants with one more year of life. Like some grimy Hephaestus[4] who used oily puddles infused with brake fluid, instead of hair conditioner, I would emerge, grunting, grumbling or roaring.

One friend amusedly reported to another, that I was unusual, in that I would get out from under the car, calmly turn off the gas torch and position it safely, pick up a hammer, and beat the living daylights out of a wall, door, or other stout inanimate object, to vent whatever frustration had built up in the rusty underworld. On one occasion I had been under my friend's van for quite some time, dealing with some particularly recalcitrant problem. No doubt the only visible part of me was my feet. A couple of days later one of the neighbourhood kids was passing by as I walked to my front door, and quizzed me.

"Dave? Was that you under that van the other day, going 'Bastard, bastard, bastard'?"

So the world of kit cars was attractive, with their aluminium and their rivets, by comparison. Most of the tribulations were cerebral as opposed to a test of neck strength. After some ups and downs, I reached the point where I took the car for SVA, Single Vehicle Approval, as it then was. At the time of writing, the SVA test has been supplanted by the IVA test. Individual Vehicle Approval. The difference between Single and Individual is about £300, something of a bureaucratic triumph, with the ante being upped from the SVA's £200, to £500 for IVA, approximately. And a tad more fear, though the test is broadly

4 Greek god of fire and metalworking.

similar. We are lucky in the UK though, to have any kind of system for this compared to some countries where self-built cars have no chance of a legitimate existence.

I drove the car to the test station, as one was entitled to do. Most sensible people use a trailer but I like living on the edge a bit. It involved more than one trip, though I remember few details now. You didn't have to pay the full fee again each time, the principle being that you take up less and less of the inspector's time on each re-test after rectifications. Hopefully.

The brake balance was one issue, as you have to lock 'permanently' any driver adjustable arrangement, which rather negates the design of some of the typical balance bars used on these types of car. At least the balance is properly tested though, which is a good thing. The inspectors are basically helpful, and despite the odd pernickety area such as dashboard 'furniture', the test is there to ensure you achieve a safe result, ultimately. So it should be seen in a positive light.

You will read of meticulous builders' cars passing first time. Some people are just too damn clever, aren't they? It's a bit like history being written by the winners. Not so many people admit their more embarrassing errors in magazine articles, so one is left with the impression that it's all plain sailing.

I wasn't too bothered about being more towards the Richard III end of the historical spectrum, as long as my worst sins were hammered indentations on the garage stool rather than imprisoned nephews. As long as it passed in the end. In due course, I received my registration document and tax disc via the local vehicle licensing office. This human element in the chain has since been deleted, sadly, and the route now would be via written or perhaps email communication with the DVLA Swansea monolith. Woe betide you if you should want to find a human at the end of a phone line. Woe betide you, and may you be armed with the forbearance of a Zen master, should you wish to try.

But this is now, and that was then, and I was finally on the road, feeling like Toad of Toad Hall in my roaring and turbulent creation.

4

Sheds of Treasure

I was driving home one night at 2 a.m. after a taxi driving shift. This was a period before I got around to paying three years-worth of tax. The taxman conducting my eventual interview said that I 'wasn't a very upstanding citizen.' They used a 'nice guy nasty guy' interview technique, with two of them on the other side of the desk. The comment on my moral worth came from the nasty guy in my second interview, who was nastier than the nasty guy in the first interview. In the end he just made up some figures, ignoring the ones in my notebook, and said, "This is what you're paying." As the figure was less than what I had calculated I should have paid, I settled for being an untrustworthy character and didn't argue.

So, with a bank balance somewhat over inflated with public money, I noticed an MGB in a car showroom as I sat at the red lights, and thought *I could afford a car like that*. I didn't need a car like that, I had a perfectly reasonable 1100cc Ford Escort van that got me to and fro to work, even if it had its quirks. I used to follow our telephonist on the way home as far as my turn-off, to make sure her Hillman Imp got that far safely, until one night she thought I had broken down as there was another vehicle following her. All that had happened was that I had got around to adjusting the headlights, so that they both pointed ahead, rather than one up and one down. You were lucky on those Fords to have enough metal on the grille panel for the headlights to stay in, let alone point forward. Nowadays of course any form of surviving Mk I Escort is worth crazy money.

I began a search for a suitable MGB. I don't remember actually going to see any other than the one that cropped up near home, which seemed to run all right. It was a GT, which was a cheaper and more practical option than the roadster, and I think we agreed on something like £925. Given that my van had set me back about £350, this was at the time an absolute fortune to me. My father was quite amused when he saw it in the garage, calling it a 'hot rod.'

I wouldn't quite describe it as that, but it was a curious machine, with potential as what would nowadays be called a 'learning resource.' I became quite adept at tuning and balancing SU carburettors, for instance, with a tube inserted into the carb mouth at one end and into my ear at the other.

MGBs at the time occupied an almost unique netherworld squeezed between 'incipient classic' and 'car that's only recently gone out of production'. The newer rubber-bumpered ones were despised, the older ones were eyelash-fluttering Jezebels leading the unwary into a dank domain of endless subterranean decay. Sorry, rust.

Mine was a chrome-bumpered one with little oblong British Leyland badges on the side of the front wings, and the slightly unusual recessed front grille. With its wire wheels, you could pretend you were an affluent motorist from the 1950s, in your *Gran Turismo* with its rorty exhaust note. MGB engines did rorty exhaust notes quite well actually, quite an achievement for an iron lump with a log-shaped inlet manifold, from a line of square and uninspiring saloons. Nevertheless, the tiny Leyland badges were a constant reminder of the car's origin in a chaotic industrial empire teetering on the edge of oblivion, every time you stepped into it.

Apart from feeling that you were almost lying down in the cockpit compared to more mainstream vehicles, the driving experience had a raw, almost vintage feel to it, as though a layer of cosseting blubber had been left out of the mechanical equation. The wire wheels weren't therefore needed in order to give the driver the feeling that he was stepping back two decades; the car itself did that.

In fact the car would have been much better off with steel wheels, as the wires were far more trouble than they were worth. Held on by a central spinner tackled with a purpose-designed spanner and a mallet, they went on a splined hub with a chamfered shoulder. This was fine until wear took place, then eventually the spinner ran out of thread to push the wheel fully on to the chamfered shoulder, so the wheel would move and wobble a little bit.

On my car, wear had taken place.

Looking at the positive side, it gave me the pleasure of commencing a search for affordable and serviceable second-hand wire wheels. In pre eBay days, this often involved the pages of *Exchange and Mart*, a fascinating publication catering for every conceivable category of leisure pastime and collecting fetish, from unusual rubberwear to narwhal tusks. Affordable and serviceable second-hand wire wheels were a little easier to pin down than narwhal tusks, but not by much.

However, I did find an MG breaker in the Chichester area, and combined a visit there with a trip to see some friends who lived in Devon. Thus the MG ownership introduced me to the world of corrugated sheds and Nissen huts hiding at the end of a hard to find rutted track that led to the back of a farm in the middle of nowhere. Paradise.

I didn't get to explore the treasures within on this occasion, as the proprietor had a couple of wheels outside ready for me.

Spoils loaded, I departed for the New Forest to camp overnight. B & Bs just weren't on my lexicon of expenditure back then. The night must have been fine, because I have no memory of it whatsoever. The following morning certainly wasn't, with the heavens opening in a mighty deluge as I drove out of the forest. Soon, I could hardly see ahead more than a few yards.

Then, I had a brainwave. This car was a league above anything I had owned before. In keeping with its appeal as a premium luxury sporting and leisure vehicle, the manufacturers had fitted it with a *fast wiper speed option*. Excitedly, I flicked the dashboard switch one click more than I had ever had the opportunity to do before. The wipers went into overdrive. Flick-flack flick-flack flick-flack. (Read this quickly.)

Flick-flack flick-flack flick-flack FLICK... The driver's wiper had disappeared, though the arm remained. Turning them off to save the screen being scratched, my view was worse than before, if that was possible.

I managed to pull over on the verge safely, and got out and ran back. Several cars had passed by the time I found the wiper blade, mangled by the traffic. Back at the car, drenched, I took the passenger wiper blade off and fitted it to the driver's side arm. Putting the passenger side arm forward into the position used when washing the car, I thus prevented the screen being scratched and carried on.

I reached a roundabout where the route out of the forest joined the main road west. It was still raining and the remaining wiper blade was still working in front of me. I don't recall whether it was going flick-flack flick-flack flick-flack, or flick-flack flick-flack flick-flack quickly. But I do recall it going FLICK and disappearing as I negotiated the roundabout.

Leaving the roundabout and pulling up safely, I ran back. Despite the presence of more traffic here, the wiper arm had survived. At that time I used to smoke, and a piece of cardboard torn off a Benson and Hedges packet, and rolled into a wedge-like packing over the wiper arm, was employed to achieve a firmer fit for the blade. This repair proved effective, and lasted for several months until I remembered to fit a new blade. The job included a modification to the arm, of a small drilled hole and some wire. Take that, Leyland.

It was not the last modification I made to this upmarket sports car, the most expensive vehicle I had yet owned. I used to occasionally go to a small cinema in the Moss Side district of Manchester, the 'Aaben', which showed some of the more offbeat movies of the day, that hadn't made the mainstream circuit. On one such visit, I was approached by a small child who asked if I wanted my car 'looking after'. I said no on this particular occasion, which was rash, as I was aware of the local refrain of 'Look after your car, mister?' from visits to the old Manchester City ground in the same area.

It's extortion really, though the children of Moss Side probably didn't think of it quite like that. Many years later, Denise and I were listening to a radio programme which explored the songs of some lesser known blues artists from the very early days of recording such material. One of the songs featured the immortal line…

'When I get out of this prison cell, ain't gonna extort no more…'

Now I'm pretty sure that guy hadn't described his activities in such precise legal terminology before coming to trial. And they say doing time doesn't rehabilitate!

Failing to interpret the words of the Moss Side toddler as a clear threat rather than the polite rhetorical pleasantry one might prefer, I discovered on leaving the cinema that said toddler was not too small to heave a brick through the back window. This was disappointing, as ownership of this luxury GT car brought with it ownership of a heated rear screen, something new in my experience. It had not been long before this that ownership of a heated rear window, for many people, entailed the purchase of an aftermarket device rolled up in a cardboard box, which could be found many years later still rolled up in its faded cardboard box, with its unstickable plastic surface and dangling wires which connected to… er, what? Oh yes, you had to wire that bit in yourself.

I replaced the shattered screen with a second-hand non-heated one, since the new replacement cost over £100. The final fitting is finished with a sort of semi-pliable chromed strip which fits in a recess in the screen rubber, and which never comes out without being bent out of shape beyond recall. It doesn't look much, in terms of material used, and comes in two halves, left and right sides, in a sort of E shape without the middle bar.

The British Leyland dealer's parts man went to find out a price; I think they were on microfiche then, in pre-PC days. The parts guys were perennially morose, probably due to all the inefficiencies and complaints that they had to put up with. And I had landed the most morose of the crew. When he came back to the counter, he told me that each half strip was well over ten quid (quite a lot of money then) and that I could have the left one. The right ones weren't available.

He looked at me. I looked at him.

Then we both laughed. I had never seen him laugh before, but sometimes the absurdities of life have to be faced full on. It was clear that British Leyland couldn't even extort properly.

The screen and chrome strip things were obtained from Barry Stafford's second-hand grotto, which was in part of an old hangar at the nearby aerodrome. He was an MG parts specialist trading initially from home, though he later opened a proper shop in Cheadle which is now part of the Moss empire.

So it was another trip down an unfrequented lane to a hidden treasure trove of dismantled gems. I was beginning to like this routine. Nowadays you can explore using the comfort of eBay, using one of my favourite searches, 'Barn Finds'. While away a few hours looking at projects which you wouldn't have enough hours left in your life to even start, let alone complete. Back then a bit of detective work and subtle pleading was required, before being led or directed to the location of the booty. Nowadays all the finds will have been found, and people are probably busy building new barns in which to 'find' all the rusting and partially stripped hulks which have somehow clung to continued existence. Somebody recently paid sizeable coin for half a burnt-out Lamborghini at a French auction. Yes, I did say half. Such is the price of nostalgia.

The loss of the heated rear screen facility wasn't too much of a hardship. I slipped back in time and used the side mirrors instead. If they weren't frozen.

I also manufactured a rear window demister. This consisted of a short, reasonably stout, branch from a tree, suitably trimmed, to which was attached a sponge by means of a Jubilee Clip and some bent coat hanger wire. Within the constraint of having to operate it whilst paused at red traffic lights, it worked well.

When the world outside wasn't frozen.

Work began on a Mark 2 version, using a scraper instead of a sponge.

It was in the MG that I first journeyed to Hull, for an interview at the university. I had scraped a couple of A level results from my squandered education at Manchester Grammar School, which was enough to gain me an interview for possible admission as a mature student, to study psychology. I had also secured an interview at York, which, during vacations, resembled the Mary Celeste on my visit. It had also been founded by Lord James of Rusholme, a big name in the history of the reviled MGS, which was an illogical component influencing my eventual decision.

That and the liveliness of a student union debate at Hull, which I attended whilst awaiting my interview appointment.

They were discussing the possibility of a sit-in as a response to some grievance or other. This was more like it.

Professor Clarke was very friendly, and understood my motivation of not wanting to be a taxi driver any more.

"You know which side your bread's buttered now." Quite.

There followed three very pleasant years, enjoying the luxury of study. Being that bit older, my grant was quite reasonable, and I extended my sojourn in the ivory towers with an extra year taking a diploma in occupational psychology. I supplemented the grant by breathing life into the odd motor car acquisition, by means of welding torch and a lexicon of suitable expletives. Life was good.

Hull was something of a backwater back then, dare I say. We were in the early 1980s. The fishing industry had died with the Cod War, and Thatcher's policy of structural unemployment was beginning to ramp up the misery for people north of Watford who weren't adept at spouting codswallop over a telephone.

Some didn't help themselves, such as the proprietor of a carburettor specialist I found locally. The attitude seemed to be, 'The answer's no, now what's the question?' Oh. Not steeped in enthusiasm for your product, then. I began to feel that to get out of Hull, the cul-de-sac at the end of a long railway siding on the board game of life, you had to throw a double six.

I never did. But at the time of writing, we're the City of Culture and have evolved as part of the modern world. Back then a fairly common method of local conveyance for a self-employed tradesman might be a three-wheeled Reliant pulling a small trailer. I once saw a man carrying out the removal of a three-piece furniture suite. His vehicle? A bicycle with a trailer on a hinge behind it. The three bulky items were variously lashed, defying the nebulous gravity of this alternative universe as he doggedly pushed it along the road.

I have now embraced the use of the word 'we' in relation to

fellow citizens, after the metamorphosis of half a lifetime. It was not always so, and my cultural progress seemed to follow the bell-shaped graph so beloved of psychologists when they talk of the 'natural distribution' of qualities in the human population. From a taxi driver, to a graduate earning a high-grade degree, to… a taxi driver.

Working the evening shift, near the centre of town, it became a pleasant surprise when the clientele included those able to articulate more than a grunted approximation of their destination, followed by "Drive", your job title.

"Tek me 'ome, draahve." Followed by disgruntlement after their drunken jokes provoked no mirth.

I exaggerate of course. A bit. One night, driving to a pick up, one of the young guys at the taxi office came up behind me. I pressed on, he pressed on. I realised that we were really racing now, and whilst it didn't last long, I considered it to be an excitement I didn't need. You can't go racing on the public highway. The maximum penalty is actually a life ban, and rightly so.

With that, I stopped and entered the doldrums voluntarily, until driving instruction, as I have said, provided a path to solvency and respectability. Poacher turned gamekeeper.

It was through work that I later met Phil, a chap who, by remarkable coincidence, was putting together a Sylva Phoenix, and had previously built one of Jeremy's Strikers. Clearly, these very facts meant we had common interests, and a friendship developed.

The mists of time, in their soothing narcotic way, have now obscured for me any memory of who finished their build first. But I know Phil's car was on the road by 2002, for that was the year he introduced me to the Guild of Motor Endurance.

5

Targa-Liege 2002

Phil and Dave's Excellent but Wet Adventure

As I stood near the Sylva Phoenix in the Toys R Us car park at York, a child got out of a car nearby, and looked quizzically at the classic lines of the heroic little sports car which had just raced all the way back from Italy, and mused to his parent:

"That car has got no roof and the people inside will get very wet."

Well, Phil, you have got to say, if a six-year-old kid can work that one out…

As luck would have it there weren't any six-year-old kids around at Jeremy Phillips' premises to point out this obvious shortcoming, when Phil handed over his cheque a year or two earlier. Thus the 19th September saw us driving north from East Yorkshire over the wolds and moors towards Newcastle, heading for the ferry, this being a cheaper option than going from Hull, just down the road. Also by leaving a little bit later than you should, you 'have to press on a bit' which adds to the entertainment.

I felt more relaxed when we were on board the boat. Phil had had to replace a rear-axle oil seal a couple of days before we set out, and there was always the nagging worry that the one on the other side could have later shown the same weakness, even though all the parts were new.

So we were over the first hurdle, and settled down for a relaxing overnight crossing, with much talk of "no time pressure tomorrow." So relaxed were we, and so entertaining were the Salsa dancing girls, that many pints were consumed. We had been warned in the event literature of occasional, 'crew failure'; my impersonation of a zombie the following day must have been an example of this. So much for having a bit of a drive in the car to get used to it; obviously the years of training I had put in were at too low a level of alcohol consumption.

Nevertheless, Phil had a steady drive to Spa and we were there for early afternoon. Amongst the various crews who had already arrived were Mark Fisher and some pals in two Fisher Fury sports cars. The Fury was originally a Sylva design, the rights to which Mark had purchased from Jeremy. I had a chat with Mark, a nice chap who had helped me with a couple of parts for a mostly-built Fury I had purchased the year before. Yes, that is correct, I did say I had bought another kit car, despite my Striker still awaiting completion. Which is a tale for later…

Among the more noticeable entries was the 'Dragoon' from Scotland, a vintage-looking special based on an AC (no, not a Cobra) 1930's or 1940's chassis and powered by a Rover V8. Matt black brushwork seemed a main feature of its ambiance. The co-driver was apparently a genuine lord and when the driver remarked that they might put the roof down and don a pith helmet, I was not too surprised to notice that on the single fine (ish) day, a pith helmet was indeed lying on the back seat at the rest stop. One would expect no less. It all put us in mind of Peter Cook and Dudley Moore in *Monte Carlo or Bust*, but the vehicle certainly motored on well for its size.

By five o'clock kit cars of many varieties were filling the

hotel parking areas, and people began to set off to the town square for scrutineering. Phil was a bit apprehensive but I had no such worries. His Phoenix was a beautifully assembled British Racing Green model, with the early low bonnet line hiding a carefully built 1600cc Ford Crossflow. The neat and simple interior also drew praise from one official insofar as it was the first cockpit he had seen that didn't look as if a bomb had gone off in it. Having stuck the rally plates on, and enjoyed a meal in the local restaurant, it was time to retire to the hotel and explore the equation: 1 Barman + nearly 100 Rallyists = Disgruntlement. But never mind. Then came the briefing, which told us of some testing roads and not to upset the locals by charging through towns (sensible) because after all your average is based on only 30 mph (which drew much laughter). Thanks were expressed to the burgomaster and the chief of police to let the event take place. It sounded a bit like the cast of a Frankenstein movie, and I was half expecting to see Lionel Atwill flag us off with his steel arm in the morning.

We began from the square, car 32, which meant we set off thirty-two (or is it thirty-one) minutes after car 1. As far as I could tell some previous winners of the event were in our small class (sports cars under 1600cc), but our team ambition was to finish the event as a priority, something which I had to remind Phil of if I thought he was getting a bit hectic. I did have to give this duty serious thought at times, as the competitive spirit bit later on.

We had one serious worry, the left rear tyre catching on the fibreglass occasionally. Trimming a bit of the inner lip had not been fully effective and at the lunch stop we raised the ride height on the left rear spring as the winning cure, having debated removing a spacer (thus rubbing the trailing arm instead), swapping wheels, etc. This had mostly the desired effect and scuffing was thereafter reduced to the odd moment on adverse bumps and oscillations. Moral of this tale is to try the car under

2-up loaded conditions before setting off, something which time hadn't really permitted.

The first day set the tone for our lunch stop strategy, which was to be 'lunch, what is lunch'. As far as the driving went we fell into a routine of me starting, steady 80% drive respecting Phil's car to mid-morning, then Phil taking over making up time 90% drive (he said) during the latter stint. As there was no penalty for arriving early at the lunch and evening controls, it worked well to have the quick driver doing this last dash. When Phil got in the mood, I don't recall anything at all passing us on the mixed and twisty sections. On the run down to Cortina later on we passed a lot of rally entrants, and then followed a white van for the last five kilometres into the town. (We knew when we were beaten.)

But that was to come. This, the first day, was the proverbial learning curve. We seemed to be reasonably on schedule as Phil tackled the first navigational stint, and I got used to driving the Phoenix. Halfway through the morning we arrived at the first mystery special test which turned out to be three laps round a track in a go-cart. Whether all go-karts are evil handling sows I don't know but after mine stalled under braking I wasn't overly impressed. I was then given what seemed like several free laps to compensate although with half the rally field waiting for their go I didn't really feel too comfortable. Never mind, we hung up our helmets to find over half the cars away, and now we were running late. Phil did a great job of making up time, but we then arrived early at one control, my watch having I think decided to gain time, thus departing from its normal slow habit for the first time ever. I could see Phil's face as he saw the chance of the Gold Award slide away, being slightly at variance with the 'let's just aim to finish' attitude we'd arrived at Spa with.

We pressed on to the next highlight, a lap of the Nurburgring. Quite an experience, a never ending variety of bends and a fair complement of nutters out and about on Europe's fastest one-way toll road. While waiting for a chance to pass the ex-Monte Carlo Rally Reliant Kitten (yes, really) who was one of the Targa-Liège bunch, we were overtaken through some esses by a hot hatch road-going Alfa who was very much on the ragged edge. Phil settled for a few gently squealy bits and eventually back we came, onto the public highway. Some fast roads through the Black Forest area ensued, with the overtaking of a recalcitrant Mercedes saloon driver who did not slow down for us to get in before the bend, being somewhat memorable. There was that loud squealing sound again, whether it was caused by the bend or the subsequent correction, being the subject of a bit of debate later. One can only surmise on the thoughts of the fat warm German in the fat warm Mercedes as he watched the drama he had provoked. But for us it was flying helmets and goggles, British Racing Green, Spitfires at dawn, and who needs the Nurburgring, as on we pressed in this non-competitive event.

The evening saw us at the Hilton on the outskirts of, I think, Karlsruhe. It began with K and was another blurred reference in the alternative universe I was now beginning to inhabit. My notes said that we had a long discussion about psychology but of course I couldn't remember a word of it afterwards. Our main memory was of Dudley the Dragoon pilot proclaiming that a good sarn't major would sort the wine waiters out.

In the car park in the morning, car 30 had appeared for the first time, having missed the start. This Fisher Fury crew who we came to refer to as 'Spike and his mate' were good company during the rest of the event as exploits were necessarily discussed, and Sylva/Fisher building and modifying experiences compared. Spike appeared to have sanctioned the modification of his girlfriend's Fury, which they were using, by his co-driver with a jigsaw just prior to the event. We thought we had problems with wheels catching!

One of the Marlins had experienced a meltdown of his expensive loom, and was sadly out, whilst we hadn't seen the wooden car since the start. I did say it was an alternate universe. So attrition was beginning to bite.

So was the weather. Into Austria was the leg where we began to wonder whether the term endurance applied more to the crews than to the cars. Fog, rain, and gloomy snow over one pass had become the order of the day. Great roads but the co-driver couldn't enjoy much of a view, and this state of affairs in varying degrees was to prevail until Cortina d'Ampezzo, when finally… it got worse.

We reached lower lands in Austria. Getting stuck behind some cows being herded was an opportunity for Phil to take a 'local character' snap with his camera, nearly forgetting that Spike's girlfriend's yellow Fury was also queueing in front of us. Luckily, further modification of its rear was averted in the nick of time. The cows were a harbinger of further things – at the next large town several cars were stuck behind a whole herd going slowly through the streets. Ringing bells and with two-foot Christmas trees stuck to their heads, they were part of a celebration, of cows being herded into the lowland barns for the winter. By the time all this was over we were running late, and Phil was watching his Silver Award drift away with the cowbells. It was interesting to see at the end of the event that the first three cars were all low numbered starters who must have got through this picturesque town before the picturesque cows arrived. Not that we were bitter being non-competitive…

We reached the lunch stop late, a quick coffee and a roll scrounged from breakfast stuffed in my mouth as I slotted the Phoenix in gear and off we went again. By now I'm talking about the second day in Austria, wet, bedraggled, and looking forward to the evening hotel, wherever it might be. We were turned back from the climb to the Grossglockner Glacier as conditions were too bad up there… we then had to find our own way to another landmark in the road book. Swapping drivers, a long haul over and down into Italy followed. Like the previous evening following a Mercedes through the fog, we were grateful to white-van man leading us the last few kilometres to the hotel. Phil's pace on both evenings had probably more to do with wanting to dry out as soon as possible, than any time targets set by the organizers.

We later heard that on the leg to Cortina, John Regan, one of the Fisher Fury runners, had had the most lucky escape. Missing the road after a hairpin, they had launched into a dark abyss. Landing in a field, they barely had time to feel relief before realizing that the field was very, very steep and they were spinning as they descended. Finally a degree of control was regained, they spotted a gap… and popped out onto the lower bend of the road in front of Mark Fisher's car, who had been running near them when they left the road! Apparently a local driver had been seen stopped at the top, hazards on, peering into the blackness wondering what had become of these crazy Englishmen who had just whizzed past them.

We arrived at Cortina to be met by marshals with a glass of bubbly. So cold and wet were we that it tasted like the kick of a brandy. We took an inventory of our bedraggled luggage and went for a welcome meal. The following morning it wasn't so much raining as continuous wetness with a little bit of air in it. We reluctantly took off the tonneau[5] and tried to get moving to avoid as much of the soaking as we could. We finally found the stadium where a special test was due to take place. Indeed it did, cars circling pointlessly round cones while we waited for our turn in the pouring rain in an open car without an umbrella. We were told to go out on the north road, and then make straight for Brescia on to the motorway route south.

5 Cover for an open sports car cockpit, generally made from waterproof fabric.

Finally we followed one of the Caterhams up the hill after time had dragged by. By now there was heavy snow and some cars had already returned to the stadium, saying they couldn't see enough. When the Caterham spun at about 10 mph, Phil decided that the continuing beauty of the Phoenix was more important than bravery and I did a sort of nine-point turn on the snowy main road with much nagging amid visions of snow-chained lorries appearing round the bend.

We regained the environs of Cortina and decided to have a go at the south road. The snow was just as bad on this route and we descended a hill thinking that we would not have got up it again had we now decided to go back to Cortina. Stranded lorries abounded, some getting snow chains out. Fortunately there wasn't an equivalent rise at the end of the descent, and I gingerly drove on. The guy at the next filling station told us conditions were easier in another twenty kilometres and indeed soon afterwards, the snow began to turn to slush and we were over the worst. A morning of mere rain ensued, and about 100 miles later (it seemed) we paused at a truck stop. I basked under the luxury of a dry grey sky as Phil changed from sodden to merely damp clothes. About three hours later we negotiated our way into Brescia after coming down the motorway. Dick, the Reliant Kitten driver, was the only other rallyist we encountered at the motorway services. He had got out via the north route by virtue of letting tyres down and wrapping bungie and rope round them.

In Brescia town square we began to relax. Some of the Lomax and Blackjack crews had already arrived having got out of Cortina early and wisely. Eventually other cars began to trickle in and early evening saw quite a good gathering attracting a lot of interest from the locals. I had a pleasant conversation with an old chap who came over to admire the car; unfortunately our common vocabulary only extended to "*Bella Bella, Mille Miglia*, Stirling Moss", but the thoughts were there. I imagined that he would have seen the original road race in the 1950s. One of the interested spectators was an Englishman who offered to bring us tea from his home at the side of the square. We then realized that his home was a Mercedes camper van. The following morning, there he was flagging the cars away.

Obviously the mayoral promise to wield the flag had wilted with the early hour. Off we went for a drive on busy single-carriageway A roads that took us to Maranello. Highlight was a Blackjack crew that caught our queue just as some lights turned to green, and sailed past everyone with perfect timing. A quick stop at the Ferrari museum was the midday schedule which for us included tightening the fan belt. It was quite a small museum but fascinating none the less. Ferrari was a man for whom the business of racing came first and foremost, and he didn't bother about preserving historic cars which were at the time just last year's model, to be sold on, or cannibalised.

Talking of racing, off we went again, taking in some of the roads famous on the Mille Miglia, such as the Futa and Raticosa passes. Not as hair-raising as you might imagine, but merely twisting roads giving some great driving. In fog. And rain. And a bit more rain. Luckily the mist was not bad enough to affect our speed but there wasn't much of a view of the highlights of Tuscany. The following day as we set off for home, we could see the hills we had come over, bathed in sunshine. Such is life at times.

And so to the final hotel stop. We descended to the outskirts of Florence. The very last kilometre and at a crossroads we were confronted by a No Entry, which the road book said was the correct way. We flailed for another option but nothing else seemed feasible, so we found ourselves behind Dudley and His Lordship in the Dragoon as they turned into the No Entry.

"What shall we do?" said Phil.

"Follow them," said I, making a quick navigational decision.

And so we made our way to the finish, following the behemoth with its Italian flag on the right wing and skull and crossbones flag on the left, the locals shouting at us, "Eh! Eh! *Contra*! *Contra*!"

And thence to the bar. We chatted to a lot of the other competitors, in particular the owner of the Beauford company who seemed a very clued-up chap regarding the kit car industry. There had been a team of Beaufords on a previous event it seemed, but this year he had participated in a Marcos Mantis – a very unusual Triumph-powered coupé of fairly massive proportions. After the hotel had rustled a meal together (hadn't they expected us to endure the full five days?), and we'd harassed the bar staff again, came the presentations. No, we didn't win anything though I must admit I'd rather hoped there would be an award for the best presented car, for which I am sure, Phil would have been a strong contender. One of the main organizers, Peter, had remarked how many complimentary comments he had received about the Phoenix when it was parked in Brescia's square. It's a pity they didn't include a few various awards on top of the normal 1-2-3s and first in class, etc. The only other one was 'Spirit of the Event', which was won by a Marlin. Correct me if I'm wrong but they have roofs, don't they? Wimps!

Everybody received a specially made wheel and tyre which to be honest wasn't all that special, being about two and a half inches diameter, but we pocketed the unusual memento all the same. All something of an anticlimax then. Two young chaps in a Caterham won the event, being one of a small contingent who got out of Cortina before the north road became completely impossible. So some lucky or crazy souls were trying to do a road stage up near the Stelvio while we had been told just to get to Brescia on the motorway. Strange, but good luck to the winners.

The following day saw us heading north, and we reached

Dijon which was just enough of a springboard to make the ferry by the following evening, saving a day on our original plan despite two wrong turns near Utrecht making the final miles a trial of nerve and desperation. Another night on board, watching Salsa dancers, and we were back in the UK. Hull seemed quite welcoming for once, despite the attractions of lunch in Monte Carlo which had been the goal of some competitors. No doubt work and money had something to do with that navigational decision, we being more Yorkshire than jet-set end of the spectrum.

I noticed my Peugeot saloon was making some squealing noises on the drive home on the twisty roads from Phil's house. It died out later though, as did the recurring dreams about time controls and dashing through various continental landscapes for some subconsciously generated bizarre reason unknown to Freud.

It was a good event and a lasting experience but such a shame about the weather really. The organizers couldn't be blamed for that as it was unseasonable, certainly in Italy, but there was some inconsistency in some of the decisions, we thought, when conditions became unreasonable. But a lot of preparation went into the event, it has to be said, organizing all the routes and marshalling. We thought it was a long drive back after the 'climax' and perhaps a more circular route finishing further north could have helped.

But until somebody invents a virtual reality environment that makes squealing noises when you're reeling in a Caterham near the Passo della Raticosa, and does genuine 180-degree spins as mere hiccups in this inexorable and inevitably successful quest, I think Phil is hooked.

6

The Middle-Aged Fantasist

Due to the frustrations involved in putting together a kit car for the first time, to be ready for the 2002 season, I became somewhat niggled, and came to the conclusion that the cure for this malaise was to enter a motor race. I can't now recall whether the car had passed the SVA test at this stage. Probably, but the SVA status was in a sense irrelevant in the face of the plain fact that the car was in no way prepared for an ordeal rather more arduous than a trip to the vehicle test centre twelve miles down the road.

We had at one point taken the car on the trailer to Blyton Aerodrome in Lincolnshire for a bit of a shakedown run. Our convoy consisted of Denise and me with car and trailer, and my pal Bob and his friend Alison on his motorbike. I had attended this venue back in 1998 when an outfit called RallyDrive offered the chance to cane a Golf GTi around a mud track, with, for a bit more money, the icing on the cake in the shape of a Sierra Cosworth around the tarmac circuit. The configuration of this part of the track was then more basic and a completely different layout from what it became in more recent years. Coming round onto what I thought was an old runway section, I lost the back end in a lairy slide. Applying correction, I got the car pointing in the right direction and was all for continuing in said direction. Howard, the instructor, had other ideas though, given that we were now in a field of, I think, broccoli. Or possibly cabbage.

We would eventually exit the field via the path I had originally planned, at a very contrite and careful speed. A few minutes later. After his shouts of "Stop!". And after he had calmed down.

The calming down involved being told to leave the engine running so as not to deprive the turbo of lubrication. This was to date the only time I have driven a turbo petrol car, as far as I know. The other thing I know is that the experience ultimately cost me many thousands of pounds, given that the taste of power had indeed corrupted, and that I have subsequently spent many years scratching that itch with the various specialist automotive products available in the speed-addict market.

In the meantime, here we were at a bleak Blyton, with its cabbages and clouds. I took the car round a few times and then allowed Bob to have a go, in recognition of his support. The last time I had let Bob use a car of mine was when he borrowed a Nissan Stanza I had for sale. He had a single parcel to deliver to Manchester, and it would be a more civilised ride than his van, as his girlfriend was coming along on the trip.

"It's got a bit of wheel wobble at a hundred."

"A hundred!?!?!!!!"

So I was partially prepared for the way he attacked the circuit as soon as he got in the driving seat, manipulating the wheel and gearstick like a whirling dervish and revving to the max in each gear as I cringed in the passenger seat.

At least it was a proper test, which worked well, with our session ending in a cloud of steam as the header tank split at the seams.

By the time we got to Snetterton for the actual real motor race, little had fundamentally changed, apart from the replacement header tank being intact. Our convoy was also similar, with Denise and me in Toyota with trailer, and Bob and Alison this time in her Rover which he had been repairing. So, staying at a Premier Inn the night before, we were all relatively comfortable.

The track though, as another former airfield late in the year, was no less bleak than Blyton. A year or two later, Bob tried to entice Alison into a motorbike excursion to watch me race at Cadwell. No doubt the icy winds scouring the plains of Snetterton race track in autumn entered her recollections.

"I don't want to stand in a field all day listening to cars go round and round."

"Denise *loves* it."

"No she doesn't. She just goes to support Dave."

It's good to get a reality check, and the race meeting itself was one giant reality check. The briefing beforehand was useful, and a special briefing was also held for those who had never raced before. I attended this with Anton Landon, another newbie. We traded nervous smiles as the official described our first target, which was to get three laps under our belt during practice and thus qualify for the race proper.

I think I did six or seven laps, so that was no problem. The sense that a smelly, steaming, wheezing car was becoming something of an embarrassment was, however, definitely a problem. I worked out where the pit lane entrance was and came in. My racing licence test had included the meaning of flag signals, one of which was the orange spot on a black background, along with a competitor's number, meaning that competitor must come in to the pits due to a mechanical problem he/she might not be aware of.

I had the impression that the marshals were just readying that flag for me, and that I had saved them a job, as I drove down the pit lane with some degree of relief. The session had been a complete culture shock, nothing like fast road driving. I was like a bumbling bee, inadequate wings inexplicably defying the laws of physics by keeping me moving at all, in amongst a swarm of angry hornets. The only bit of the track I remembered at all was a large bridge at the end of an interminable straight, after which came a 90-degree left. Into this turn would sweep a phalanx of cars, two or three deep and three or four abreast, seemingly every lap, as I clung to the right-hand side in my earthly progress, unable to comprehend the spaceship velocities of those with whom I shared the track.

After struggling to load the pummelled car onto the spindly single-axle trailer, I visited the race control office to inform them that I would not be starting the race. The clerk thanked me for explaining that I thought a rethink might be necessary, and asked with a smile, "Will you be coming back?"

"Oh yes."

Was I mad?

Probably.

But then, what has motor racing got to do with tedious sanity?

Over the previous year or two I had got to know Doug at Pioneer Tuning in Hull. Bob had been doing some engine development for a grass track Mini racer he knew, and Doug had helped by making his rolling road available for evening sessions. So I had started taking my ordinary cars there occasionally.

Now I popped by with the Striker, regarding the cooling issue. Taking one look at the radiator, Doug pronounced, "That'll never cool that engine."

Aha. The wisdom of a different and experienced eye.

The radiator was patterned after a Ford item, adapted for the angle it lived at in the Striker. But the 2.8 was a bigger lump than conventionally used in the Striker (by sensible people). Johnson's Radiator Works next door to Doug didn't seem too interested, as they had become focused more on sheet metal fabrication at that point.

I approached Serck Radiators, only a street away, a national concern who kept a thick catalogue of automotive radiator specifications, over which we pored. I decided on a customised Capri rad, same shape but with extra cores compared to the existing item. I think it was 4-core rather than 2. Not twice as good, due to the heating of the airflow before it reached the rearmost tubes, but good enough.

Sometime later, I was down at Doug's with the Striker. We had the bonnet off, chewing the fat. The guy from Johnson's was passing by and had a peer at it.

"We made that radiator."

Serck had farmed the job out to them!

With the cooling issue solved, but with minimal appetite for tackling an engine overhaul as the clock marched forward, I took the car to a meeting of the 750 Motor Club Kit Car Championship at Oulton Park. We were into May 2003 by this time, and the series had already completed four rounds at various other tracks.

This time the briefing reminded us that no matter how well we performed, Ron Dennis and Frank Williams would not be calling us on Monday morning. Good advice.

We were lumped in with various V8 Morgans and Porsche 911s from the Roadsports Championship, who were a bit low on numbers. Thus with them, and the kit cars from Class A, a reasonably sized grid was formed. The grid. I was on the grid!

Steve Jones, the photographer, began a fine tradition of seeing me coming with my money, and provided an excellent shot of me ahead of a Morgan and a Porsche. Obviously they were on a different lap. We were using the short version of the circuit and I think the leading Morgan lapped me four times before the race finished.

Conscious of the increasingly asthmatic engine, I avoided the use of high revs, the more so as the race went on, until at the end I was circulating in fifth without changing down at all, thankful for what was left of the V6's natural torque. Then the chequered flag came out and I circulated in a state of overjoyed delirium, waving back at the marshals who held up hands and clapped in admiration of my special effort of survival. Naturally, with experience of more than one race, it becomes clear that they always acknowledge each competitor at the end of every race, but for now I was steeped in the melodrama of an alternative reality, actually playing a part in this vivid world rather than being a passive witness.

Like a monochrome cartoon suddenly bursting into colour, expanding into 3-dimensional life, and leaping off the plodding page of my earlier existence, I was filled with passion and excitement. I had got to the chequered flag and only the anticipation of the next race seemed to matter.

It came at Cadwell Park, just fifty miles or so down into Lincolnshire. We were again with the Roadsports competitors, bringing a wide range of semi-exotica including Porsches, TVRs, Ginettas and two Renault Spiders. Remember them? (A bulbous Lotus Elise rival.)

Phil had taken pity on me and sold me the Mk II Granada he had been running about in, for a generous, in the sense of low, price. It was actually quite a tidy car, so another crime against the future was perpetrated as I hoyed the engine out for the Striker, depriving Ford aficionados of one more basis for classic or modified status further down the line. But racing was all, and no Terminator figure loomed out of the dry ice of time travel to stop me beavering to replace the first tired V6 in the month between Oulton and Cadwell.

The meeting was fun, getting used to the routines of a racing day and enjoying a car that didn't feel as if it might expire at any moment.

I even managed to relax enough to climb out of the car before we drove to the grid, when we were held in the assembly area due to a mishap in the preceding race. As Cadwell's assembly area overlooks the start/finish straight down below, we stood and chatted as we watched several damaged hatchbacks being removed, the result of a kerfuffle at the start of their race. Typical hatchbacks, was the general feeling.

Graham Dash, a very quick Sylva Striker driver, was amused by the vintage looking buckled leather straps I had fitted as a fail-safe to augment the rather pliable SVA compliant catches on the bonnet. When we finally got going on the green light (standard starting procedure back then) I passed him, as he was parked on the grass, about to get out and run back to retrieve his bonnet, which was lying on the verge some way behind.

Nevertheless he caught and passed me, his best lap the quickest of the kit cars, some eleven seconds faster than mine and on the shorter circuit at that. I couldn't resist reminding him that his result would have been yet more impressive had he fitted leather straps similar to mine. It actually mattered in the long run, when Steve Taylor pipped him to the overall championship in the last race.

As for myself, I was delighted to achieve a respectable last place on the day.

During our race, Clive Turner, a fellow user of the Ford V6, though the 3-litre 'Essex' as opposed to my 2.8 'Cologne' (it matters!), found a loose panel of aluminium or fibreglass, moving around in his Gemini's cockpit. Deciding it would be safest to jettison it, he managed to grab it and fling it out to the side. It was caught by the slipstream or wind, and Nick Craddock, following, found himself staring up at this tumbling aerial threat as he accelerated away from the hairpin. He elected not to try to pass Clive for the rest of the race, if such were the lengths to which he was prepared to go…

Bryan Healey, a former champion in the kit car series back in the early 1990s, and now competing in the Zetec engined Class B, turned out to be the Bryan Healey I had gone to technical college with in my first job after school, when we both worked at the same quantity surveyors. We would alternate the weekly driving, me with my mother's A35 van, Bryan in a rather smart 1950s Sunbeam Talbot saloon, quite a tail-happy machine. Shades of Jim Clark.

Bryan asked me what gear I took the hairpin in. A rather lazy third, I confessed. As he incredulously explained that he used first, I supposed that there might be a bit more to this racing lark than I had seriously considered.

The next meeting was at Pembrey in South Wales, over near Llanelli. You join the M4 near Newport, thinking, not far now, yet there are still about 100 miles to go. I booked a B & B and Denise came along for the weekend. We had races on both the Saturday and the Sunday. I was using a sixteen-year-old Toyota Supra at the time, which I had purchased for my usual 3-figure sum. It came with the bonus of a towing rig, and with a 3-litre motor, pulled the trailer comfortably. Having developed a tendency to lose water, it was not to last too much longer, but for now we were OK.

Being a large coupé, the Supra had long doors compared to saloons, and as Denise re-embarked at the services on the M5, the edge of the door caught, fairly lightly, the side of the car in the next bay. The owner was regrettably on board, and began to huff and puff. Denise, to whom cars were merely metal devices to get lifts in, had no conception whatsoever of paintwork and pride of ownership, and just shrugged. Watching the clock, and feeling that any altercation would serve little purpose, I executed an 'Apologetic Gallic Shrug' gesture, and pulled carefully away. See what happens. Nothing did.

On the Saturday we found a pub a little way down the road from the B & B, where we were able to get a meal. Talking with some Irish guys at the next table, who were staying at the same B & B, it turned out that they were scrutineers for the Irish Formula Vee Championship, who were enjoying a weekend of races away from their usual haunts across the Irish Sea. They regaled us with some hilarious tales of what tricks their competitors got up to, including one guy hiding bottles of water up his sleeves during the pre-race scrutineering, to cheat the weight limit rules. Notwithstanding the obvious bulges, he was given away by the water running down a wrist, from an inconvenient leak.

"Sweating a little, are we, sir?"

For my part, I told them about the hatchback incident at Cadwell. My brother had been watching that day, and said that, as they set off, one car appeared to turn sharply through 90 degrees for no obvious reason, triggering the melee.

"We've got a few like that," said the Irishman. "It takes years of practice."

The meeting was good, nice and sunny after a damp practice. By now we were well into July. With only one race per day for us, I had time for a chat with Bryan again. I had been following a Porsche 968 Turbo in the qualifying session, and remarked that I could see him braking before the second part of the Esses, whereas I got through without using the brakes.

"He probably needs to."

Ah. I supposed that there might be a bit more to this racing lark than I had seriously considered.

Denise formulated a plan to bring folding chairs in the future, after spectating alongside the wife of Gary Goodyear, who was so equipped. The plan made no reference as to whether any folding chairs would fit easily into the rather limited luggage area in the Supra.

Gary was another new competitor that year, in a green Striker with an innovative use of the 1600cc Toyota engine.

The first race featured a coming together of several cars

at the hairpin, which is at the end of the start/finish straight, lending a certain inevitability to such occasional occurrences.

"I think that green car caused it," said Denise.

"I think that was my husband," said Julie.

I noticed that one particular competitor, during the qualifying session, had gone straight on at the hairpin, and seemingly without much slowing down, ploughed into the tyre wall at the end of what appeared to be another old runway, a frequent feature of many British circuits.

During the period after the qualifying, he set to, to repair the damage. Seeking a coolant hose, he asked if I had any, and I was able to find something in my box of spares. I watched as the welding equipment came out of his van, figuring that it would be a good idea not to get too close on the track, to somebody who brought welding equipment with him in anticipation of some sort of collision.

The second race of the weekend was the more exciting, as I got into a dice with a lad in a Clan Crusader, which is a small fibreglass-bodied coupé, fairly rare. With a Hillman Imp engine in the back, his engine capacity was about a third of mine, which with the nimbleness-blunting iron V6, made us fairly evenly matched. My times were nearly four seconds better than the first race, as I chased and harried him, and ultimately his car's rear end, with its engine weight, came round a bit too far and he was off backwards.

Afterwards, I was ecstatic.

"I beat someone."

"No, you were last," said Denise.

"I did, because I forced him into a mistake."

"That doesn't count. You were last."

Presumably, if the Clan had managed to restart, she would have been lost in admiration.

The next race was at Silverstone, using just the 'National' circuit layout, which is a bit of a glorified triangle really, enlivened by the Luffield 'complex' at one corner of the triangle. The entry fee for Silverstone tends to be more than many other circuits, but that is so that you can say, after you retire, that you raced at Silverstone. It sounds better than saying that you raced at a glorified triangle.

We were allocated space in the paddock adjacent to the Austin 7 based racers and specials. The drivers of these old machines are magnificently dedicated to their preservation and continued use in the heat of competition. It might be true to say though, with great respect, that they constitute a more mature age group in the 750MC pantheon than, say, hatchback drivers.

So perhaps the sample was a little skewed, and perhaps some of the more senior racers from other formulae happened also to be wandering nearby, as Denise cast her eye around the paddock. Evaluating the preponderance of portly men in racing suits, she paused. Turning towards me she pronounced judgement.

"Hmmm, there are a lot of middle-aged fantasists here, aren't there?"

The race was absorbing, and therefore fun. Afterwards, I had a Steve Jones photo in pride of place on the mantelpiece for a long time. It shows me just ahead of Jeff Ball, another Striker driver, going into Luffield. The photo itself is less than striking, with the empty stands constituting the unavoidable background from the vantage point used. However, it captures a moment after I had actually *overtaken* someone. He repassed me later but we'll skip over that.

Post-race, Patrick McDermott and I were summoned to race control. Our cars were both underweight! Penalty was a slapped wrist and exclusion from the results. I didn't feel morally bankrupt, as I had quite innocently gone off the weight shown on the SVA test summary, which showed it as falling over. I can only assume the car had my toolbox in when they weighed it at the vehicle test station. Never mind. Patrick and

I got to know each other quite well whilst we waited for Viv to pass judgement and complete the paperwork. It's fair to say that no race meeting could go ahead without the dedication of the officials and marshals.

After bolting a substantial amount of roofer's lead to the passenger floor to further slow the already comparatively sluggish car, I 'enjoyed' a rather rainy trip to Lydden Hill, at the far end of Kent near Dover.

My plan to erect the tiny one-man tent crumbled instantly as I arrived in teeming rain at a dark, damp paddock which was basically a terraced hill with a rickety wooden toilet block constituting the sum total of the available facilities. Leaving the trailer, I drove to a village, which had a pub, which had the address of a B & B, a few miles away on tiny lanes populated with scurrying badgers.

The racing was fine, the most notable moment being the semi-outbraking manoeuvre on Andrew Owen, a former champion, during the qualifying. It was more a case of swerving to miss him, when he braked earlier than I had expected, than any rational planning.

We returned to Cadwell in September, and here history records that I finished 'not last' and with a race time over six seconds better than the qualifying time. Progress.

Two races at Mallory Park ended the year, finishing ahead of Jeff in the first, tables turned in the second despite a half second improvement on best lap. Patrick was just ahead of me on both occasions. So, a good tussle and two good outings. Ending up thirteenth in the championship and fifth in Class A was a fairly meaningless statistic, mostly due to the skill of turning up and finishing.

But, feeding greedily upon this mere crumb of credibility, I now felt like a seasoned veteran.

7

Targa Brighton

I have earlier alluded to the purchase sometime in 2001, of a Fisher Fury, in spite of having an unfinished Striker in my garage. It is difficult for most members of the population to understand this logic. If you do understand it, you are probably subject to the same affliction as me. If not, then it is unlikely any amount of explanation will change your view. Just think of it as collecting, and we will progress with the tale.

Even collectors sometimes feel the need to justify their purchase, if only to themselves. In this case, the almost finished sports car would be saleable for a profit after I had completed the small jobs required. The Fisher is a derivative of the Phoenix, which is in turn a derivative of the Striker, with which I was by now very familiar. So it would be easy to sort it out as 90% of the work had already been done.

The other part of the logic that the general public find difficult to understand is the lack of storage space, given that I had only the one garage. This of course is laughably easy to solve. Simply rent another lock-up from the landlord you used to rent lock-ups from before you moved to your own place and felt that you would no longer need to rent lock-ups all over town.

The 'easy' finishing of the Fury build took a while longer than anticipated, after I had first obtained SVA and legality for the Striker, and could enjoy the logistical challenge of swapping the garaging between the two cars. Experience with the Striker didn't entirely overlap with the new snags thrown up by the Fury. The most frustrating was the nearly perfectly accurate speedometer which read very, very slightly under the road speed. So that you might think you were doing 30 mph but actually doing 31, for example. Hardly trumping mad Frankie Fraser for villainy, but that's the law. You can have a fairly massive over-reading, but the one in the car was the wrong side of what is allowed.

The car ended up at Doug's along with a collection of about four other speedos I had accumulated, from various Escorts, Capris and the Granada. He could try them on the rolling road after fitting each one. When I visited to see how he was getting on one evening, it was to see the dashboard hanging loose, wires all over the place, and to hear his judgement that the car had been built with no thought whatsoever for future accessibility. Oops. Even though I wasn't responsible for the dashboard installation, still oops. As a man who exhibited considerable patience, most of the time, with the vagaries of production car layouts which are built to achieve easy factory assembly rather than with any thought for the mechanic's task, this was the nearest I had seen him to what I call rational rage.

With that issue at length solved, it was on, I believe, the second SVA test that the car disgraced itself by dumping its coolant all over the ministry's rolling road. Exhausted mentally, I declined the examiner's kind offer of time in which to fix it, and limped home to fight again after that and various other minor niggles had been sorted.

So. Not quite the quick fix I had hoped to achieve, but by the time 2003 came around I was the proud owner of a sweet handling sports car of cute and diminutive proportions. It had the benefit over the Striker and Phil's Phoenix of a proper full windscreen, the same as fitted to the early Lotus Elan. And two opening doors!

So when Phil expressed the thought of doing the Footman James London Brighton Kit Car and Classic Car Run in his Phoenix, the thought of doing something similar with the Fury started to germinate. After the Targa-Liege the previous year, I think there was an element of kit car vacuum that was niggling to be filled. No way could we afford or spare the time for the 2003 Guild two-week event, which in the end was cancelled anyway. London to Brighton was hardly in the same league, but it was an easy little jaunt.

Denise was amenable, to a surprising degree, to sharing the pleasures of kit car life in the Fury, and so we phoned up and entered. She would be able to visit her son Ben on the way in London, and we would stay there on the Friday and Sunday nights, although for the Saturday I booked a Travel Inn near Woking so we could easily get to the Brooklands start on Sunday morning.

Plans were made with work. Friday 6th, afternoon off. Monday 9th, day off.

Sunday June 8th. Brighton Run.

A few days before, luggage rack designed and built for Fury. Oil, water, lead additive, tools, spares, all organised.

Simple.

Except it didn't turn out that way.

There was one proviso. Sometimes Denise threw in a proviso. It was usually just a quiet mention to start with, which meant there was a 90% chance that it turned into a change of the original plan. No problem.

This time the proviso was that a bouncy castle had to be delivered to her grandson, little Thomas. Fine. I had been thinking that the Fury needed a boot rack. Then she said she would go on the train with the bouncy castle. Now I insisted that a boot rack would be made. How can anybody contemplate train fares when there's a roofless Fury to be enjoyed!

The dimensions were 22ins x 16ins x 8ins I think, perfectly accommodated within my design parameters for a rack that would clamp to the roll bar using the spare seat belt mounting threads and a couple of appropriate exhaust clamps at the top to triangulate it, and no need to cut into the fibreglass.

So there we were on the Friday; I picked Denise up in the sensible car after the morning at work, along with luggage and bouncy castle, and we tucked into some sandwiches at my place while I loaded the Fury. Make sure small bag of tools are in, make sure hats and goggles are in door pockets along with spare contact points, etcetera, etcetera. Bouncy castle strapped on rack, one bag each therefore to go longitudinally on transmission tunnel until London, it will be an interesting challenge minimising the amount of gearchanging during the trip. Denise come on we're nearly ready. Plan A doesn't work, tie one bag on top of bouncy castle; luckily I had upgraded the left hand mirror to 'spot black cab with neck twist' spec from the previous 'for decoration purposes' spec. No problem.

Sit in Denise. Could you just put this bag on your knee for a little while? Are you all right like that? (Please.) We'll stop often for you to stretch and rest your bad leg.

Okay. Check back door. Check both key sets. House and sensible car on one set. Fury and garage and padlock for sharp, recently erected boundary gates on another set, don't ask me the logic except that I had too many cars to ever have a single bunch.

Check sharp, hopefully thief-deterring welded creation is padlocked. Denise is sitting with bag on knee bravely only 20% on the sulk-suppression meter. We're ready. All I have to do is go.

Out of the access alleyway past the local kids. "Like your car. Where are you going?" Onto the main road. Accelerate with the two o'clock traffic. Not bad for time, only an hour late on our ideal departure time, as usual.

Have you got your handbag? WHERE'S YOUR HANDBAG? Not in passenger space. Semi-vicious U-turn through dual carriageway gap. Back to house. Search high and low. House. Backyard. Road. Corner shop, has anybody handed anything in? Could've slid off back on vicious U-turn. Run back to house. Up and down main road to U-turn site. Nothing.

Denise cancels all credit cards. Reveals her innermost ability not to flap while I descend into deep depression. What about her keys, she then says. Anybody finding the bag would be able to find something in with her address. So I now have a task to interrupt my despair. Drive to Denise's house and lock the inner front door with a key not in the handbag set.

In Fury. Up to end of road. Can't see so edge forward, but stop for traffic. CRACK! I feel the bump at the rear. I drive left and leap out of the car, noticing that my ranting and swearing glands have fully kicked in, with afterburner. Luckily the culprit had his wife as passenger, who helped mediate. But it was extremely fortunate that the point of impact was the reverse light lens and no fibreglass had been damaged.

So a tenner changed hands (£12 for the unit at Harrogate kit car show eventually, but never mind), and off I went again. In Denise's door was a note – found your handbag on Anlaby Road, ring Ron, with a mobile number. Try the number, can't get through. Back to my place. Denise has just finished cancelling her credit cards. Ring Ron. Success! He sounds a regular guy, he can bring it later on. But of course that's no use to us now, so it's into the Fury and off to Beverley to Ron's house, now in the rush hour traffic. Ron's a nice guy, we've got a banknote ready but he wants no reward, except that we must promise not to do it again.

Back to Hull. Ring Ben to say we're not currently near

Totteridge as he might expect, but just leaving Hull. Full steam ahead. The little Fury's running well, all the better since I'm not listening for missed beats with the customary mild paranoia.

Peterborough area. Petrol stop at the services; BP, which seemed then to have LRP quite often, but not this time. So I tried high octane unleaded and put some additive in. Off we go again and really on song now. An enjoyable blast all the way to Totteridge. A couple of whiskies and chat about kit car racing with Ben. I'd just finished my first ever race in my Striker a couple of weeks earlier, although limping around at the back with a knackered engine might have been a more appropriate description than racing.

We woke on the Saturday. Refreshed. We would need to be as things turned out. The morning was spent pumping up the bouncy castle while Denise sat in the Fury with Thomas while he experimented with the dashboard controls. Ben had just sold an MGB which Thomas was allowed to sit in whilst it had been a fixture on the driveway. So I just kept an eye on the two-year-old apple of everybody's eye as he demonstrated his motoring skills.

After a while it was decided we would drive down the road and obtain breakfast in a favourite café. Thomas was to come with me in the Fury and the child seat was installed. Off went Denise and Ben in the saloon, with us following. The car park was less than half a mile away.

As we turned in, up a slight slope, a stutter, a flutter, and then nothing. Flick the starter. Nothing. Mr Retired *Petit Bourgeois* in his new Toyota *petit bourgeois* carrier immediately started tooting. This was London after all and he had been kept waiting two seconds.

Although my creaky enraged leap from the car was getting better after the recent practice in Hull, it was easier on this occasion to simply lean my head back and bellow.

"Do you think I'm doing this on purpose, you d★ldo?"

A man walked by laughing to see such fun and a young lady

offered to help me push. Thomas remarked, "We go for drive now? We go for drive now?" as we pushed, and no doubt the dish ran away with the spoon, but I wasn't looking.

Had the fuel regulator been disturbed whilst I was showing Ben the engine bay? I turned it up a bit.

We got the car to a parking space and went and had a pleasant breakfast. On our return it started and got us back to Ben's. Perhaps the fuel regulator then.

OK we'd better get on now. Drive south-west from Totteridge, avoid the M25. Seemed OK at first but my old kit car passenger, Mr Mild Paranoia, was travelling with us again.

We started stuttering, going up a hill. HT[6] problem? Started keeping an eye open for motorist shops on the route, a dying breed in these days of Halfords. Yes, a bit of luck, a little motorist shop in a small parade. The owner was working out the back on a customer's car. I purchased some oil for top up, and some plugs and leads. Luckily I had the contact points myself as he didn't have them on the shelf. He kindly fitted the electrical stuff and timed it for me. A very reasonable fee changed hands and off we went.

All seemed well. It had lost the rolling road tune up setting but seemed steady. Down towards Hayes then… Uxbridge? Why were we in Uxbridge? We'd missed one turn and had gone several miles at 90 degrees to my plan. Well, we were virtually on the M25 now, the car seemed OK, the alternative was to go back through the suburban traffic.

About eleven miles on the M25 needed to be covered. After six it stuttered and cleared. After eight it stuttered and cleared. Mr Mild Paranoia grinned evilly as he sat on my shoulder. Now we were near our junction. Just a bit further to our jun – ju – ju – junc – ju – silence – ju – ju – silence – coast, coast, coast to the side.

---

6 High tension electrical wiring, e.g. to spark plugs.

I looked down at the petrol gauge. It had gone from a quarter full to zero in about seven miles. I'd been so bothered about the traffic I hadn't watched it.

"Denise, I'm going to have to walk for petrol."

"Well I'm having a pee firstly."

Other drivers laughed to see such fun and kept straight despite the moon.

Denise was given her safe motorway waiting instructions. At least it was a bright warm day. Off I marched. What is a short amount of seconds in a car is surprisingly lengthy on foot.

Eventually I got to the roundabout. A taxi passed by with a passenger on board but I put my hand up anyway. The following vehicle, a Freelander, saw me and stopped and asked if I needed a lift. Thanks, mate.

He took me to a garage and a can and a gallon were purchased. Borrowing their phone I kept getting an Asian man on the line, I think he was in the garage office. Eventually the counter assistant managed to get through to a taxi company.

Off we went in the taxi. Of course the first junction after the marooned Fury was impossible to turn at, so further north we went, then round and back 1.9 junctions. Twenty quid, cash in pocket getting rather depleted by now. He waited while I put the petrol in and it started. Fine.

Off we went. It stuttered. It stuttered and stopped. I couldn't coast up to the roundabout and we rolled back like Eurydice[7] into the Underworld. I leapt out (getting good at this by now) and pushed it back to a wider, safer part of the hard shoulder.

It was time for the RAC to start repaying my investment. This was after I had taken the top off the Dellorto and checked

7 Wife of Orpheus in Greek mythology. In his quest to rescue her from Hades, he had a moment of doubt and looked back to see if she was following, breaking the condition set by Pluto. Thus he was doomed to see her slip back into the Underworld. In some accounts she vanishes instantly, but the inexorable slow descent as the shades pull her back seems more indelibly agonising.

any easily accessed jets, which all appeared clear. I had meant to read up the Classic Ford article on Dellortos but of course never had time.

Let's just use the motorway phone and turn the brain off for a while. The woman at the other end came back on saying that the RAC said I hadn't paid my membership. Gulp.

Need to keep a cool head. Err. Gulp.

"I'm sure I did."

"I will have another word with them."

Funny how time starts to lose meaning when you run out of decisions and solutions.

Limbo. The neutral zone. Traffic roars by four yards away like the tree falling in the forest that makes no sound. I have run out of thoughts.

"Hello. They will come anyway and sort out the membership issue later."

"Thanks."

Walk back to reality.

It later turned out that I had paid although the act hadn't lodged in my memory. I think there is some multinational corporate conspiracy afoot to manoeuvre people who don't set up direct debits, towards Third World status.

In the meantime I still had access to the man with the orange van to soothe my worries, a step up from the old days with just a bag of tools and Mr Mild Paranoia to accompany me in various bangers.

I explained to him the whole saga so far with my various theories, most of which he sensibly ignored and began to check the vehicle in a logical manner from first principles.

Whilst he checked under the bonnet for a circuit I operated the key, and noticed that the ignition light was going on and off at random moments. Armed with this information the RAC guy homed in on the ignition switch itself, a Sierra item. It seems the connecting plug is known for having less than tight connections a few years down the line from Dagenham. Mine possibly mated at that point to the Escort MK2 loom which might not have helped.

A judicious squeeze of a female connection later, we were back in business. That was all it was and of course if the thick rim of the small steering wheel had not obscured my sight of the ignition light I would have noticed it flickering and not been sidetracked to the fuel issue. As I wrote to conclude the original version of this tale nearly a year later, the fuel gauge was still defunct, and must have failed coincidentally on the motorway.

We ran to a quiet road, behind the RAC van, and he tightened up the connection better when there weren't three lanes of roaring traffic nearby. A hero, for being prepared to go head first under a kit car dashboard, not to mention a contortionist. He even guided us to Brooklands behind the van for a few miles, to make sure the fault was really solved.

Which it was. So thanks, Thomas. Thanks very much. Saboteur with the angelic smiling innocent face.

Ben never quite believed that his little boy was responsible for all this when we told him the tale, though his point about the position of the steering wheel and warning lights was valid; "It's the difference between design and bodging."

So there we were at Brooklands, long after the afternoon gathering had dispersed, but at least we knew how to get there in the morning, which was knowledge worth having.

Off to the Travel Inn. The restaurant next door a godsend, stress gradually dissolving.

Back at Brooklands on Sunday morning we joined the merry throng of kits and classics. A well-heeled and well-wrapped lady disembarked from her husband's Cobra next to us and said drily "I imagine this will be one of those days where I will be frequently told how much I am really enjoying myself."

We had time for a quick look round the museum, well worth a visit. Bought a postcard featuring the holographic racing car driver (an amazing thing) to send to Ron, our handbag rescuer.

Highlight for me among the kit cars was a Tornado Typhoon, a beautiful early 1960s sports racer in red with something of the 58 Testa Rossa look about it. Few of this model were produced and this one was brought back from the USA, in amazingly unmodified condition, by the owner, whose father was the works manager at Tornado when it was made.

So to the start; Denise was given a two-minute introduction to route cards, Stirling Moss flagged us off and away we went. Phil, whose idea it had all been, had non car-related problems back in Yorkshire, so it was just us flying the impecunious Hullensian flag, so to speak.

It was a pleasant day as we motored along, and at last we were exploring leafy byways and villages south of London, the kind of picturesque spots where you might see the Saint's Volvo or Emma Peel's Elan appearing in black and white times, searching for the villain's hideout.

One such village contained a modern addition in the shape of several mini roundabouts.

"Seven miles to the next junction," said Denise.

"Are you sure no roundabouts are mentioned?"

"No. Seven miles."

"It should mention in there that there have been junctions."

"No. Seven miles. I am right."

After another couple of junctions passed without comment, I stopped for a review. It turned out two pages had been turned at once, although Denise had done well hitherto.

Oh well. The dodgy low-slung rear exhaust had been grounding too much for my comfort anyway, not helped by the choice of the grip-offering 60 profile Yokohamas on the back instead of the 'bar of soap on a draining board' 70 profiles that came with the car. So we were riding lower especially with two on board. So a less undulating main road route was chosen which got us nicely to Petworth House for the lunch stop.

We got our book marked, this being the only on-route checkpoint. Hardly the Targa-Liege but that wasn't the point of this jaunt.

A look round at the interesting cars, the grounds, and Petworth's quantity-based approach to sculpture collection. Most people have figurines on the mantlepiece, but here the large hall looked pokey, crammed as it was with giant white figures variously writhing. If it was a kit car it would be over-chromed.

A pleasant meal was available in the café, followed by a stroll back to the car park through the grounds. How relaxing it all was, compared to Saturday's walk along the M25, thus proving the value of tribulation in heightening the relative pleasure of normal experience. Do motorists without kit cars realise the paucity of their ration of bliss as they draw up smoothly to the tourist goal of the day, unbuffeted?

On we travelled through the Sussex Downs, the navigation now easier with more major roads than before. Denise liked major roads. She was once sick out of the door of my P6 Rover 2000 after an energetic drive through the B roads of Holderness. This was in front of some students who were walking alongside the traffic jam in which we had found ourselves in Hull town centre.

"Uurgh," they said in unison, and walked on as we sat in the queue. After a while the traffic moved and we came to a stop just ahead of the group of students. Denise opened the door and was sick again.

"Uurgh," they said in unison.

So I liked major roads too when she was on board, and especially with the exhaust which desperately tried to hug the underside of this Fury, to little avail at the end of sharp dips on the small lanes.

One positive effect of Denise's occasional travel queasiness was that she liked the harder ride of sports cars and was prepared to refine her technique for climbing into and disembarking from each model I have owned, mainly older MGs before the kit car bug bit. However, she never forgot the incident at the single-file roadworks on the North Circular some years previously, in a Midget which featured hip-hugging seats that I had found at a bargain price. It had developed a problem with grit getting into the needle valve seatings after fuelling up in Bedfordshire, and I had felt that I should prime her about possible evasive action now that any tendency towards overflowing in the fuel bowls would not be mitigated by the engine revs, now that movement of the car was intermittent. Even though I emphasised that I would be dashing round to her side of the car, in any possible occurrence, to pull her, cork like, up from the grip of the contoured bucket seats, she subsequently had the tendency to ask me, when looking at a vehicle I had purchased,

"You are not going to ask me to be ready to get out of this one if it goes on fire, are you?"

We carried on via the Devil's Dyke area and down into Brighton, my old stamping ground, although not much of the countryside remained in my mind as more than an imagined landscape such as one might conjure whilst reading *Watership Down*[8] or some such tale.

Brighton seemed a little more interwoven with grimy reality as we queued to fill up the now unpredictable tank at a suburban garage which had become a mini Tesco at some stage in its evolution, and was as busy with shoppers, it seemed, as with people wanting fuel, with a commensurate queue.

At last, with only one wrong turning, we arrived at Madeira Drive and joined a line behind various classics and kits. A commentary was given as we got our book stamped at the line,

8 *Watership Down*. Richard Adams. 1972. Published by Rex Collings.

telling the spectators some background about the Fury model. I think we were the only Fisher Fury on the run, of which I was aware, so I hope we made a reasonably competent looking sight and that they were gazing more at the front and sides of the car than at the bulky Rover silencer slung transversely at the back of the car. It was a bit like Dr Fu Manchu – fiendishly ingenious but also well able to spoil your day with a nasty scrape awaiting the unwary.

We parked on the front and I had a quick look at the other kits and classics, but without wasting too much time we were soon off to look at the Pavilion and the Lanes area of Brighton. By the time we returned to the car many of the entrants had departed on their trip home, and the seafront road was beginning to look emptier.

The little Fury sat faithfully waiting, our lifeline to a comfortable bed in London. But first a short detour for nostalgia's sake, to see my old flat in the basement of one of the posh Georgian houses overlooking the sea. Not that the motley crew who lived there were in any remote sense posh, but that's a totally different story.

Further down Madeira Drive is a side road that climbs steeply up to join the top seafront road, which would bring us out virtually opposite Sussex Square. Off we went.

At the top is a Give Way, at quite an awkward angle. This was where the gear stick came off in my hand.

Time to leap out and snarl at the motorist behind. We needed room to roll back to a safer place to examine it. No, I didn't call him a d*ldo but that was the reserve position should his disgruntlement have escalated.

Hastily Denise was instructed in use of the handbrake. Should she slip up, Madeira Drive awaited several hundred feet back at the end of something like a 12% gradient. She would be going quite fast by that time, backwards without even being in the driver's seat, not that she drove in any case. I envisioned this scenario as I contemplated trying to stay on board the car with one hand on the steering, one foot on the footbrake and one foot outside the sill pushing, but realized that I wasn't a giant octopus, so with a Fury, it would be difficult.

Naturally no one got out of their car to help as we inched back with frequent cries of "Handbrake ON" until it was pointed to where I could get back in and control it on the footbrake as we rolled back to the right-hand side of the road away from the junction, where a pavement was available.

I soon found that the screwed collar holding the stick in place had wound its way loose, not an unknown trick for Ford 4-speeds. After several attempts with fingers squeezed through the small square gap in the aluminium tunnel top which removal of the gaiter had revealed, the thread was started satisfactorily. It's a thin so-and-so of a thread pattern, easily crossed when only the extremes of your fingers can get anywhere near it. Incidentally, why did the survival of the submarine Seaview, in all those *Voyage To The Bottom Of The Sea*[9] episodes, always depend on Seaman Kowalski tightening a nut behind a hatch that only permitted him extreme arms-length access to the vital connection, usually with about three minutes to work with his adjustable spanner (which he would always drop once), before critical flooding or nuclear disaster occurred?

But I digress. A big screwdriver for a drift, and tapping round with a hammer, completed the repair, and we were in business albeit gaiterless, the rubber having joined the various old plug leads, bungee straps and empty water bottles on the passenger-side floor. Not concours, then.

We stopped at Sussex Square and took a couple of photos and then it was off to London. Press on before it gets too chilly; we were now into quite late afternoon. A fairly uneventful trip

9 An American TV series originally for the ABC network from 1964. Based on the earlier 20th Century Fox movie of the same name. Produced and directed by Irwin Allen. Starring Richard Basehart and David Hedison.

until London, when a tinkling noise underneath developed. Taking a look I saw a U-clamp adrift, but as it seemed to be performing no function that other clamps were not taking care of somewhere else, we pressed on. I was surprised how busy the roads were through London even at 7-ish on a Sunday. The Fury drew some interested and appreciative glances from the multitude of Londoners all going somewhere at what I thought was a quiet time of day.

Eventually we reached Ben's and told our tale. The offending U-clamp was removed on Monday morning; it wasn't until MOT time some months later that I remembered it, when the MOT tester spotted the denuded fabric strap from which it had hung before it picked a fight with one speed bump too many.

We had a lovely sunny drive back up the A1, and paused in Grantham. There was a small museum there where Denise popped in to use the toilet. No problem, said the curator. Hang on mate have you forgotten you're British, you're supposed to scowl and become excessively territorial when confronted with a stranger wanting a piss?

We got talking about our experiences, recalling our visit to Brooklands, as the themes of the Grantham museum related in many cases to the 1930s. We told of the holographic racing driver and the Napier Railton and such like, and the curator was sparked into an interesting tale of his time working, as a young man, in a bank in Grantham which was used by BRM, and where great ingenuity had to be employed to get around currency restrictions on what the team could take abroad in the 1950s and 1960s. It seems the bank manager had at some stage been shocked into a submissive role after being driven by Raymond Mays[10] on a trip between Grantham and Bourne,

10 Ex-racing driver instrumental in setting up the BRM company after WW2.

"straightening every bend on the way," said our host. Mays claimed he was a safer driver at eighty than the majority of the public at twenty, apparently. Miles per hour, that is. Different days.

We drove on, the more scenic route over the bridge into Hull. Nice and early for once. People were out enjoying themselves in the sun in the park near where I kept the car in the lock-up. I dropped Denise off at home and went to get something from a shop, deciding to use a small loop road at the park to do a U-turn to reach a parking slot.

Some drinkers were at a bench nearby. About four young men and two young women, the men topless in the sun. I turned in the loop and had to pause at the Give Way line. The most boisterous of the bunch whooped and charged over to the car, leaning on it, grasping the roll bar and luggage rack, which I was now glad of fitting.

I weighed up the odds and the dickhead quotient. I knew I could leap out, enraged, quite well, after all the practice, but also knew that leaping back in and making a quick getaway would never be an option, as the days when I could 'do suppleness' had been consigned to history, even back then.

I was sitting with an accelerator pedal available and the baboon on the back was making sounds but none of them equated to intelligible English words.

Bearing in mind Health and Safety, I said "I am going to set off now, if you are still holding on you will fall."

I revved and went, the rock ape letting go of the car and prancing back to his cohorts at the self-same instant.

It had been a long and eventful weekend. Already I was looking back at it with a rosy glow of incipient nostalgia as I became enveloped in the familiar everyday environment of the streets of Hull.

The slight air of menace. The mopeds with three twelve-year-olds on board. The two-year-olds playing in the back streets where boy racers tried to flatten the speed bumps at fifty. The buses coming towards you in the middle of the road because the kerbs and white lines were designed by people without a driving licence.

The baboons…

Kit car run to Brighton with mechanical challenges stressful?

Nah…

8

Phoenix Rising

2004 started in March at a wet and windy Donington, a scenario that became something of a tradition over the years. There was still a healthy turnout of twenty-seven entrants despite the icy squalls. In qualifying Matthew Lewis, in a V8 Razer, was a victim of crosswinds on the back straight near the old Dunlop Bridge, and the car was too badly damaged to continue. I got off more lightly after experimenting with a wider and faster line into Redgate corner. The experiment, on lap three, ended in the gravel, but luckily my back wheels were just about on the track when the rotation had finished, and I got enough traction to get going again. Lap 6 saw the loss of coolant, a bottom hose having worked loose. A lesson learned but sometimes forgotten in years to come.

The race was fine, beating Jeff after putting on a spurt near the end when I saw him catching up. Relaxing enough to have to put on a spurt is not what motor racing is about, really.

The meeting was called off early due to increasing wind velocity, so much so that I avoided the Ouse Bridge M62 route on the way home.

Missing a meeting at Snetterton, perhaps due to the mental scarring of 2002, the next meeting was Brands Hatch in May, an ignominious debut at the Kent track, when the scrutineer deemed my seat belts to be too high. This was on the grid just prior to the start. He instructed me to come in after the first lap, whereupon he assisted me to get the crosswise belt down nearer to my waist. Given that it was sitting so far up that it was reminiscent of a waistband on the voluminous trousers that one sometimes sees worn by grossly over-rotund middle-aged men, he had a valid point. So after missing a couple of laps, the outing was more of a practice session for me at this new track.

June brought us to Cadwell, where I was just half a second quicker than the previous year. I had grappled with changing the axle ratio during the winter, having to make up a crude slide hammer from a scrap propshaft and brake drum. Success was hard won, but the half shafts finally gave in and the differential was freed. I changed it from the Mark II Escort's 3.9 to 1, to the 'longest' Escort ratio of 3.54 to 1. The smaller the number, the more long-legged the gearing. Normally on a race car you go for a shorter gearing, to get better acceleration. Graham Dash's Striker, for example, used the rare 4.4 to 1 ratio. But the V6, with its torque, was a different kettle of fish. Half a second improvement around Cadwell was inconclusive though. Until the race, when I found another three seconds.

The second race resulted in a heady eighth place, after several competitors became confused by a white marshal's flag and came in to the pit lane, and were thus not classified. So it is a matter of journalistic slant as to whether 'eighth place' or 'last of the finishers', is offered as truth to the wider world.

Last out of thirty-two starters in qualifying for the next outing, Brands Hatch again, was much more convincing. In the sense that you couldn't argue with it. Something told me that I would not be able to rely on fifteen people getting confused by a flag signal, to match my impressive Cadwell placing.

Nonetheless I was twenty-third, with several failing to

finish, or even start. And I still enjoyed it, despite being unable to get the car below a one-minute lap, no matter how hard I tried.

The next venue was Pembrey. Good fun, featuring two entertaining scraps with Patrick as we fought over last place (or penultimate place) in both races. His car more powerful, mine more planted on the road. I was chuffed to come out ahead on each occasion. We might not have won any prizes but it was still proper motor racing on a challenging track at a real place on a real day. Not Scalextric, not Gran Turismo, not Ferrari F40 in an arcade. Magic.

Mallory Park was another track, like the short Brands circuit, where I should have, but couldn't, break the one-minute barrier. The weight and lack of power in the car created an impenetrable ceiling. Although it can be handy, as a race driver, to have a built-in excuse every time, there is a limit.

Spirits remained high. Denise was along on this trip, and we enjoyed a nice pub hotel in a nearby village and an excellent curry in Leicester on the evening before the racing. The tow car was the fairly respectable Peugeot 405 which had come for a slightly bracing figure at the auction, in the rarefied air between £900 and £1000. I used to look around the lot for a tow ball, then assess the vehicle to which it was attached.

And I had more good news to impart, to one or two of my racing friends who cared to listen. I had bought another race car!

At that time the 750 Motor Club used to send out a monthly bulletin to members. Printed in colour, it was large enough to make a satisfying ker-plunk as it fell from the letter box. On the last page were shown, 'Cars For Sale'.

There was a white Phoenix peeping out with its quaint blunt nose. 'Read further', it seemed to say. It was common around then to find Sylvas occupying nine out of the first eleven, or even thirteen out of the first fifteen places on the grid, whether they were Strikers, early Phoenixes with the flatter nose, or later, prettier Phoenixes, along with the occasional similar, Sylva derived, Fisher Fury.

The ad for the Phoenix had a Hull telephone number. The car was in Skidby five miles away. I found this out by ringing the owner. There was no reason to ring the owner, as I already had a racing car. Once I had spoken to the owner, there was no reason not to 'just have a look'. Once I had 'just had a look', there was no reason not to buy it. Except the bank balance, an obstacle overcome by talking to my mother about an early instalment of my eventual inheritance. So no reason not to abandon my principle of self-sufficiency either. This was racing, and the strictures of normal life do not necessarily apply.

The car just had an aura of competence about it. A proper racing car in a different league from the cobbled together hot rod I had come up with on my own. It had been originally built by Martin Stewart, who worked at Caterham Cars at the time. He had won the Kit Car Championship with it, twice, in the early 1990s, just after Bryan Healey I believe. The build quality, as Bryan said to me, was 'second to none'. Even Denise, viewing it in my garage after the poor old Striker had been relegated to a lock-up half a mile away, was moved to declare that she understood why I had to have it.

So, gentlemen, if you wish to be seduced by curves in mid-life and suffer no recriminations, I can recommend a racing car as a possible way forward. Don't blame me for the time and money side of things though.

The debut was at Silverstone. The old non-favourite triangular National Circuit, where I was ironically to experience some of the more dramatic outings of my racing days, on the occasions I did decide to part with the premium price for a race entry.

Starting now.

Practice was rather alarming, with the alternator charge light staying on. There ensued a panic as I wondered what to do about it. Sorry, did I say panic? I meant to say, carefully reasoned and logical response, but very rushed.

A chap called Mike Topp, who had been a successful competitor in the kit car series previously, used to attend our race meetings then, with a van full of assorted spares. Luckily, he had an appropriate alternator. Out came the credit card and the spanners.

Some people seem to thrive on the buzz of working on the race car at the track, whether making adjustments or even quite major repairs. Changing engines at the meeting is not entirely unknown, even at our level.

I was of the opposite school of thought, and have always detested time pressure when it involves anything mechanical. However, there was no choice. Although our race was not until mid-afternoon, the qualifying had also been quite late, and one or two snags cropped up with the alternator fitment.

By the time problems associated with the different diameter pulley wheel had been overcome, I had to rush to get into my racing overalls and get the car to the assembly area. Getting to the grid, I tried to calm down, noticing that we were on a curved part of the track, where it was awkward to see the starting lights.

Off we went, my relief at the extinguished ignition light rapidly forgotten when we had to cope with an early red flag due to a kerfuffle amongst cars ahead. Ages were spent rearranging cars on the grid, as they had to be replaced in the order they had passed the start line before the lap when the red flag came out.

Being last after a careful qualifying, my task was simple, but I still had to wait as the manoeuvring took place, so I flicked the ignition off. When it looked like the restart was imminent, I flicked the switch on again, and pressed the starter. Hearing the engine come to life, I relaxed a little and focused ahead.

I could hear a siren somewhere. One of those warning klaxons, I thought. This was posh Silverstone, so they probably used a klaxon to say 'five minutes to go', and suchlike. It was very loud though. And continuous. And very close.

Hang on. I think it's the horn, on this car. The rules then said the cars 'must be capable of passing an MOT'. I beckoned the marshal who was still manning the grid.

"The horn is stuck on. Can I get out and pull a wire off?"

"Yes. You've got two minutes."

I had seen where the horn was, when working on the alternator. Down near the left front wheel. I leapt out, still being just about capable of a leap in 2004. Fishing around with my hand behind the left front wheel as I lay on my back, I was unable to locate the horn and its wire. One minute of the two had gone by. I got up and leapt back into the car. Ish. Did up the seat belts. Took a deep breath. Listened to the horn. Found where the start lights were. Took a deep breath. Watched the start lights. Put it into gear.

The lights went to green. The clutch came up. Oh. I had found reverse. Behind was the course car which was primed to follow us on the first lap. A medic would be aboard in case of any early disasters. The red Jag loomed, filling the mirror as I reversed towards it, massive in comparison to the minimalist Phoenix.

Hurriedly, I braked and selected first. Off I went again. The field were quite a way ahead by this point.

I now began to access the performance enhancing drug known as 'red mist'. I caught and passed three cars who had qualified ahead of me, after giving them a decent start. My next target was Anton Landon, my contemporary newbie at Snetterton all those eons ago, and I began to close, horn constantly blaring, until I ran out of laps and the dosage of red mist became redundant.

So... Different. It was great to have a thoroughbred racing car to play with. Even better when it came with its own supply of red mist.

I later discovered that the ignition toggle-style switch was a 3-way switch, not a 2-way one. Nobody would use the horn, but it had to be provided to satisfy the rules. So Martin had wired it so that the ignition operated in position 2, and the ignition plus horn in position 3. I respected Martin's work, as a careful and more meticulous builder than me. The switch was changed.

Oulton Park was next. The full proper circuit. Superb.

And superb.

I passed Jeff Ball and John Clayton, in a Fletcher Hornet, who had qualified ahead of me. Then experimented with not lifting off, going into Druids. Then experimented with sitting broadside on to them after the spin, hoping they would not drive into me.

More successful was the Allcomers race which I also entered, featuring Lee Noble in his eponymous car, several kit cars, and a couple of MINI Coopers (the modern type). With only ten starters, and the first seven spread out quite quickly, the main interest for the spectators was the ding-dong battle at the back, between myself, John, and one of the MINIs.

Swapping positions quite frequently, we entered the next to last lap with me behind the two of them. I changed that going into Old Hall, using the inside line to pass both of them at once. Holding on for the 'victory' of eighth place, I crossed the line punching the air in animated joy. Special.

I finished the season at Cadwell in late September, eschewing the Snetterton nemesis option in mid-October. On the full circuit, I was down to 1.49, beating a previous best of 1.56 in the Striker. I believe Martin had achieved 1.45 or so with the car in its previous single, not twin, carburettor guise. So let's keep things in perspective.

But I was now, in my own deranged world view, not just a seasoned veteran.

I was a faster seasoned veteran.

9

A Ballet and a War

Denise was diagnosed with breast cancer in about 1998. Looking back, it's clear that when things began to get more serious and difficult around 2002, it coincided with my increasing involvement in racing and sports car activities.

Perhaps the highs counteract the lows, though fundamentally it was circumstance that had never allowed me to try these motorsport activities earlier in life. Whatever the correlations, she never stood in the way of it, to the extent of enrolling a close friend to go with her when she had an operation during my trip to Florence with Phil in 2002.

Over the years to come, the treatment rollercoaster would underpin the ebb and flow of our lives. I think it was my father's friend, a retired surgeon, who put it most plainly. Radiotherapy, chemotherapy, surgery. Burning, poisoning, chopping. She would have to cope with them all.

We enjoyed wonderful holidays in France in 2002 and 2003, motoring through the Loire Valley and to the west coast, and to Aix-en-Provence and the Camargue, in an old saloon car with a tent. So life was lived rather than endured. But by 2005 circumstances had altered.

Denise had been less than impressed with some of her

treatment, and had sought a second opinion. Anybody has a right to do this, though few avail themselves of it. Perhaps just as well for our embattled health service. With strong family connections in London, including a lady who worked in oncology research at UCLH, commonly known as the Middlesex Hospital, she decided to undergo a course of treatment based on the medical opinion down there. The original oncologist who saw her was a woman very well regarded in her field, apparently quite famous. Denise could stay in north London with her son Ben, or Ray, his father-in-law and a close family friend, during her visits for treatment.

Things evolved into having chemo, prescribed by the oncologist at UCLH, to be administered in the hospital at Hull, so that she needn't travel so much. It wasn't too long before the arrangement hit the buffers. I will always remember sitting in the Hull oncologist's office, as we were told that he was in charge and would not necessarily be dictated to by the London specialist. I have the opinion that he simply would not accept being subservient to a woman in any way. It was strange, that day, to walk out of an establishment which has the *raison d'etre* to help people in distress, feeling that a vindictive dictator had tried his best to remove that lifeline.

With Ben in the middle of house renovations, a friend offered Denise accommodation in her house in Dulwich, and she moved there for her treatment, which continued at UCLH. It was a rare weekend when I didn't motor down to London on a Friday evening, returning on the Sunday. The previous year had involved us in a lot of toing and froing to London for appointments anyway, so life on the A1 was not exactly new. Don't ask about trains. Petrol was cheaper, and often more convenient. I had a 160,000-mile Nissan Primera from the auction, an ex-taxi, and a Mondeo from the salvage yard which

I had repaired (a cracked bumper). If one broke, the other was on hand. Neither ever faltered.

Denise could claim travel expenses, and we did have a couple of expeditions on the train. The last of these endures in the mind as being one of the most bitter battles. We had booked a hotel, to enjoy some luxury near the West End, not prevail upon friends and family this time, just be together. It turned into the most horrendous night; illness and misery, a glass of water spilt all over one of the beds, no sleep to speak of. Her saying that if she died, I would just have to deal with it.

I can't even remember if all this was before or after her chemo session; logic says probably after. I recall a sojourn in A & E, with a man in just a pair of shorts in the adjoining bed to Denise's, surrounded by staff and security personnel. From time to time he would roar and rant, a frightening experience when you could see his powerful physique. Denise was unmoved, completely unfazed by the nearby psychodrama.

She was discharged after a long wait. It seemed that the staff were partly distracted by the nearby ruckus. Denise thought so; determined to escape the confines of the hospital, she saw the roaring giant as the 'tsunami' that had come to her rescue, pushing the doctor into relinquishing responsibility for her care, and transferring it into her own hands. To clear the way for more desperate people. For the staff it was probably just another weekend night in A & E. God.

We were reaching the 'more pain than benefit' stage of treatments, in the latter half of 2005. I know that Ben felt that she was becoming something of a guinea pig for the oncology profession. She had been keeping a diary and writing of her dismay about how the early interventions in her illness had been poorly judged, even cack-handed. Her feisty nature needed something to focus on, I believe. People vary in how they confront the ultimate battle; Denise was the epitome of Dylan Thomas' defiant cry, 'Rage, rage, against the dying of the light'.[11]

She had formed a close friendship with another patient at UCLH, Maggie, who was undergoing similar treatment. It is Maggie's analogy of cancer treatment as akin to being in a war, which still rings true for me. Whilst Denise was emphatic that I should do enough to keep my job, everything else in normal life was secondary, orbiting around the dark star of unwinnable medical conflict.

For some rare people, memories must be like newspapers, records of minutiae, consecutive and detailed. For me, they are gratifyingly random, overlaid as in a Jackson Pollack morass where some elements achieve an enduring existence, whilst others wither to leave space for the clutter of daily coping. What lived on, of 2005, were two almost independent strands of life, adrift from chronology, momentous yet unanchored.

The racing I can only piece together with the help of records. It continued in its own universe, independently of our other struggles. A provider of positivity, a haven in which we were briefly spared the view of the gathering clouds of the other life.

Mallory. March. Two battles with Jeff. One victory each, if you ignored the nineteen or twenty cars ahead of us. Under the one-minute mark, finally.

Donington. Qualified twenty-ninth out of thirty-six. Overtook Mark Matthews, in the Marlin 5EXI, after he had qualified ahead of me. A well-planned pass which stuck, with which I was chuffed. Mark was a hard-working and friendly fellow, who ran the Marlin company at that time. Sadly,

---

11 'Do not go gentle into that good night…'. Dylan Thomas. From *The Poems of Dylan Thomas*, published by New Directions. Copyright 1952. Originally found in *In Country Sleep and Other Poems*. 1952. Dent.

I discovered a few years later that he had died of illness as a relatively young man.

In June we came to Cadwell, which was one of those 'double-header' meetings where we had one race on Saturday and one on the Sunday. With the track only being some fifty miles south, I was able to commute and spend Saturday night at home. And Denise was happy to come along just for the Sunday race, which was less tiring for her.

The Saturday was vivid fun. On a high after qualifying twentieth, which meant that there were no less than *four* cars behind me, I got a great start for once and was up to eighteenth by the end of the first lap. Steve Edwards, in a Ford Crossflow Striker, probably 1700cc, and Bruce Brown in a 2000cc Ford Pinto-engined Luego, were my main rivals here, as they had been the year before. Along with Mark Matthews in the rear-engined Marlin, with a 1600cc Rover twin cam engine.

My eager little car, with its 1600cc version of the Crossflow, felt wonderful and at no disadvantage, as I pelted along, ahead of all three of the guys I wanted to beat on this auspicious day. Super keen as I flew down the hill from the Gooseneck, super keenness turned into super rotation as I came into Mansfield corner just a *teeny teeny bit* too fast. After the spin, on the grass, I was pointing the right way, so just carried on without further ado, laughing.

Though Steve and Mark got by, I still finished ahead of Bruce, so I was pleased by the result. I suppose some people in the same position might feel it to be frustrating, but I always thought, if you have proved something is possible, there is always another day to try and achieve it…

Even the Nissan went well on the way home. Executing a couple of swift, safe overtakes on fancier cars, the journey just flowed as I remained in a smooth, fast groove, hardly held up by anything on the challenging Lincolnshire lanes.

The Sunday was relaxed, in terms of no car issues to be

dealt with, but less auspicious in terms of the weather. A good proportion of the late morning was spent staring at the threatening sky. We were due out just before lunch. There was no worry pertaining to tyre choice, as Yokohama 032s (I think) were mandated as a 'control' tyre for the kit car championship. They weren't perhaps the strongest wet-weather tyre, but it was the same for everyone. So you didn't have to worry about choice, you could just spend your time, as the sky darkened further, in a pure and unadulterated form of... worrying.

We finally got out, as the rain started, still light enough to provide hope that we might not get a deluge. With conditions different from Saturday, and it being a different day anyway, we got a green-flag lap to go round and see where the puddles were. Somebody contrived to blow up on the green-flag lap, leaving oil and bits of piston on the corner below the 'Mountain'. He wasn't a popular bunny. He may or may not have been a popular bunny before, I don't know. But he wasn't a popular bunny as we sat on the grid getting wetter, as the concrete dust came out for the marshals to mop up the mess.

Eventually, it was decided to move the lunch break forward, and we were guided back to the paddock. This would give them more time to mop up, and our race would be the first after the lunch break. So we could relax for a while. No we didn't. Obviously few felt like tackling lunch, so we relaxed by chatting, worrying, wandering about aimlessly, worrying and chatting. And looking at the sky.

Which darkened more.

After we got to the grid again, I can't remember whether we got another green-flag lap on the basis that conditions were even more different now. I don't think we did, but I took the first racing lap fairly carefully anyway. As we came back round downhill on to the start/finish straight, I felt confident that I had assessed any dodgy bits of the circuit, and could now get on with catching and passing some other cars. My first target was Mark Matthews, who I could see just ahead. The record shows that Nic Scott, in a fast Striker, was uncharacteristically running at the tail end, in close proximity to Mark. I don't really recall this, as I was focused entirely on the bright green Marlin. I would pass him, then catch my next target, pass them, and so on. It would be a good race and I would be able to make up a good few places before the end.

As I pulled out to try to pass Mark, I was in third gear, flat out, which gives about 95mph ultimately. There was more of a wet glassiness to the line I was on, which I hadn't seen hitherto because of the presence of Mark's car. The lap chart shows that I was within a second of Mark and Nic as we went over the start line. They will have drawn away after this, on the basis that they were facing forward so probably making better progress than I was.

I wasn't facing forward. I have the feeling that I converted an anticlockwise spin into a clockwise spin with an instinctive reaction, but this may be fanciful. It was definitely a spin though. Gratifyingly, the faithful little car kept going in a straight line. But spinning. Again. And again.

As I saw the side barrier going by at each rotation I had two main thoughts.

This is embarrassing in front of everyone.

The car will be in bits when this finishes.

Luckily, very luckily, it ended only in a glancing blow against the barrier as I went backwards up the hill where the straight curves into Coppice corner. I think it had been two and a half rotations in all. The uphill grass and the nudge on the barrier had brought the drama to a relatively benign conclusion. As I sat and breathed, a marshal leaned over the barrier and asked if I was going to rejoin.

Er, what?

"Does the car look OK?"

"Yeah, it seems to be."

"OK, I'll get going then."

There was no mad rush to turn and join the track, so I carefully got moving, coming to some terms with my astonishment at finishing virtually in one piece, and trying to feel if the car was exhibiting any unusual handling traits. I could see the rest of the field going down into Mansfield corner, way over to my right. Coming round on the next lap, the view of the rest of the field was pretty much the same, providing the realisation that I stood no chance of catching up in a slowish race where we would only be completing seven laps, or six in my case. So I motored on with the sole intent of reaching the finish.

It was fortunate that I did so, for although Denise had missed the incident she knew something had happened to me, from the tannoy. But then she saw me come past.

The incident had caused more than a few open mouths. Anyone can spin on a corner of course, but to pirouette several times from a straight line start, giving a passable imitation of the prima ballerina at Swan Lake twirling vigorously across the stage before disappearing behind the curtain and plunging into the backstage props, takes an inordinate amount of natural talent, I feel. As soon as the race ended I breathlessly enquired, of the spectators I knew, who had been eager to discuss the physics of racing car ballet, where Denise was. I think it was Patrick who had seen her in the clubhouse café. With thanks and apologies, I dashed away from the transfixed throng (two or three people can constitute a throng, can't they?), and rushed to find her to calm her fears relating to my drama. Glancing up briefly from her seat, she calmly resumed her absorption in eating a baked potato. That's one of the things I loved about Denise. Priorities.

After a reasonably enjoyable weekend at Pembrey, meetings at Mallory and Silverstone in August were skipped, and I found myself at Brands Hatch in September, for two scheduled races. In the first, I came down the hill after Paddock Bend, to be confronted by an almost stationary Paul Harvey, with his Phoenix in the middle of the track. I can't remember if he had spun or had been forced to brake for an incident ahead of him. It is evidence for a non-photographic memory but otherwise doesn't matter.

I had three choices. Go left, and probably end up in the gravel. Go right, and almost certainly spin, given I had not quite straightened after Paddock and would be tightening my turn again at high speed. Or brake, to gain a split second of decision time, then go left or right. I went for this third option, and the dilemma was solved when I spun anyway, with the braking demand being enough to tip the car over its available grip.

I ended backwards in the infield on the right, which was fine, as I hadn't hit any other cars. And in fact I was able to carry on, catching and passing Natalie Hardy, a newcomer to our ranks. But it was not ideal, as any excursion off the tarmac is going to introduce some buffeting into the equation. It's a good idea to carry out a spanner and visual check of the car after such an incident. Whatever I did do in this regard was, in view of how the second race turned out, not thorough enough.

The second race got going OK, but there was some sort of melee ahead, with a red flag coming out. The record shows several non-starters for the restart, which proves the point. I was also listed as a non-starter, despite being on the re-formed grid.

On the re-formed grid, I was watching wisps of smoke drift out of the bonnet top air intake. Yes, this was from my car. The slight smoke now started making a dim correlation in my mind with the slight whiff of fuel after the day's earlier spin. Which I clearly hadn't *quite* solved with my spanner check.

But I was in driver mode, not mechanic mode, by now. What's more, it was red mist driver mode, from the interrupted racing and the nervous impatience of being gridded up again after the red flag. And through the red mist I could see only one thing. It was the sequence in Frankenheimer's film *Grand Prix*, where James Garner's car catches fire, but he manages to make the finish and get his result, due to the slipstream blowing the flames away. If we could just get going NOW, the movement would blow those flames away and I could have a race. But get going. Please. NOW.

The red mist had been psychologically selective and had conveniently edited out the later part of the Garner sequence where he has to leap from the car immediately after taking the flag.

As I sat there, there was to be no green flag, and all that happened was that the smoke became whiter and more profuse. Time to snap back to reality and wave my arms vigorously. I saw Steve Ford, the scrutineer who had made me return to the pits to tighten the seat belts here in 2003, making towards the car, alarm on his face. He must have been thinking I was a right bozo by this time. As I got out after flicking the kill switch, a couple of alert marshals arrived with extinguishers, and with me undoing and edging the bonnet up to get the jets aimed a bit more accurately, fortune smiled and the car was saved.

After the 'Phoenix from the Flames' drama, I scrounged usage of the jetwash at work to remove as much of the corrosive extinguisher residue as possible. Other than the loose fuel pipe, the car was, amazingly, relatively unscathed. When the Phoenix had been built a 1600 Crossflow with single downdraught carburettor was the front running combination for the old class B rules, and as this set-up had come with the car, I was able to replace the fire-scorched twin Dellortos to get out for the next meeting, which was at Snetterton in October.

Here the qualifying was less than auspicious, being several seconds adrift of Natalie in qualifying, which seemed to be more than just wariness on my part. Was the car simply outclassed on this circuit with its two long, long straights? The answer came in the first race, in which I did only seven of the eleven laps before parking on the grass along the back straight. The car had been going noticeably slower just prior to this, and in fact was not outclassed, just knackered.

It turned out that the skew gears on the camshaft which drive the distributor and oil pump had chewed up. It seems to be the Achilles heel of racy Crossflows, in my experience. Does the high-pressure oil pump start to seize, causing the camshaft gear to be gradually stripped, or is the skew gear too weak to cope, having to drive two components? Chicken or egg? It doesn't matter. Snetterton remained my nemesis for the foreseeable future.

In spite of it all, we enjoyed our outing. We met up with Mel, an amusing Midlander with a fund of hilarious tales from his days working at the chaotic British Leyland in the 1970s. I had formed a good friendship with him by way of Denise's friends and family circle, first bumping into him when we visited a mutual friend in Norwich. He lived now near Bungay, about thirty miles from Snetterton, and the years ahead would feature a regular meet-up when I raced at the venue.

This time though, was to be the last meeting Denise would attend, after which she became too ill for me to spend time on racing car repairs. We would bend our will towards the trials of the other life, in the time that remained.

10

Just Getting Too Complicated

2007 dawned for me, racing wise, at a dark, wet and windy Donington. Crawling into the cramped confines of the Mondeo estate, I was still looking forward to the morning and the chance of something positive.

Denise died in March 2006. Her battles had included an effort to get to Switzerland to end her life on her own terms, when the quality of life turned to endurance rather than joy, from about November time. I was to go with her on a train; she had asked her children not to make the trip, not wishing to play the part of a grim pied piper. I had to organize the collection of an oxygen cylinder, to help her manage the journey. At one point Bob had even offered to help in the hiring and driving of a motorhome, to solve the various issues involved in crossing borders and so on, but she had wanted the train.

I was walking in Regent's Park after visiting the pharmacy who would supply the cylinder, when I got a phone call from Dignitas. Necessity had propelled me into the modern world and I was thankful for the mobile phone now. There had been a problem with the paperwork. They are super finicky about the detail, for obvious reasons. Something relating to her ex-husband's details needed clarification, which would mean revisiting the Crown Court offices in Hull again.

I sat in the park for a while before going back to see her. She was sitting in some sort of private clinic room somewhere in the hospital; there were chairs instead of beds I think, for the most part. It could have been any room anywhere, divorced from any sense of time or connection with the bustling city.

Her reaction was disappointment, quietness. The feistiness now subdued.

There followed a journey north. Tears as we sat in the dark car park at Tibworth Services. Revisiting the court building. Rubber stamp. Phone call to Dignitas. Macmillan nurses. A sojourn in the hospice. Attempting to visit the bathroom whilst dragging a heavy oxygen cylinder trolley instead of summoning the nurse, typical Denise.

Back home. More nurses and carers. The time had passed, when she could have made it on that train. When I would have come home with an oxygen cylinder for company, and listened uncaring, to whatever music had to be faced.

I would have had it easy…

The funeral was a joyful occasion, as far as these things can be. Amusing stories which she had written in her last months, family, friends, reminiscences and tales. Memories of a unique and bright spirit.

I went down to London a few weeks later, to return the oxygen cylinder. Visited Maggie in Brighton. Later I visited Mel and we went to see the kit cars race at Snetterton. Without my usual racing pass, we had to pay to get in, but got a discount when he announced us to the girl in the kiosk as 'two coffin-dodgers'.

Then I went back to work and normal life resumed, in its way.

I rebuilt a V6 that I had bought from a guy in Tamworth. It had reportedly had £3000 spent on it, though my outlay was down in three figures, a few hundred. It is important to get these V6s balanced properly, but I took a bit of a chance if I'm honest. It was also a bit daring to fit a performance rotor arm, one which doesn't limit the top revs like the standard one. After installing it in the Striker and taking a road trip to Silverstone in the car to bed things in a bit, and watching the kit car race before heading back, I was feeling ready to tackle one or two races later in the year.

These plans hit the buffers when the gearbox lunched itself on a test run. I had a pleasant hour watching the birds of prey in the sky above a quiet East Yorkshire hill as I waited for the tow truck. After Doug heard the tale, he questioned whether I had been blackballed by the RAC yet. No problem, I explained, as long as it's always a different fault.

So after a mad and abortive effort to install a V6 4-speed, which didn't fit past the tunnel and which is a heavy type of box anyway, I was back to a second-hand Type 9, the 5-speed. It was September when I finally got out on track, at Donington. Confident after a reasonable qualifying session, I upped the pace as we set off in the race.

The 'good' V6 lasted two laps before a con rod made a bid for freedom. When somebody spun on the oil, the resulting red flag meant I didn't even get a point for starting. At least Ben was amused. This meeting was to remain the only one where he had seen me 'race'. I later tracked down a photo of the car enveloped in white smoke as it blew up, which I gave him for his garage wall.

So now here I was, back at Donington. I had £40 for the marshals' Xmas party in my pocket, as contrition for the oil spillage. I also had a Crossflow 1700 in the Striker, and the hope of better things.

Not that it was that much better to start with. The car ran like an asthmatic dog and I would have been quicker in the Mondeo. I nearly retired from embarrassment after being lapped three times by the leaders, but decided to stutter to the finish, bizarrely ending up with a respectable looking eight points due perhaps to a slightly meagre entry list.

We later discovered a broken brass component (starter jet holder, I think) was giving rise to massive overfuelling on one carburettor, hence the running on two feeling. A bodge sorted it for Brands in mid-May, meanwhile I fitted the single carb set-up which had come with the Phoenix for Snetterton and Cadwell, and at least achieved some reliability if not outright pace.

The 1700 Crossflow choice had been made after the demise of the first 'non-standard' V6. With the Phoenix untouched with damaged engine since 2005, I had started to look for alternatives. The Zetec Sigma 1.6 (Focus/Puma engine) looked attractively light, but Mark Alexander-Williams, who had fitted it in a Phoenix, seemed to have suffered some reliability issues. I decided against it, wary of being a guinea pig for anything new, on my limited budget. As the year wore on, Mark seemed to either win or suffer some sort of blow-up, more often the latter. The only other competitor who had run this engine, Natalie Hardy of *Totalkitcar* magazine, didn't appear to have suffered such problems. Then again I could usually keep ahead of Natalie but couldn't catch Mark…

Nevertheless, chatting to Mark's engine supplier, he had a second-hand racing Crossflow which could go straight in the car, so that's the route I took. Somehow I ended up at one point driving to Jeremy Phillips' home on a black and rainy evening, where we loaded up a Striker which needed delivering to a customer in Norfolk. I was on my way down that way to stay with Mel and get some tyres for the race car at Snetterton, from Mr Polley the Yokohama agent. With the barter deal from Jeremy, of a set of second-hand twin Weber carbs, I was up and running!

However, we had a major struggle getting the Crossflow timed up at the rolling road. Eventually Doug got the engine out and deeper investigation revealed a broken skew gear on the camshaft. Sounds familiar? Motto – try to find the time to strip a second-hand engine whatever the background story. Luckily Doug was able to fit a 244 camshaft I had ready for the Phoenix engine rebuild, a couple of days before Donington. Then came the carb issue…

But Snetterton and Cadwell were better, and very satisfying that the car was at least responding. Despite being near the back I garnered eight and six points (twice) respectively, there being two races at Cadwell. My brother and some friends got to Cadwell, and I stayed with Mel again on the Snett visit, so the social side was jolly. And I had finally finished a race at Snetterton. Amazing.

We were at Brands on May 19th, and I stopped off at Ben's in North London. Although I could have stayed, I like to be ready at the track in the morning, so got on the M25 after a meal. Congratulating myself on picking up the A20 (easy to get M20 by mistake) I then forked left instead of ahead at the roundabout at the bottom of the long hill. Fork it! No matter, I would find a right, look for a signpost with a place name on it so the road wasn't too narrow, it would then come out on the A20.

Well, I went through the 'place name' village but then the road became narrower and narrower. Eventually a T-junction promised escape from the single-track nerve shredder. The map revealed a maze of white roads, but left was definitely wrong so right I went. At last a two-lane road albeit not particularly wide. As I progressed along this dark road, there was an entrance to a posh hotel on the left, but the road was unlit. Two oncoming vehicles passed me without problems but a third… was coming fast. Was coming *very* fast. I think he only had sidelights on. I couldn't move any farther left.

He passed very close to the car and my fervent hope that the guardian angel was on the case was not enough. The guardian angel cannot change the laws of physics and an almighty metallic thump heralded the trailer's demise, as I stopped fully and disembarked to see both of its axles pushed back with one completely severed trailer wheel lying in the road. And a Mercedes coupé now on my side of the road, airbag deployed, with a rather dazed driver standing unsteadily beside it, asking if I had a trailer on.

"Yes," I replied. "You've just wrecked it." Confining our conversation to this and a brief enquiry to see how he felt, I got on the mobile. Luckily we were outside this Brands Hatch spa hotel or I would have had no idea of location. The police found he had had a few drinks. Whilst waiting, I was pondering the wisdom of imbibing a small glass of wine at Ben's. Motto – you know the motto. Luckily I registered zero.

An hour or so later I had unloaded the Striker and seen the remains of the trailer hauled onto a breakdown lorry, not without a struggle on the driver's part. I managed to get hold of Rob Johnston on the mobile, to get him to ask if anybody in the bar who had not had a drink, could help. Andy Hiley was the abstemious volunteer (was this the secret behind his championship win?) and I drove up to Brands and met him, then we doubled back and I drove the Striker up to the track. After a cup of tea with Andy's family in his motorhome, I retired in reasonably high spirits. After all, I still had two of the three four-wheeled devices I had set out with.

In the morning Rob Johnston's dad Alec kindly did a nifty aluminium repair on the small missing part of the rear wing where I reckon the Merc's wing mirror had torn through it. I was back on the twin Webers for this race and the difference was noticeable, other competitors remarking on it. A sixth in class finish but much faster than before, although I couldn't stay in touch with the Zetec runners for long. I was even planning to lap Natalie but then the car went off song two or three laps from the end.

Looking at it afterwards, the exhaust manifold was clearly leaking, so I attributed the misfire to this. More pressing was the task of getting the Striker home. Fortunately one of the Hot Hatch competitors, Andy Robinson, had brought his transporter lorry to the meeting and there was plenty of space on it. He was on his way back to the north-east, but first had to load his badly damaged Peugeot which had collided with a Caterham on Paddock Hill Bend. On the evidence here, Caterhams are suprisingly strong!

Andy dropped the Striker at Ferrybridge Services. I had phoned Bob, asking him to meet me there. I had expected his van and a towrope, just in case, but Bob and mate John turned up on a motorbike! The Striker would have to behave then. Sixty or so miles later our convoy of three reached home in Hull; I got out of the Striker bent double. Brands Hatch seemed a lot smoother than the M62.

The next meeting was a double header at Mallory Park. With a week to go I replaced the exhaust manifold gasket where it had been leaking, no problem.

Problem! The car still wouldn't run right and time wasn't plentiful now. I had a good-looking pair of Dellortos obtained from Richard of the Northern Roadsters kit car club, but hadn't previously solved why they weren't working as they should. So in a bit of lateral thinking I installed the Dellortos that had been in the Phoenix when it caught fire in 2005. This involved swapping the diaphrams from the 'good' Dellortos, working from underneath the car on the Saturday morning before travelling to Mallory. Lateral thinking or mania? That's what racing does to you, despite my aversion to working on the car so close to travelling.

I went in an old Granada that I had bought from the salvage as a back-up car. This was now coming in handy, as the Mondeo's tow bar was bent from the accident. At least the Granada didn't break down and I stayed in a hotel on the Saturday night.

Sunday wasn't so successful, the car was worse than with the Webers and I limped round in the role of mobile chicane. six rather depressing points due to some attrition in the race. Nic Scott (Crossflow Striker) had blown up and Paul Boyd (Vauxhall 1600 Striker) had collided with him as they both spun on the oil. Before the second race Tony Gaunt (Toyota 1600 Phoenix) pitched in to help try to tune the Dellortos. To no avail though as now it was so bad that I merely did half a lap and retired, as I didn't even have enough reliable power to avoid being a danger to other competitors.

Less than overjoyed on the journey home then, but I resolved to try the single carb once more as an experiment. It was immediately clear on a test drive that this had done nothing to change things. So instead of barking up the carburation tree, I replaced the distributor with the one bought from Burton's when battling timing issues at the start of the season. Doug had refitted the original dizzy after identifying the camshaft as the source of our woes, and indeed it had performed well up to Brands. This season was beginning to develop a habit of challenging obvious assumptions.

Back on the twin Webers with the new dizzy, I blasted round the outskirts of Hull. A great advantage to having a road-legal racer, although this change was obvious by the time I reached the top of my road.

So to Pembrey, a meeting I always enjoyed despite the six-hour journey. I got down early on the Saturday after travelling overnight Friday, in order to get some new tyres from George Polley at the track. He was only there on the Saturday although both our races were on Sunday. John, a local farmer, turned up on Saturday to collect a Weber DGMS for a V6 which I had sold to him. Although the tickets I had sent him were valid all weekend, he said Saturday was a better bet as the forecast for Sunday was appalling! Uh-oh.

Rain on the roof of the Mondeo (now back with insurance agreed tow bar replacement) was incessant and depressing that night. But the morning dawned a little better. A damp practice for the Allcomers race, which I had entered on the strength of the car finally coming on song, saw me achieve a respectable grid position and on a drying track, likewise for the kit car races. I even stayed in front of a couple of more powerful Caterhams for a lap or two in the Allcomers, so was now on a high.

The kit races were fun, not quite hanging on to Tony Gaunt in the Phoenix but having a darn good try. In the second race I left Carl Swift's Zetec LA behind but he caught up towards the end. Not knowing Carl too well I decided against the normal line into Honda Curve as he looked like he was going for the inside. So he got through and I ended up on the grassy line, but I always tried to play percentages when it came to possible car damage; Schumacher and Senna didn't have to repair their own solitary car after their uncompromising and well-documented incidents.

Carl told me I had been able to pass in the first place because his car had stuck in fourth gear. The fact that he had eventually caught up on a track that includes a hairpin highlighted the struggle that a Crossflow now had against the modern generation. The only one out there that seemed to be keeping up was Nic Scott's, but it did seem very highly strung and missed a lot of the season with reliability issues.

So… back home in high spirits. The weather had held, amazingly, and with the new tyres and the 1700 on the Webers running right, I was five seconds better than ever before at Pembrey, which was with the 1600 Phoenix.

Just as we loaded the cars up the heavens opened and the journey back heralded the terrible floods of the following days. My spirits couldn't be dampened, but poor Charles Stirling with the V8 Dax had not been so lucky, his car catching fire in a big way after, I think, hitting some tyres coming up to Honda Curve. Charles was unhurt, but not so the car which suffered a lot of damage.

2007 was turning into a year of attrition and at the next meeting at Snetterton things really hit the fan. At the first corner Simon Childs got into a slide, Steve Taylor behind him had to back off, Steve Owen behind him had to back off, Jason Stirzaker behind Steve Owen tagged him, Steve Owen was spun off the track and speared back on to be T-boned by the next car to arrive. Poor Charlie Sterling was also involved in the chain reaction. Back out in a Phoenix hastily fitted with Paul Boyd's engine, I believe, in a bid to keep his Class A challenge alive, the car sustained extensive damage. Bruce Brown in the Luego and one or two others were caught up in utter carnage. When I arrived I saw Steve's car broadside and took to the grass as the lesser evil.

When we gathered at the assembly area for the second race of the weekend the following day, I counted just seventeen cars, when twenty-three or twenty-four had started on Saturday. In a meeting to discuss next season's regulations, Keith Messer, the technical advisor for the club, had warned us that an average entry of eighteen is necessary for a formula to survive. With this in mind, together with the fact that the car was basically behaving well, I kept my entries in for the last two meetings, Silverstone and a single race at Snetterton to finish.

Having said this the car didn't perform well over the weekend, rotor arm coming adrift in the first race, and despite triumphantly brandishing a margarine tub containing rotor arms, selecting one which caught on the electronic module in the second race, producing much the same effect. If I had not dropped to second for Russells chicane exit, I might have gradually reeled in Natalie's car. But the burst of revs was too much for the rotor arm's tenuous grip on the shaft, and I made the quick decision to coast into the pit lane. A wise decision, because watching the first five or six runners slipstreaming within inches of the pit wall, after I got out, it was not a place I would've liked to be in a stationary car.

I think in retrospect these two DNFs[12] put paid to any chance I had of third place in Class A in the championship. In itself, that such a thought was even possible was quite stunning, and only a result of all the attrition we had over the year. In the end Tony Gaunt got the third in Class A, and eighth overall, well deserved.

Tony didn't attend the next race at Brands and a mere sixteen were on the entry list. But our ranks were swelled by the surprise return of Graham Dash with Matthew Lewis's old Razer V8. We hadn't seen him since he won Class A in 2003 with the Vauxhall powered Striker (now owned by Paul Boyd).

Yet another incident just after the start saw Stephen Ward with his hand raised, and I had to slow as Natalie came past. But I was able to overhaul her before too long and with only five starters in Class A this meant I was now third in class, as Graham reminded me after the race. I now had to grasp the concept of asking for a trophy as well as the results sheet. On the mantelpiece it would subsequently sit. Not sure how many £1000s it cost to acquire, but it is REAL!

So to Silverstone, which I didn't usually bother with, as the National Circuit is not too challenging at our speeds. Nevertheless I had history with the Phoenix of working frantically on the car before the race and then doing well in the race propelled by red mist. This time was to prove surprisingly similar.

The drive down went well; I dropped off a gearbox to a man in Worksop so was holding folding, and I now had a Renault Trafic van, bought from the foreman of the scrapyard. I had

12 DNF. Did Not Finish.

only gone there to look for an SVA-compatible steering wheel for the Phoenix. The outlay of £350 seemed reasonable, as it got to Silverstone and made for a luxurious night compared to the Mondeo. It's a motorhome, Jim, but not as we know it.

In the practice, the end of the exhaust can blew off. I saw it lying on the track next time round. Fortunately so did everyone else and nobody ran over it. Somebody was being black flagged but it wasn't my number so I thought I'd do another couple of laps. I stayed out as it was running OK, if loudly. Then it went suddenly and emphatically off song and I pulled over exiting Copse. End of meeting I thought, as I was towed in.

After having lunch trying to look cool, I got the car in the garages which we had the run of on the Sunday. Already prior to practice I had had it on stands battling with a leak from the fuel sender blanking plate. Now it was hands-on time again as Tony came over to help. The distributor was the culprit again, if I remember rightly, the screw holding the upper part of the central shaft. I reluctantly agreed with Tony that it would be easier to take it out to deal with it. Noticing that Tony and his wife Heather looked remarkably relaxed eating their sandwiches, I thought they had spare energy and sent them to race control to retrieve the exhaust cone, which had not yet been picked up when I had enquired earlier on.

Tony returned with the exhaust cone *and* the packing, which looked like a racoon that hadn't made it across the road. Losing the timing settings meant getting a trial and error setting on the distributor, and I ended up with bits of fibreglass packing stinging my fingers, too rushed to put gloves on. Tony did some sterling work with a ballpein hammer and finally we had it riveted back. Although we weren't racing until 4.00, time was now getting on.

Out in the assembly area, just time to catch breath. Thumbs up to Tony and Heather. The car was running, I was wearing a racing suit, and the finish was thirteen or eighteen minutes away. Time for the red mist…

After an indifferent start, I was behind Bruce. The 2-litre Pinto is fast but the Luego doesn't handle as well as a Sylva. Silverstone is quite wide so I tried all sorts of different lines in the corners. By a strange coincidence, Bruce seemed to favour whatever line I had chosen. Finally I got a good run on the back straight and took the inside line. Leaving the braking a bit later than Bruce I was first into the Luffield complex (one left and one very long right, not very complex really) and just had to wrestle it round and stay ahead.

Tony had in the meantime drawn away but a spin meant he was within range after I got past Bruce. A lap or two later I had got past him in exactly the same way I had overtaken Bruce. I was expecting him to come back at me but it didn't really happen. Just keep on it to the finish… Towards the end I saw the marshals getting blue flags ready. This was all the incentive I needed to push on. The leaders were NOT going to catch me and indeed they didn't. A mega satisfying result. Tony's car was not quite as sharp as usual, he said, but I was still chuffed to pass him. As for Bruce, he requested some of the drug I was on…

At the final meeting at Snetterton I would have had to be second in class I think to catch Tony; even then he would stay ahead after dropped scores. I had a good tussle with a new competitor who was renting Mike Topp's LA Gold car for the meeting. Discovering afterwards that the car had a Zetec in, I was quite pleased that I had caught and passed him. However, a time consuming off at the end of the pit straight, missing the turn in for Riches corner, meant a ploughing interlude and the end of any deluded hopes of catching Nick Craddock (Crossflow Striker). It also enabled the LA Gold chap to overhaul me at the end which probably made his day at least. I guess I had begun to relax by then or he had found out how to get out of the corners quicker. Whatever, Nick got the third in class this time, his first trophy after several years of competing in kit cars.

That was it then, a grand total of eighty-six points, ninth in the championship and fourth in Class A. Andy Hiley (Taydec) was the overall and Class B (Zetec) champion with Gary Goodyear taking the Class A honours in his Toyota-powered Striker.

I had not only got more points than my best previous effort (fifty-six in 2004) but had exceeded it by some margin. So I felt all the effort to get out there had proved worthwhile. Although others had suffered bad luck, I had got to all and managed to finish most of the races. Next year, as my reward, I would be able to display the number 9 on the car. Paying for only one digit would save ninety pence so that the racing budget would hit the ground running. McLaren, eat your heart out. Incidentally, I noticed that the previous year at the British GP, Lewis Hamilton had to try to save his engine for the next race. Join the club, mate.

And then the Striker was sold, when I got a serious enquiry from Ireland in the November. As a result I trailered it to Holyhead and Dave and Claire met me there and drove it onto the ferry. Claire's intention was to eventually race it in a one make Striker series they had over there. It would have to be fitted with a Zetec. It was nice to think it would be racing on.

It joined the Fury in the cull. That had gone towards the end of 2005, when I got a call on the mobile somewhere near Grantham on one of our frequent pilgrimages along the A1. Luckily I was near a lay-by at the time and able to initiate a dialogue. The chap had form in racing, funnily enough, having won the title in the 'Sports 2000' series some years before. The secret of success, he said, was working hard to get the car out there after mishaps.

He wanted to use the Fury as a project to install a motorbike engine. Not quite my cup of tea, but each to their own. As such, he didn't need the Ford Crossflow, and we negotiated that I would keep it. This involved meeting up at Bob's factory unit on a Sunday morning, where spanners twirled, and between the three of us we got the car on its way on the trailer, engineless.

I felt a bit of a pang, although I was generally fairly unsentimental about parting with cars. But life was just getting too complicated...

Never mind. There was still the Phoenix.

1. My infinite world of motoring.
Photo: Hugh Roberts

2. Bigger cars, lesser space. Not moving on…
Photo: Dave Roberts

3. The Fabergé egg…
Photo: Dave Roberts

4. … and the hatched beast.
Photo: Steve Jones

5. Mother applies the vital adjustment to the sticker.
Photo: Denise Hyde

6. It's a motorhome, Jim, but not as we know it.
Photo: Dave Roberts

7. Phil fettling Phoenix. Somewhere in Europe, 2002.
Photo: Dave Roberts

8. The Porsche had to brake…
Photo: Steve Jones

9. Ignition at the Cherub's mercy. Brighton run, 2003.
Photo: Dave Roberts

10. A good start at Brands Hatch, 2007.
Photo: Steve Jones

11. With Rob Johnston. Cadwell Park assembly area, 2007.
Photo: Rick Roberts

12. An unmolested Phoenix.
Ahead of Mark Matthews, Donington, 2005.
Photo: Steve Jones

13. The Black Donkey trying hard. Snetterton, 2011.
Photo: Steve Jones

14. With Tony Gaunt and Bruce Brown. Silverstone, 2007.
Photo: Steve Jones

15. The hairpin dance. With Spike Buckland
and Lesley Wilson. Pembrey, 2013.
Photo: Steve Jones

11

At Least You've Got Nothing

There is no timetable for grieving. And thankfully no societal pressure or convention, that I know of. People are just glad they're not in your shoes, quite understandably.

I had a sympathetic manager at work, for which I was grateful. I had gone back to work after a few weeks, ready to be doing something. 2006 became 7, became 8. I still talked about her a tad overmuch, to any willing or captive ear, still pulled over in the car on the way to work for a few quiet tears, when something like 'Shine on You Crazy Diamond'[13] came on the radio. Or on the CD which I had of course selected myself.

Such habits didn't worry me, but there came a time during 2007 when I made a specific effort to widen my circle, and perhaps get fitter, by going to a class for salsa dancing, quite a popular activity then, and probably now. Although my parents had been keen ballroom dancers, in the Latin style, and I feel I have at least a slight degree of musicality, it was hard going sometimes, and on occasion I had to force myself to get out of the door on a Thursday evening. Nevertheless, 'Beginners' was

13 'Shine on you Crazy Diamond'. Gilmour,Waters, Wright. From *Wish You Were Here*. Pink Floyd, 1975.

a pretty good physical workout, and a class consisting of myself and eight or nine women was not untypical, which I viewed as quite a promising long-term ratio, so to speak.

The difficulty came when one felt ready to move out of the upstairs room, to the nitty gritty of the 'Improvers' downstairs. Here there was more explanation, more variety of moves, and with all that, more headache. Towards the end of the week's routine, there would often come two or three moves involving passing over or under the partner's arm whilst rotating oneself or the partner. After which the opportunity to soothe the overheated brain cells once the routine was 'learnt', by queuing at the bar, would usually be a most welcome hiatus in the proceedings.

Very occasionally, I would enjoy an energetic dance with one of a group of three or four ladies who had originally attended Beginners at the same time as me. This was in the 'free dancing' period after one had topped up at the bar and recovered from the octopus-tentacle phase of the taught routine. Jenny and her pals, being quite good at this by now, were able to participate in dancing some of the few moves I did remember, and enjoy, which was I suppose a taste of what things could be like.

They had progressed promptly, through Improvers and on to the dizzying heights of the 'Intermediate' class at the far end of the downstairs dance floor. Goodness only knows what esoteric levels of skill were required to be elected to any 'Fully Competent' class that might exist, presumably at a confidential time and place known only to its initiates.

For the most part, I was content to chat and have the odd tentative dance with some of my fellow Improvers. As well as our teacher, Ian, there were just a few men who had learnt enough, here or elsewhere, to be able to lead a partner in a good variety of flowing moves. I would watch them implacably, inwardly seething with resentment and frustration, wishing I could remember enough to turn fumbling aspiration into confident expertise.

In any class situation, as time races by, week by week or day by day, it will be found that the members of the cohort will tend to diverge, according to varying levels of ability. So unless there is a will, on the part of the teacher, to ensure the slower learners are given enough help to attain whatever the goal of the class might be, they will drop back, become dispirited, and in an uncoercive situation, eventually vote with their feet.

I devised a plan to manipulate the odds, in an effort to remain on the playing field of armography and cucarachas, without being overwhelmed by terminal despair. The teachers, Sue and Ian, ran classes at two other venues during the week. If I went to the Tuesday one at a nearby meeting hall, I could turn up to the Thursday one at the social club, and get a second bite at mastering the week's routine, with the head start. In this way I might seem vaguely competent to the ladies with whom I conversed on the Thursday. My goal was modest – not to dazzle, but merely to avoid the demeanour of a complete nincompoop.

The plan had some success, though I can't remember now whether it was instigated as a direct result of one particular moment of awkwardness. This was when I was dancing with one of the friendly Thursday ladies and we ran out of room on the floor. As she moved backwards, the contact with someone's foot put her off her stride, since the someone was not a fellow dancer, but a spectator sitting on the bench seat at the wall. With the two of us fumbling after my inadequate leading, she ended rather inelegantly on her knees at my feet, in preference to finishing up in the spectator's lap. Apologetic and somewhat mortified, I could see no positives, other than her attitude towards me remaining mercifully unfrozen.

I'm now married to her.

Fancy that.

After managing not to vote with my feet, in a dance class, and witnessing my future fiancée not allowing being knocked off her stride, to put her off her stride, I began to climb out of my morass of muddied metaphors, and enjoy an influx of positivity.

Our first excursion together was to an evening of dancing, organised by the salsa club. No tuition, just dance as much or as little as you liked. We spent much of the evening chatting, getting to know each other a bit better.

This was on the day before my birthday, as chance would have it. By further chance, along with a bit of judicious decision making, our wedding occurred exactly one year later. In our fifties, knew what we wanted, bam. Done. No fannying about like these kids. And the chances of me forgetting the anniversary had been minimised.

Several of our early assignations took place with me using a Mercedes E-class saloon. Although I had been in steady employment for some thirteen years at this time, old habits died hard and I could not resist the odd flutter at the car auction, such as using a tidy Skoda Octavia for most of 2006, before generating a respectable profit from it and moving back to looking at tow bars and buying the car to which one was attached.

The Merc was a pure punt really, as I had the scruffy Mondeo estate for daily driving. Another one that had come from the salvage yard needing only a repair to the bumper and a second-hand radiator grille before it was back on the Queen's highway. The Merc, by contrast, was very well presented, if a tad old. It sat plutocratically with its gold paint, in the auction compound, as if challenging the hoi polloi who clustered with their burgers and polystyrene coffee cups, to dare to contemplate ownership.

With the budget in my pocket, it would be this or a Nissan Primera, the performance version, smart in unblemished turquoise. Unusual colour, but somebody might love it.

As the cookie crumbled, it was the Merc which glided

into the hall first. £1600 changed hands, and I was the proud owner, hopefully temporarily, of a straight six auto luxobarge. I've always been a sucker for a straight six. It was large as well, something like a 4.2 I think. Petrol of course.

Now all I had to do was find a would-be pimp or drug dealer to be tempted by it.

I popped down to Doug's to ask him to do an oil change, as the megalithically proportioned filter required a special tool.

His premises were accessed via a single roller shutter door. The main garage within opened out after a few yards of dark dinginess alongside the office, which was wide enough for only one vehicle. It was in this gloomy tunnel that I parked briefly, there being no room on the street.

Doug broke off from whatever he was doing as I disembarked, peering into the ill-lit gangway with determined concentration, as he sought to identify the interloper who was silhouetted against the sunlight of the white-collared outside world.

"Is that you?"

"Is that yo-ooou?"

"Is that *you*?"

The juxtaposition, of myself and Merc, was clearly hard for him to compute after the preceding years of bangernomics.

It was in the Merc that Janet and I later had an outing to Bempton Cliffs, having been meeting up for a whole month or so at this stage. Bempton is the home to a multitude of sea birds in late May and early June, and lies just a few miles north of Bridlington and Flamborough.

The road from the village to the sanctuary is quite narrow, and, just before the car park, divides into two single-track tarmac sections. A one-way system, one in, one out.

The 'in' road has a substantial dip in it, not just a brief

compression but a steep downhill stretch of road followed immediately by an equally steep uphill stretch. As we levelled out at the bottom, there was a nasty clang underneath the car. However, a visual inspection in the car park revealed nothing hanging or dripping underneath, so we proceeded to enjoy our walk, holding hands and gazing at puffins. Aaah! As opposed to aaargh which is quite a different sound.

After our walk, there was still no evidence of anything untoward below the car, though it was hard to be sure on an earth surface dampened by recent rain. We motored towards Bridlington, where fish and chips awaited.

On the outskirts of the town, the auto box started to behave abnormally, as if with clutch slip or too high a gear selection. When we parked, before I could even crouch at the front of the car again, a pedestrian pointed out that "something's coming out of your car, mate." It was the auto gearbox fluid, which is cooled on many vehicles by passing through a separate chamber at the bottom of the main radiator.

There was no choice but to call for recovery, via the RAC. Go out in a Merc, come home on a recovery lorry. Welcome to my world.

As we waited for the truck, munching fish and chips, Janet laughed. Clearly it would be wise to tempt this amiable woman with matrimony, whilst such escapades were still a novelty.

The insurance claim turned into a saga. I drove up to Flamborough a few days later after work. There must have been a big pothole at the bottom of the dip, hidden by the angle of the road. This looked to be the case; however, it was also the case that very recent roadworks had filled it in.

After several letters, finally resorting to the threat of the small claims court, East Yorkshire council held up their hands, and we progressed to a valuation of the damage. The engineer that came was very pleasant and polite, but too much of an engineer as opposed to an assessor.

Gleefully, he prescribed a course of action. To get the car via recovery truck to my garage (i.e. Doug), bypass the gearbox coolant part of the radiator, and see if the car ran all right. It might only need a replacement radiator!

What?!

Mate, this thing's already been playing up. The damage to the gearbox has occurred. Not to mention the battered panel below the radiator, which was evident upon closer inspection. He seemed to think this 'might beat out'.

I bit my tongue and went along with the crazy idea. It was as if the assessor was operating on the principles of bangernomics to save his own money.

Doug got Gary from East Hull Recovery to collect the car, and it sat at his garage for a week or so, until he phoned asking if I had a spare key for it. Well I did, amazingly enough for an auction car, but only one which was dodgier than the dodgy one I usually used to start the car. Small batteries had been replaced in both, with zero effect on their random effectiveness.

Naturally, the second key produced no joy down at Doug's, and we were at something of an impasse. He could not commence to follow the insurance assessor's edict if the car could not even be driven into the garage. The transponder in the key sends a signal to an ECU, in the driver's mirror of all things, on that model, and electronic permission to explore the UK's excellent road network is then granted. I missed the days when anyone could get into a Cortina with a screwdriver and drive away by the simple expedient of touching the correct ignition wires together. My habit of taking the rotor arm with me whenever I left the car unattended for any length of time was a bit of a chore, but not half as enraging as possessing a sophisticated limousine which remained moribund at the whim of a recalcitrant transponder or microchip.

There the car sat. I spoke to the Mercedes agent. A new mirror would cost £300. Time went by.

I went back to Doug's. The car sat outside. Silently. 1600 quid's worth of aggro locked in paralysed mockery.

"Doug, I think I'm going to have to get the car to Mercedes and fork out the 300 for the mirror. As it stands, I've got nothing."

He looked at me, sympathetically yet with the hard-edged realism born of many years in the increasingly over-technologised world of modern vehicles. There wasn't an ounce of sarcasm in his voice as he pronounced his wise verdict, in the manner of a Zen master offering an answer to his acolyte, in the form of a riddle.

"At least you've got nothing."

I went away to meditate upon the teaching.

What he meant was, you will take it to Mercedes. They will change the mirror. £300 please. Sorry, that didn't work. We will change something else. More hundreds of pounds please. And so on.

He once told me of a nearly new Vauxhall, top of the range model, which sat in a garage in Grimsby, its wiring all stripped out, hanging everywhere. Nobody had been able to solve its niggling electronic issue. Doug's thesis was that the man clever enough to isolate the problem was too busy designing such systems, being paid five times as much as a lowly garage 'technician', to be available to tackle such an individual glitch. The logic is inescapable. Every so often problems crop up, which exceed the capability of those employed to solve them. Meanwhile white-shirted reception staff act as gatekeepers and credit card hooverers while the hapless customer is forced to accept the corporate shrug.

I later tracked down some Mercedes specialists, two lads who had worked at Mercedes and later started their own company.

Bob and I got the car and keys to them and they managed to effect a soldered repair within the 'good' key, enough to get the car mobile again. Doug did the radiator bypass and we had at last reached square one.

A payout was forthcoming, with the added bonus of somebody from Lancashire, a taxi operator, buying the written-off car from me for spares, for a surprising sum. It must have been worth it to him, immaculate but unusable with its wrecked gearbox. The lengthy episode had been a trial, but overall perhaps easier than winkling out the requisite pimp or drug dealer to clinch a sale.

My other project, around this time, was to get the Phoenix road legal. With the Striker, I had driven to MNR Racing for a set-up session, after chatting to Mark Norden at the kit car show in Harrogate that year. The difference was marked, with the car far more compliant and thus more usable afterwards. The corner weight settings would have been ruined when the Crossflow took the place of the V6 for 2007 of course, but that year only highlighted the advantage of being able to drive the car locally, even just to find out whether sparks or fuel was the area to work on before investing in track time. And of course you could go to work in the car now and then for a bit of a pose. My colleagues appreciated the source of amusement.

Convinced of the benefits, I set to; proper seats were made up, with wooden bases and the help of upholsterers. I trailered the car to Jeremy's works, now in Horncastle, where he made and welded in some SVA-friendly seat belt mountings and straightened a slightly bent chassis member which must have dated from the Cadwell prang.

Amongst the plethora of mechanical clutter from two lock-ups, re-homed after the departure of the Fury and the Striker, I uncovered the Fury's engine, a ready-made fit for the Phoenix, with successful SVA provenance in its previous location.

I bought an old Capri from a university student, to cannibalise it of four wheels. Their old style higher profile tyres helped to raise the critical headlamp height, and with the camber adjusted to the extreme to provoke at least a modicum of self-centring on the steering, the SVA was negotiated. Incredibly, I recall no snags thrown up by the test.

I then remembered that there was a 750 Motor Club Kit Car Championship going on, and turned up at Cadwell in May. A standard tune Crossflow in a very light kit car makes a fairly nifty device for enjoying the country roads, but is however completely outclassed on the racetrack by equivalent cars that have larger, more modern, or race-tuned engines. My progress, particularly on the 'Mountain' uphill bit, was akin to the children's parable of the steam tank engine pulling far too many carriages, as it chuffed up the hill.

"I think I can, I think I can, I think I can…" Cheerily, I kept to the side and waved at the passing contenders.

Anglesey followed, another picturesque and enjoyable circuit where I had plenty of time to watch the world go by as I learnt the track. It was a jolly expedition, enjoying the luxurious accommodation of the ancient Renault Trafic van. It was fine as long as you were prepared to stop along the way occasionally, to check and possibly top up the coolant. Nothing dampened my spirits at this time. One day, a week or two later, Janet, seeing me staring wistfully into space as we relaxed in an intimate setting, questioned me with a smile.

"What are you thinking about?"

"The best line through Rocket Corner at Anglesey."

I did get away with that one.

Once.

During the race meeting, I confided in Patrick, that I had a new dalliance. He kindly offered advice based on the benefit of his experience. Just remember, he said, the three little words that will enable you to maintain a harmonious relationship. The three little words that every woman longs to hear.

"Yes, my dear."

I skipped a Brands Hatch meeting in favour of the cheaper option of everyday life, and turned up next at Donington.

Unabashed by the pedestrian spec of the power unit in the car, I did my best and had fun. I was thrilled that I was capable of reeling in the penultimate running car – on the downhill Craner Curves section. Of course there is an uphill section shortly afterwards, and given that the rest of the track is at least approximately level, the benefit bestowed by gravity on a very small proportion of the circuit did not enable me to unsettle the front runners. Or in fact anyone.

So I would have to do something. This was a year in which the rules had been changed to accommodate the up and coming kit car engine of choice, the Ford Duratec. We now had three classes – Duratec plus the V8s; Zetecs; and 'everybody else', a small bunch including myself. In fact I believe I was almost the last surviving Crossflow participant at this stage, apart from Nic Scott.

Nigel Brown, our formula official, had been the pioneer in installing a Duratec, and was talking about selling his Zetec stuff. I spent a very pleasurable trip home from Donington convincing myself that taking the opportunity to modernise my set-up would be a good move. In fact the speed demon on my shoulder didn't have the slightest difficulty in convincing my rational self; it was simply a matter of being seduced by the idea and enjoying the experience. The miles flew by.

On arrival home, I contacted Nigel, only to have my hopes dashed. He had already done a deal to trade his newish Zetec engine to Andrew, a lad who was competing with us that year. His car had the Ford CVH engine, which was a bit outclassed. Whilst outclassing mine of course, but I doubt that was much consolation to him.

Sometime later, Nigel was back in touch. He *did* have an older, but useable, Zetec. Was I interested in that? Had the Pope had a mild flirtation with Catholicism as a possible career choice? Nigel would buy his engines as a new item before making the necessary mods to run them in the race series, as opposed to being a disciple of the 'it's done 100,000 miles in a taxi but it'll probably be OK' school of thought. Actually, I've had good luck with ex-taxis as road cars but that's hardly the point. The engine was a known quantity, even though it was his earlier one. So the planets lined up and a trip to Birmingham was planned.

At the bottom of the garden behind Nigel's home, I was shown a large garage where he would work on his race car. This building extended far enough back to accommodate six cars fairly easily, in two lines of three. This was theoretical, as one side of the garage was filled with multifarious mechanical clutter including older race cars, semi-disassembled. Gratifyingly, at the far end, a large shelf had been constructed; this was home to another chassis and/or bodyshell. I think. It's a few years ago now. Plus of course the obligatory dusty boxes to obscure the treasured objects and further intrigue the casual visitor.

In fairness, the objects perhaps weren't necessarily 'treasured'. Rather, they had probably 'ended up there'. It doesn't actually matter. One can only leave such premises filled with a deep and abiding admiration for a man who is prepared to construct a shelf to store one car above another. Magnificent.

Nigel's nobility as a *garagiste* extended to offering a more than fair price for the engine, and I headed north with carburettors, induction and exhaust plumbing, and some coolant hoses into the bargain.

The Zetec installation would have to wait until the close season, as I had found the time to rebuild the 1600 Crossflow race engine, which would slot straight in. A bit of an oddball hybrid (in the original sense of the word), it used flat-topped pistons from the 'pre-Crossflow' Ford engine of the same family. This would not normally work, as the Crossflow has the combustion chamber formed in the top of the piston, rather than in the cylinder head as is more normal. However, by using con-rods from a 1300 version, the piston doesn't come up so far, which leaves a very shallow cylindrical space at the top of the travel, to act as the combustion chamber. It was a backstreet tuners' mod from 'back in the day'.

Fascinating, but only to petrolhead anoraks, as my future bride made clear. Strangely unimpressed, she confined her car knowledge to the use of an ignition key. Precise use of technical terminology, if required, extended no further than the word 'scoosher' to describe the screenwash system.

Undaunted, I slotted the race engine back in, crowned with the Weber downdraught carb on a 'crossover manifold', the latter being another period mod which had worked OK on the Fury. Testing the car with a pleasurable summer run to spectate at Harewood Hill Climb, it felt quick and perky. I allowed myself to bask briefly in the cleverness of having made the car road legal.

We went to the next opportune race meeting, which took place at Oulton Park, one of my favourite circuits. Although she had driven independently to watch at Donington (key, turn, go) this was the first race where Janet accompanied me on the journey. We stopped over at my mother's in south Manchester.

The paddock chat was convivial. The atmosphere jovial. Less so after practice. The car was awful. No matter what I tried. Nothing had changed since the trip to Harewood. It missed, picked up, and missed again. The air turned blue. Not from oil fumes. My future bride laughed. She explained to Steve Taylor, who had paused to sympathise, that I would be allowed a further fifteen minutes of chuntering. Max. And then had to behave in a civilised manner. In the absence of further ideas, I used about thirteen of the chuntering minutes before resignation set in.

The race was no better than practice. Miles off the pace and last again. This was still good enough for fourteenth, not too auspicious for the formula, as the break-even point of an average eighteen entries was hanging like a Sword of Damocles. To an extent, in club racing, the more popular formulae can subsidise the strugglers, but such elastic does not stretch forever. Maybe the recession was biting. The hysteria of greed-obsessed bankers halfway across the world had impinged on our idyllic little scene. Ninja mortgages, how does that work? No Income, No Job At-all. Investing in the prospects of becalmed and desperate people with less sense of fiduciary responsibility than a lobotomised mongoose.

I concluded that the carburation was the culprit. Whilst fine on a fast road run, a race was a different matter, with such a high percentage use of full throttle that the induction system simply could not cope with the demand. So, a lesson learned, but an annoying one, as Oulton had been and gone, and was a rare occurrence on our calendar. With my whinging time exhausted, I was forced into an attitude of at least resigned acceptance, if not outright jollity, as we journeyed home. Behaviour modification. Probably better for the blood pressure in the long run.

Whilst unloading the car and driving it into the garage, I became aware of a new issue. No oil pressure! Cognisant that low pressure is not the same as low level, I nevertheless poured a bit more oil in, to see if it made a difference. And a bit more.

The pressure came back, but at the cost of an overfilled sump. The engine should really have come out, but without much time before Snetterton, I hadn't the heart. It was only one race meeting…

It won't take a vast leap of the imagination for the diligent reader to jump ahead and conclude that the season was to end with the, by now familiar, ignominy, parked on the grass at the side of the back straight at Snetterton. And although practice was OK, and I managed six laps of the first race, that is indeed what happened. Nic Scott, the other Crossflow runner, managed less than one lap. The end of an era.

I later sold the engine to Phil, a Crossflow aficionado. He thought he might use it in a kit car one day. At the time of writing, nearly ten years later, I don't think he's yet got around to stripping it. House moves, domestic upheavals, life… I'm expecting that he will find that the oil pickup, a clever rotating design that swings with centrifugal force on cornering to combat the risk of starvation as the oil surges in the pan, has some sort of crack in it, which was submerged by the overdose of oil. But there is a reason why dipsticks have an upper marking, which is the drag factor.

Whatever. Here we were again, towed back to the paddock at Snetterton. With technology, and life, seeming to move on ever faster.

12

Diamond Rings and Other Things

Denise had quite rightly bequeathed almost everything she possessed to her four children. The only exception to this was a ring with a substantial diamond in the middle of it, which she gave to me. Her father, an entrepreneur from Libya who progressed from being a bookie's tic-tac man, via importing cotton to Manchester, to eventually owning a department store in Kingston, Jamaica, as well as a quarry and other interests, had left it to her mother, a working-class Mancunian woman who had never really coped with his high-flying lifestyle. Divorced and in the doldrums, she clung to this ill-starred talisman, which Denise felt had brought nothing but jealousy and avarice to the maternal side of the family. Hence Denise's desire not to pass it on to her children.

We found an old-fashioned little shop in Hatton Garden, almost a time warp setting amongst the sharp bling of the glassy modern showrooms. The proprietor was prepared to offer us a price. A Hungarian émigré, he was a wry and worldly-wise character whom we liked. I think the amount was in the region of £1650.

And I spent most of it on the Crossflow. Which did not

complete one successful outing. Perhaps the diamond was indeed a bringer of sadness.

That and being too bloody lazy to take the engine out.

But time and life move on, which is a blessing, since there's nothing else. The slightly cavalier attitude towards engine development was falling down a bit too often now. Especially at Snetterton. But I had a distraction, another activity to concentrate on. I'd never played the 'Will you marry me?' card before, ever. Perhaps in this arena I would have better luck.

And so it proved, the bonus part being that for the next seven months, I could manipulate conversations around, at every reasonable opportunity, to include the words, "My fiancée". It was a once-only opportunity, a period which would never come around again, during which I could use the superbly mellifluous phrase, and I was determined to make the most of it.

When we told my mother, she paused to weigh up this momentous news, before delivering her verdict in the understated and dry manner I knew so well.

"It took you long enough."

Some of the winter period was usefully devoted to clearing the decks in the garage and installing the Zetec. More involved than the Crossflow job, but not too daunting. The main demand being for persistence rather than perspicacity…

I had sold some V6 bits to Chris, a guy with an old TVR, who lived a couple of streets away from my house. On his side of the main road, the council had provided funding to enhance the area, with many of the houses receiving new frontages involving UPVC windows and front doors, as well as neat walls at the pavement, and brickwork where needed. He advised me to hang on in my house, as there was a feeling that my area would eventually receive the same treatment. Firmly anchored by a garage full of clutter and an abiding inertia, I had cleverly done nothing, and, sure enough, the grant had come through. Builders' vans and red and white barriers proliferated along my street.

There was one 'snag'. This grant did not extend to UPVC window frames throughout the street. Rather, cheaper cosmetic improvements, plus the odd new wooden front door, were the order of the day.

But wait. I knew the top of my bay window was suspect. A tradesman working for my neighbour had seen the dodgy state of it when up on a ladder. Thankful for the tip, I had responded with further inertia. Use of a metaphorical bucket of sand in which to bury my head had also been my trusted strategy when considering the encroaching rot in the window frames themselves.

The policy of doing absolutely nothing paid off in a big way. The bay windows, both up and downstairs, were deemed by the surveyors to be in too poor a condition to be repaired. And because there was no budget for UPVC, complete new window frames in the original material, wood, were deemed necessary. One off, bespoke items made from scratch for my house. Work that one out.

Because making and renewing the bay windows wasn't a five-minute job, the house had to be made secure whilst the windows were out. The contractors achieved this by securing large boards to seal across the front lounge and front bedroom, dividing the space in the rooms by half. This meant moving all furniture back into the remaining halves of the rooms, and in the downstairs, into the rear lounge area as well, to compete with the existing clutter.

I would come along in the evenings after work, and in a tiny remaining one-metre-square of space in the rear lounge, change into several layers of old working clothes, whilst absorbing what heat I could from the wall-mounted gas fire nearby. Then do an hour or two in the garage, then come back to my little square changing area, before going back to Janet's house. Sometimes she would meet me at my house if she had been working at the hospital nearby. There would be Little Jack Horner, in his corner, changing as rapidly as possible, in view of the prevailing temperature, from garage gnome to normal human being.

Despite the Arctic conditions, this gnome-alone period was fruitful and even perversely enjoyable, working in small but focused sessions. And it also had the useful secondary effect, as the future Mrs R watched me shiveringly change out of my woolly hat and outdoor layers in the gnome corner, of demonstrating to her my true proclivities. Having seen all this, she could have no future complaint that the demonstration of marital goods had in any way misled regarding the terms of the Night-time Use of Garage Act.

The engine transplant was completed in good time and the car was ready for the season opener, Snetterton in March. One modification was to the bonnet, where it had to lose the svelte lines from the Crossflow period. Not wanting to mess about with fibreglass sculpting, I grabbed some aluminium sheet and formed a more substantial 'power bulge' to cover the Zetec, riveting it in place. This would lead to comments in the works car park alluding to having assembled the car from 'bits of an old washing machine', which I felt to be somewhat cruel. I at least had a ready reply to a colleague who wondered if it was a convertible. Laughing as he asked, I presumed the question to be banter.

"No, Gary, it's open *all* the time. There's no roof, so it can't convert to anything else."

I remember almost no detail about the season, which indicates a good degree of reliability in the car. Turn up, drive, have burger, have banter. Just the way I like it.

Snetterton saw only ten finishers. More worryingly, from only eleven entrants. Ninth was good, beating Anton in the first race, though with him being two laps adrift, he was clearly grappling with a mechanical issue. But finishing at Snetterton was fine with me, and a proper ninth in the second race saw me ahead of Bruce Brown.

Mallory saw a similar showing, not really denting the Crossflow lap times from 2005. History then records a 10th May outing at Cadwell, which will have necessitated a relatively short honeymoon, having been married the weekend before. Great day by the way, Janet.

Entries were still around the sixteen mark, even for Brands later on, which didn't bode well for the kit car formula. A second weekend of Cadwell races followed Brands, a perfect calendar both geographically and in fun quotient. Icing on the cake followed in the shape of a meeting with the NSSCC Championship at Oulton Park. Like Cadwell, challenging and not too far to get to. Two races, swapping positions with a Seat Ibiza, Toyota MR2 and Fiesta XR2, were great fun.

In the mixed bag of runners here was my old mate Brian Healey, who had tired of one too many nudges near the front of the 750MC kit car melee spoiling his weekends. Also Paul Collingwood in a Sylva 'R1OT', who would later join our championship, and Chris Huntley in a Subaru. At the time Chris's name didn't mean anything to me, but that would later change.

I skipped single outings at Silverstone (expensive), Snetterton (holiday in France) and Mallory in October (cold). And that was it.

A good season, though I hadn't found a marked difference in pace. The car would have been a bit heavier, but more power outweighed that. Was I coming up against a self-imposed glass ceiling, a limit to what I was comfortable with? Enzo Ferrari, as we have said, famously thought his drivers lost an edge once they became seriously embroiled with a woman. Surely not?

I was still having fun, especially at the Oulton outing, where a tussle with others added a bit of spice. And the way I looked at it was this: I didn't feel that I was especially slow. Just that quite a lot of others were quite a bit quicker.

13

Behaviour Modification

I made a considered decision not to race in 2010. My mother needed to move to smaller, sheltered accommodation, so there was a lot to think about. I knew we'd be over in Stockport a lot, and so it proved, three weekends out of four in some months, organising, visiting or removing. When not occupied on that side of the Pennines, we began the renovation of the parts of my house in West Hull which had hitherto been used to store car bits, such as a spare, decoratively challenged, bedroom, a downstairs extension that had once been a bathroom, and indeed the kitchen.

My old slab-fronted Renault Trafic had gone, replaced by a slab-fronted device called a Vauxhall Arena. Which was a badge engineered Renault Trafic. Since it was an Arena, and since my football-playing teenage neighbours were always kicking a football in its vicinity, I christened it 'Wembley'. I'm not in the habit of naming my vehicles, but this opportunity was too inviting. The local would-be Beckhams, when challenged, claimed that our street was a valid stage for their window-threatening antics owing to the preponderance of discarded syringes in the local park a mere ten minutes away. I suspect, rather, that the ten-minute walk demanded too much commitment, but it was a difficult argument to refute without spending time on park research, time which I did not have.

I plied across the M62 in various conveyances; the Mondeo, my wife's more comfortable Picasso, Wembley, or occasionally a larger hired van if we were doing a focused run to Bredbury Tip with my mother's old but valueless furniture. Wembley was only a short wheelbase, and his 1.8 litres made him a plodder compared to his LWB 2.2 Renault predecessor, even including the latter's pit stops for coolant. And hired Transits, and especially Ivecos, were like spaceships in comparison.

The one place it didn't matter was what I called the lobotomy zone on the M62, twenty-five miles or so of roadworks lasting several years, with a 50mph limit, during which the thoroughfare was converted to what I think they call an intelligent motorway or smart motorway. This involves making the former hard shoulder available to moving traffic and providing the odd lay-by for emergencies. So if you own a vehicle which may conceivably break down (which equates to any vehicle, notwithstanding modern advances in technology), then you do need to plan your breakdown to coincide with one of these safe havens. If not, you become a pawn in a game of wakefulness between a CCTV watcher and an East European lorry driver who last slept two days ago in the bar of a ferry from Zeebrugge. At the very least, get out of the vehicle as quick as is humanly possible for yourself and your elderly and infant passengers.

Back in the days when I ran about in classic bangers as opposed to just bangers, I once found myself travelling from the north Manchester area back to Hull, in the small hours. Nowadays I pay the insurance known as RAC as I am more able to afford it. Then, I habitually relied on a bag containing a cross-section of tools, chucked in the boot. Wary to the point of superstition, I would never dare to declare to a passenger that 'the car's running really well', after the words had been followed in short order, on two or three separate occasions, by the stuttering, shuddering, misfiring, imminent total disobedience of a recalcitrant mechanical servant who had hitherto been treated with nothing but love.

In this instance, I had broken my normal rule of travelling only in daylight, and dallied with the pal I had been visiting, for some games of snooker. Hitting the road at about eleven, the MG Midget made it as far as Pontefract before expiring. MGs of that era had electric fuel pumps thoughtfully positioned inward of the right rear wheel, where they could be peppered with as much grit and mud as reasonably possible. The *right* rear wheel, note. Maybe MG felt that since nine out of ten buyers, incredibly, were American, the law of averages would better serve them if only hapless Britishers were obliterated by slightly off-line juggernauts whilst lying next to the carriageway trying to reach a loose wire somewhere just inboard of the back wheel.

I think the only reason I was brave enough to wrestle with the fuel pump until about 1.30 a.m. was because the traffic had become quite sparse by then. I remember thinking, I've had a good run. If it does end here. A good life. If a lorry veers over a bit. It'll be quick. Over quickly. And I've been lucky. Where's the wire? Luckier than many, can't complain.

A train of thought (the squashy bit) I had never had before, and have never, touch wood, had since. Thanks, MG.

Thanks to a ticking noise when I moved the live feed one more time after over an hour of struggle, I was able to seize the chance to bumble through another twenty years of life, for which, notwithstanding its doldrums and tribulations, I was unreservedly grateful. And here I was now, trundling along in Wembley, with plenty of time to think.

And what I thought about quite often was where the racing was going. This was what I term leisure thinking rather than work thinking, house-renovation thinking or mum's-house-removal thinking. I've spent many happy hours returning from race meetings over the years, whiling away the miles with leisure thinking, often involving the revision of air ducting to brakes. We all have our fetish. Blasting out *Exile on Main Street*, or, if particularly weary, the Ramones at high volume, and having a eureka moment about where to locate an intake and associated pipework. It's like being at one with the universe in a Zen bubble. Admittedly quite a specialised universe.

Some of the entry lists in the kits had been sparse of late, and I felt that the formula was, sadly, under threat. My deliberations began to focus on possible alternatives. A train of thought which built up a head of steam on a downhill gradient.

Within the 750MC there were three categories of interest. RGB (Road-Going Bike-engined) were in a way, the next class up from kit cars, faster and more frenetic, with the light, high revving motorbike power units. They had started, back in 2002 when I was first coming to 750MC meetings to watch and dream, as a 'toe in the water' class to see if there was enough interest. I remember seeing an RGB race at Cadwell with about twelve entries, virtually all Westfields and Fisher Furys. In other words, kit cars adapted to take motorbike engines. The category rapidly attained championship status, and was now heavily populated with rear engine Le Mans prototype look-alikes, purpose designed. Something like eleven grand would have to be found to join in using anything remotely competitive, bringing with it the great joy of learning curves relating to bike engines, paddle shifts, chain drives and the like.

The next on the shortlist were Locosts. Based on the book *How to Build a Sports Car for £250* by Ron Champion, these were bare-bones Lotus 7-esque cars with a basic 1300cc Ford Crossflow power plant. The £250 amount was by this time only really achievable if you had a factory unit full of square tube, welding kit, and an old Ford lying in the corner, rusted beyond all hope of revival. But the thought was there, and they were, in a way, the next step down from kit cars. The fact that they all had to run identical low-powered engines, and have identical bodywork with the aerodynamic finesse of a de Dion Bouton, meant that momentum was all, with a lot of slipstreaming. And it was not uncommon to see more than one Locost being unloaded from the recovery truck after a race, with a front or rear corner in crumpled semi-detached condition having been savagely deprived of its newness.

I gravitated away from the kit-like choices towards Toyota MR2s, for which there was a thriving class. Most were the Mark 2 shape, substantial coupés which looked to offer a lot more metal between the driver and the accident than Locosts or Formula Vee single-seaters, the other 'same spec for everyone' classes.

By pure chance, I had acquired an MR2 from a colleague at work, Pete. This decision had taken form in a sort of evolutionary manner without much logical planning. In fact without *any* logical planning, really. I suppose I was aware of the existence of the MR2 class in 750MC when I bought the car, but that was as far as any track-based thoughts went, when I was walking towards the car park with Pete one day after work.

I mentioned that I had seen a Nissan 200SX for sale on eBay. In spite of it being an unusual non-turbo model, according to the description, it still looked like a smart example of a model I had always fancied during its nineties youth. Ready to plunge with my 800 quid, I had contacted the seller, but had been beaten to the punch by another punter who had seen the advert before me. Que sera.

Pete said that, if I was interested in that kind of thing, why didn't I buy his old MR2? He used to come to work in it, but had now moved on to an Audi TT, so the MR2 languished. I could have it for £200.

I was 'interested in that kind of thing' in the way that domestic cats are interested in a mouse if they can't find a bird, which they will mess about with even though there is a perfectly good plate of Whiskas or Felix which meets their dietary needs. It was easy to go and see it, it was easy to get 200 quid from the cashpoint, it was easy to enjoy the thrill of the chase, even though I hadn't been putting much energy into chasing anything when the prospect suddenly dangled. My wife tolerated it all with the puzzled demeanour of a normal citizen who believes that ownership of one vehicle is enough to meet her transportational requirements.

I think 'going to see it' may have been included in 'going to collect it with cash in pocket', since I knew the vehicle from the works car park anyway. No matter. Janet ferried me to Gilberdyke, a few miles away. The car required a jump start, there being a known battery issue. The current from the leads must have magically transferred itself to Mrs R's eyebrows, which raised in direct correlation with the operation of the starter. Money and car changed hands and she followed me to the nearby petrol station. Pete had pointed out that a tyre or two might benefit from the life-giving ministrations of the service station airline, which was mercifully in working order. She sighed as she watched me crouching next to the new object of worship, no doubt feeling that Pete, the rogue trader, was meanwhile counting his £200 with a devilish cackle, having unloaded this perfidious jalopy onto her naïve and innocent spouse who had drifted into his carefully cast net like a herring.

We left the fuel station and headed home. Janet followed me for a mile or so, before peeling off to visit her sister, who lived nearby. I had made the decision to use the ordinary back road, rather than the A63, which would have taken me home more quickly. Although a busy dual carriageway, it did not benefit from a hard shoulder. With the car a bit of an unknown quantity, I felt the quieter road might offer a safer plan B.

The car got as far as the top of a hill near South Cave, before dying. Pleased with my plan B, I was also fortunate to be near a grassy entrance to the compound of a communications tower which is situated there. I coasted into it, there to enjoy the company of the odd disinterested rabbit whilst I pondered my next move.

Grateful to be part of the mobile phone age, I began dialling. My second call was to Janet, still at her sister's.

"I'm up on the hill by the transmitter, waiting for the AA. Watching some rabbits."

I then had to wait for a reply.

Probably four or five minutes. I could hear, in the background, that Janet was explaining the scenario to Lynne and her family. I could hear the gales of laughter.

Eventually she came on again, still laughing.

"Could you maybe come this way on your way home, just to see if I'm OK?" The pathetic plea made her laugh all the more. Little Jack Horner, still in his corner. But a very pleasant corner. Peace and quiet. Summer evening sunshine. Rabbits. And the odd sheep.

Janet curtailed her visit to Lynne's by zero, but did finally turn up, and we sat in her reliable car to chat. It wasn't too much longer before the arrival of the AA man, who soon spotted the frayed electric lead which dangled near the exhaust. The lambda sensor feed, I think. After rigging a temporary connection, he kindly followed me home. I was at this point on the family AA membership, which I later discontinued after an incident where Wembley locked me out of himself with his engine running. I rang for them to come to the house with an expert door-opening implement, but ended up putting a brick through the quarter light when they never showed. Wembley had become hot and bothered owing to his rad fan failing to kick in, and was never quite the same afterwards. After some postal tirades, the AA paid me to go away with my grievance, at which point I felt it politic to bow out of the family membership, lest

Janet and her daughters were forever compromised by my fleet of patrol-sapping degenerates.

With the MR2's wiring issue sorted, attention turned to the battery problem. After studying wiring diagrams and battling to find obscure fuse locations, the culprit was tracked down, being the switch which triggered the boot lamp. The bulb had been permanently on, enough to drain the battery when the car was left for two or three days.

There was a cost to this satisfying victory though. After crawling in and out of the car several times to mess with under-dashboard plastic covers, I was tipped over the edge and flung a small black bit of cosmetic plastic to the floor, where it shattered into nasty sharp bits which I had to track down on hands and knees. This normal level of penance was augmented. The accompanying colourful turn of phrase quite shocked Mrs R, who had been in the nearby kitchen. I was now living with her in genteel suburbia, and my prowess at stringing six swear words together without repetition, seen as mere eccentricity in West Hull, could no longer be viewed as tolerable. Behaviour modification.

Although the endearing small coupé, with its red paintwork lacking a degree or two of newness, had now been rendered reliable after the replacement of a couple of tyres, the whole episode was to have a lasting legacy. The car would forever afterwards be known as Donkey, a christening gleefully latched onto by Janet's neighbour and friend Tina and her two daughters. I later formalised the piss-take by sticking a decal found on eBay to the side of the car. It was similar to the black bull AGIP trademark, but was a donkey. Not a bull.

With Wembley and Janet's reliable Citroen Picasso ('Pablo' obviously), things were now getting silly for someone purporting to be unsentimental about vehicles. The original blame lay with Janet's daughter Rachael, who owned a Rover. Ralph the Rover, I ask you… The only bastion of common sense was a green

Peugeot 406 I got at the auction. £200, towards the end when a lot of buyers had drifted away. Tow bar, naturally. And all it ever cost me was the replacement of tyres and exhaust. It would forever go by the name of 'The Peugeot'.

After the retraining concerning forms of verbal expression, and the redundancy of the term 'MR2', I was able to start enjoying the energetic charms of Donkey on the way to work. Was that really 90mph on the 'Cadwell Park simulator' stretch of B road? Surely not. So by the time I had a chat with Patrick Mortell, proprietor of Rogue Motorsport, whilst spectating at a summer Cadwell meeting, I was ready to be convinced of the merits of joining the 750MC MR2 Championship. Patrick was heavily involved with it, providing or looking after cars for several competitors. He explained that my car was an early version of what I call the 'Mark 2' shape, within which there were several 'revisions' over the years of production.

Mine being an early one, it had a lighter bodyshell. (Good.) No sunroof. (Good.) No power steering. (Good or bad depending on your point of view.) The 138bhp single cam engine, not the later twin cam with 172bhp. (Bad.) Fourteen inch not fifteen inch wheels. (Probably bad.) And so on.

I went away to think about it. Leisure thinking was still allowed and could not be policed.

14

Tin Top Terror

The seed of MR2 perusal having been firmly planted, I spotted an ad on eBay for a cheap MR2 which could be rebuilt for track use. This turned out to be posted by Chris Huntley, the guy who had been racing with NSSCC at Oulton when I was there. He ran a business in the North East based on breaking and repairing MR2s, which were then in the affordable price bracket between recent production and collectable sports car. Hence the strength of support for the 750MC race car series.

A trip north was arranged, and he showed me the advertised car, which somebody had managed to squeeze between two trees on its way to the ditch. It was a Category C insurance write-off. Categories C and D are, broadly speaking, cars written off as being beyond economic repair, by the insurance industry. However, they can be returned to regular use, possibly subject to an inspection at a ministry site. The two Mondeos and the Granada I had run in recent years were such cars. It's a fairly cheap way of motoring if you don't mind the repairs, which may be just cosmetic, and the compromised resale value.

The close arboreal encounter had been with more than just the layer of bark, judging by the re-sculptured doors, and the underside of the vehicle, seen from under Chris's ramp, had also taken a pummelling from more than the odd large dandelion. Explaining that the bruised woodland wanderer would be 800 quid, Chris mentioned another car that had come in since the advert was placed. This was a Category D, more lightly damaged.

In fact, I could hardly see the 'damage' to the front bumper on this second car until it was pointed out, and compared to the first example it was like a new car. The only drawback was the 'Targa' roof – two removable transparent panels either side of a steel spine which ran over the cockpit in a nose to tail direction. The race regulations prohibit glass panels, so they would have to be replaced. Notwithstanding this, the extra £200 on the asking price over the first car seemed a small price to part with. The 1000 quid had effectively burnt through my pocket on the short walk from the workshop back to Chris's office.

There followed an extensive discussion, effectively a planning meeting. I would buy the car, and Chris would do the work necessary to get it race prepared. The major issues were the installation of a roll cage and the replacement of the Targa roof. And much detail including paring down the wiring and providing basic ignition and cut-out switchgear. It was a new approach for me, but I knew if I tried to do even just the detail work myself, it would drag on and I would miss half the season. A happy bunny drove south along the A1 later that day, with much leisure-thinking fodder to munch on and fuel the delightful plotting.

The weeks that followed included a trip to Demon Tweeks in North Wales, taking my mother for a ride out from south Manchester. I think she enjoyed the change of scenery, waiting patiently on a seat in their showroom as her hopelessly addicted son allowed his bank balance to be syphoned. Rule changes compelled a replacement helmet, new overalls were a good idea, and a race seat was chosen to be shipped up to Chris. Mother's reserved inscrutability had, if anything, increased in these years, and it was difficult to be sure what she made of it all. For someone with a tendency to stockpile smoothed-out brown paper bags from the local bakery, it was probably like visiting another planet.

Chris managed to sort the roof issue with the help of a bodywork specialist, by cutting the equivalent roof sections from a non-Targa scrap car. Neither was the roll cage, though obtainable as a component item from a specialist, a straightforward job for him. His view of that supplier was usefully noted for future reference, shall we say. I was increasingly glad of my decision to delegate these things to someone who had time, experience of the model, facilities and expertise.

Chris felt that there would be no weight penalty by going with the Targa bodyshell, since there was no obvious extra strengthening by the Toyota factory, as viewed from below, over the plain roofed model. Having said that, we never got the car down near the minimum weight allowed in the regulations, so there was something funny somewhere. When I saw someone at the first race meeting, with an earlier car, who had fitted the spare wheel in the front luggage area as ballast to help the handling, I wondered a bit. But it was too late by then to change track.

I agonised for ages about the heater equipment, which is naturally quite a weight, finally acquiescing to the weight-saving argument and giving Chris the go-ahead to remove it all. Racers I later saw had fitted little ducts and vacuum cleaner motors to blow 'hot' air somewhere near the screen. Reinventing the wheel as a threepenny bit. With my car being Category D, it had the bonus of being easy to make road legal, in fact if I recall, Chris got it MOT'd up there before it was delivered to me. And it was quite fun to drive on the road. When the weather was dry. Which meant it was unuseable for half the year.

I later (much later) took a half day off work and extracted

heater matrix and pipework from a scrap MR2 in the salvage yard near York, in order to rectify this shortcoming. With this Targa-bodied car being down to nearly a bare shell, I could see the extra steel in the overhead spine part – maybe this was where some of the extra weight was. Oh well, spilt milk. Obviously the earliest model mated to the last engine would have been the way to go. You live and learn. As seasons fly by… A basic rule for life and motor racing.

I've still got that heater matrix and pipework in the garage, come to think of it. If anyone wants it…

Another tip for your track-day builds, if you are of that fraternity, is to avoid race seats with high sides at the hip, especially if your car has a roll cage which impinges on the door profile. The item looked good in Demon Tweeks' showroom, with sensible extra support for cornering. In the low-roofed MR2 bodyshell, it engendered a head-first ingress, going over the transmission tunnel to start with, then reversing lower body parts down into the seat in whatever order could be crammed after they had first been folded into the car's confines, octopus-like. With none of the astonishing ease and fluidity that an octopus will display in its natural habitat.

The egress, as they might state in a Haynes Manual format, is the reverse of ingress. And the less said about that, the better.

The various tribulations were overcome in due course, with Chris labouring valiantly amongst welding and grinding kit, hand tools and workshop dust, whilst I sat in warm lorries with trainee drivers to earn the money to pay for it all. One auspicious day, the last spanner was twirled, the final payment made, and I awaited its arrival. The lad with the recovery truck was efficient and chatty, and we unloaded it on the street outside my house before I drove it around to the garage. It had even had a tickle with the polishing cloth, and I basked briefly in its gleam. It's not every day that you can say you've just had your new racing car delivered. Old boy. Even if it wasn't actually new.

Once I'd got the legal details organised, and the car was useable on the road, it migrated up to the marital residence in the suburbs. There it would sit on the drive, its shiny black paint easily outgleaming that of the faded red Donkey. Poor faded red Donkey! There was just one snag. It was still an MR2, and Tina and her daughters, unaware of the finer points of its mechanical superiority, wasted no time with a christening which they saw as entirely appropriate.

Poor Black Donkey!

The advent of this prized contender led to thoughts of how it might be transported to its track-burning destiny. With Wembley now out of the picture, sold to the salvage yard, I needed a more substantial vehicle. The Peugeot saloon might be fine towing a kit car on a trailer, but the MR2 was probably twice as heavy as the fibreglass racer, and those pesky laws of physics might feel inclined to prod the tail into wagging the dog. So the tow vehicle had to be something heavy, which meant a four-wheel-drive land cruiser style thing, or a Transit-sized van. The latter would offer small hotel capability, so the choice was easy.

With Ivecos ruled out by Mrs R on the grounds of hugeness, and the Renault/Vauxhall family barely considered, I paid a visit to my brother north of Manchester, and spent the following day at one of the big auction sites in the Ardwick area. A vast area was devoted to the moving of metal; in fact it was on or near the site of the old Belle Vue Zoo, if my geographical recollection was accurate. Appropriate for seeking a travelling companion for the anthropomorphic Black Donkey. A small white whale, perhaps?

Two fleets of Ford Transits were going through, so it wasn't like travelling to see one at a private house, or two or three at a dealer's. And they would find their true value as determined by the swarming dealers and odd private punter. No overblown asking prices or unrealistic expectations. There were crew vans with seats and a table, in the older 'slopey-front' shape, and standard high-tops with the following year's 'slopey-front with more sinister-looking headlamps' shape. All with tow bars. The later ones had the additional benefit of being shelved inside, though with doors locked so you couldn't inspect the detail.

I ended up with one of the latter type, hand up, card over the counter, deal done. Possibly the newest vehicle I had hitherto owned. With about five years-worth of peppering from grit and stones in its previous habitat on work sites near railway depots. I paid the bit extra for delivery, and met the driver outside Bob's workshop unit a few days later. He must have been chosen from the expert level of auction drivers, who are qualified to cope with not having much of the left side mirror left.

A replacement mirror unit wasn't too dear, as it was a model which eschewed the powered adjustment option. Shrugging at the minor inconvenience, I moved to the back doors, newly presented key clutched in eager hand. The shelving was interesting. It did consist of wood joined together, but I was not convinced that it merited the status and title of actual shelving. Sure, there were enough pieces of wood positioned *almost* vertically and *almost* horizontally to see that someone had made an effort to assemble 'shelving'. That someone was obviously a drug-addled monocular vertically-challenged person wielding a bent set-square, and saying the 'shelves' were *almost* horizontal was, frankly, being rather kind in its description. The whole edifice brought to mind one of those artfully designed trick rooms where a disguised taper makes the person at the far end of the space seem as though they have drunk from Alice in Wonderland's bottle.

Blinking and shaking my head, I closed the door on the embattled scene where all principles of perspective had met their tragic demise. Redesign might be necessary. At least there would be the pleasure of knocking it all out with a hammer, to enjoy. And not a particularly weighty hammer, as it turned out.

The van was gradually sorted, with Doug giving it a service and check over, and eventually the addition of some large marine ply panels which folded up onto the inner sides of the van when not in use. The original wood panelling was not by the shelving guy, and stout enough to support extruded aluminium brackets with bolts, over which the panels would slot, to be held by nuts. They could be folded down, hinged onto substantial wooden 'legs' bolted to the floor at the sides of the van, and another panel hinged downwards from them to form a central support. The two supports would then be bolted together so that the 'bed-shelf' could not collapse, and we were in business. Tool boxes went underneath, so that inexorably, I became more organised, and probably ridiculously over equipped, on trips away. It was strange to gradually abandon the 'chuck in whatever you can think of at random' school of packaging, which had served so well for several years.

The first meeting, for this slick new *equipe*, was to be Brands Hatch in April. Mrs R chose not to attend, feeling comfortable within a smaller diameter range when it came to van transport. Running in good time, I paused at Peterborough services for a snack. When I came out, the most newest factory-built vehicle I had ever owned would not start. Old Toyota Supra had always started. Newer but still old Peugeot 405 had always started. Ex-taxi with moon-mileage Nissan Primera had always started. Ford Mondeo estate from the salvage yard had always started. Ford Granada from the salvage yard had always started. Renault Trafic van that sat at the entrance to the salvage yard and hypnotised me into buying it had always started. Wembley had always started. Peugeot 406 in a shade of green that wasn't quite Racing Green but a Slightly Slower Green had always started.

And the newest most new with the least newness worn off it vehicle I had ever owned, just sat there. Starter churning. Basking in its five-year-old lack of oldness.

I phoned the RAC. Followed by Mrs R. Remember the tale of Red Donkey, when I phoned from the top of the peaceful hill? How the phone was put down whilst laughter took place? Laughter didn't take place this time.

"Er, Janet. It's me. Whilst I'm waiting for the RAC, could you just find and book a hotel near Brands Hatch?" Laughter most certainly did not take place.

It turned out to be a hairline crack in the fuel filter housing, causing a loss of pressure. The most newest new new vehicle I had yet owned, with its high-pressure common rail diesel technology, went on a recovery flatbed, to a garage in Peterborough, with the trailer on tow behind. Having got the racecar off the trailer whilst waiting for the truck, and chucked a few tools and a couple of fuel cans into it, I now set off for the A14 with a jaunty demeanour. After all, I still had one of the three four-wheeled devices I had set out with.

The Premier Lodge Inn place that she found was fine, with a restaurant next door. Perfect. Setting off early for the track next day, I found the MR2 area and had a walk round, trying to find a gap next to a sympathetic face. The sympathetic face was that of Mr Lennon's grandfather, who was helping with his grandson's car. Perhaps the competitive gene had skipped a generation. This kind fellow, Bob, later helped me with repositioning the transponder, which had failed to give a good hit rate in practice.

My main focus in practice was, fairly obviously, to keep the car in one piece. History shows a whopping six cars behind me on the grid, but neither was I remotely near the front. The first race was a heat. Given the popularity of this championship, there were to be two heats, which would then determine the fastest runners to go into two final races. Or something. Events became rather disarrayed later, as we shall see.

Off we went in the heat, which was like any normal race, but with the knowledge that you had to finish really at least halfway up the field to stand any chance of competing in the first 'final'. There were a few Mark 1 MR2s in the race, one of which was driven by Nina Fountain, a pleasant young lady who was more frequently to be seen at meetings in the orange overalls of a marshal. Today she was having a go at the sharp end, and was sharp enough to get ahead of me in the first lap argy-bargy. I would have to overtake in order to set off after a few more cars in the vain hope of qualifying for the final.

Now, you would think that Nina, with her marshal's expertise, might be aware of the general rule, on the subject of blocking, that, put succinctly, if you are ahead of a competitor who is trying to overtake, you are allowed to zig, but not subsequently to zag. I still remember her skill in completely ignoring this rule every time we came up the hill to Druids corner. Accepting that this cavorting was merely rubber-stamping the inevitable outcome of my forlorn hope to overtake about half the field, I still had a good chuckle as we zoomed round. At least I was getting my hand in again after a year off.

After a bit of rest and refreshment, I decided to watch the first MR2 final, and made my way to the grandstand which overlooked the start/finish straight and Paddock Hill Bend. The front runners were battling in close proximity over the first two laps. I had already heard, in paddock chit chat, that there was a strong rivalry, to the point of 'needle' between Chapman, the previous year's champion, and Bgatov, a Russian driver. These two were running three abreast, with Wilkinson, a fast lad in a Rogue Motorsport car, as they approached Paddock Hill at the end of the pit straight on lap three. Wilkinson was sandwiched between the other two, with Chapman on the inside.

Not one of these three seemed prepared to compromise and back off. It was getting late to make the decision. This was club racing, for goodness' sake.

Chapman started to move to the left to take a wider line for Paddock. Only trouble was, he was not fully ahead of Wilkinson and his tail end caught the front right of the Rogue car. Tipped left, he came across Wilkinson and now contacted Bgatov. Becoming locked together they left the track in an instant. Bgatov, now beyond control like Chapman, was squeezed between his rival's car and the barrier, and somehow got launched. I have a vivid recollection of seeing the underside of his car for a brief instant as it went by below me.

Chapman's journey to Paddock Hill ended in the gravel after seemingly going end over end, the car finishing, wrecked, on its wheels. He was later seen around the paddock with a mere bandaged forearm.

Those of us watching from the grandstand didn't see much of that accident though, being transfixed by the unfolding horror of Bgatov's flight. He was high off the ground, the car a missile, in a grim demonstration of the amount of kinetic energy that can be released by a 100mph racing car when everything goes totally wrong. There was in fact a very high wire fence here between the paddock area and the track; but there was also a gap in it, to allow recovery vehicles and the like to get onto the track. The car flew through this gap and finally landed in a tarmac area beyond. It was an area where the track vehicles would park, I think, but people could freely wander through it. Thank goodness none were doing so at that moment.

The car landed upside down. Thankfully there was no fire and the driver was eventually helped out and taken to hospital. Some days later, he was said to be on the way to a full recovery.

Mooching about for a while, talking it over with other racers and their friends, I thought it all over. Racing would be stopped for a while, clearly. There was a meeting of the MR2 competitors called. With Bgatov's situation apparently not life threatening, a vote was taken, to see if they wanted to carry on.

Most did. Once the gathering was over I walked to the admin office and told them I would be withdrawing. The prospect of a qualifying heat held no appeal. It was a long way home and a lot had happened.

I got on the road north, noticing the cracked windscreen that had been the result of a flying stone. Not exactly an incident-free weekend.

The next meeting was at Snetterton, the first time out on the new '200' circuit, where basically the fast and challenging Sears corner onto the back straight had been turned into a hairpin followed by a nadgery 90-degree left, for no particularly good reason. The rest of the circuit was the same except for Coram curve having a bit of interest taken away with a new line. Oh, well.

Janet made the trip this time, and Mel took advantage of the free ticket I had sent, so joviality was the order of the day. I didn't advance up the field much; it was beginning to feel like there was a bit more to the car specs than met the eye. There was a guy next to us in the paddock who was even more 'middle-aged' and slower than me. Quite a feat. He was absolutely disgusted with it, convinced that it was not the level playing field it should have been.

It had always been the intention, when Chris and I were planning, to just go out this year and get the feel of it, before spending money on modifications. There were things that were allowed with springs, for example; I felt that lowering the car as far as possible within the rules would be a sensible first move. Some people put thicker oil in the standard shock absorbers. Bilstein upgrades could be fitted, but they were very expensive. Engines were supposed to be to standard specification. Supposed to be. I think it was at this meeting that the winner's car, after the second race, was said to have blown the engine as it was driven on to the trailer. How highly strung was that then? I told Nigel Brown the tale later.

"Perfect," he said. "Perfect." He was right. It's the ideal goal for a race car. To be so highly strung and fast that it just lasts long enough to win the race before it blows up and falls apart. The acme of refined design, to *just* achieve its purpose. As long as you've got the funds for a replacement next time out.

But the day was fun.

Some people were trying very hard. Wilkinson managed to beach his car on its side near the end of the back straight, where the bridge is. There was then a flurry of activity in Rogue's paddock area to straighten the car out before a commercial windscreen-fitting company arrived with a replacement screen. If you think about it, getting a Mark 2 Toyota MR2 to end up on its side, when you look at its curved flanks, is some achievement. Yes, quite a feat.

I missed an outing at Mallory. Come to think of it, I had taken the car down there to a pre-season test day early in the year. So perhaps the van's average reliability had been a little better than the one breakdown every 100 miles that I figured after the Brands trip. I went to Peterborough to retrieve the van and trailer, after the repair, in Red Donkey, putting the car on the trailer for the return trip. Very civilised.

Whether the test day at Mallory had put me off racing there in the MR2, I can't recall. There were certainly a lot of people in hatchbacks, in our tin top session, doing their very best to exceed the limits of their braking capacity into the hairpin, so that they could get some welding practice and late nights done, before the season started.

We were probably just on holiday that weekend. Whatever the reason, the next outing was at Donington. It was to be a single long race, for double points. A double-edged sword. Which, since I didn't care about the points anyway, was in my opinion just a chance for things, if they went wrong, to spoil your weekend more thoroughly.

Janet came along, as did her other daughter Hannah, who had a ride down from Manchester with her boyfriend. They would join Ben in the ranks of people who came to see me race at Donington, or even race at all, but didn't.

Practice was hectic. After the corner known as the Old Hairpin, which isn't a hairpin at all, people were accelerating away from me fairly easily. I was convinced that it wasn't just down to corner exit speed. Perhaps I just wasn't caning it enough. It's always difficult to isolate the detail, to get a definitive conclusion within the minefield of ego involvement. Not to worry. I would just keep doing my best and see what happened.

What happened was an interesting start. Qualifying low down the board, I had most of the field ahead of me on the grid as we lined up. Taking a deep breath as the red lights came on, I psyched myself up. Half an hour of intensity lay ahead. It would be hard to concentrate for so long, with my limited attention sp… er, sorry… oh, yes, attention span of a gnat.

Off we went. The car was accelerating well, full throttle. But… everyone else was accelerating better. Getting away. My revs weren't dropping though. Far from it. The penny dropped. I had momentum, but wouldn't have it much longer. Clutch.

Now I was able to make a good decision. This shows how experience is helpful. In 2006 I had dithered as I came round onto the pit straight, with the engine already rattling, and missed the pit entrance. Then after a piston made a bid for freedom from the engine block I had dithered again about whether it was safe to park at the pit exit lane, and left more oil on the track until I peeled off into the gravel at Redgate corner.

Using that learning experience, I now used my meagre momentum to get over to the left and dive in to the pit exit lane. Safe enough in the circumstances, nobody there. Parking the car at the side, I got out and told a marshal what had happened. All that remained was to use the concentration span to push the car back through the paddock. And wonder if some people actually have a racing career where they never have to push the car back through the paddock.

We enjoyed the rest of the day, anyway. A bit of a trip away to do a bit of car pushing with friends and family is often fun. More involving than fishing, for example.

When I got back, the car was taken to Doug's for clutch replacement. One drawback of the MR2 as a hobby car is that the engine has to come out from underneath, very hard to arrange safely in a home garage. On the other side of the coin, it's relaxing to have to delegate to the professional mechanic, with his hydraulic ramp, while you have cups of tea at home.

Chris could obtain a race-oriented paddle clutch from the USA, for not too much more money than the standard item. Without experience of such things, I was a bit dubious to start with. A normal design of clutch had always sufficed with the kit cars. When Doug got the engine out, he contacted me regarding the clutch. I had "better come and have a look at it."

The thought of going with another standard clutch died out as soon as I saw the remains. Even the metal pressure plate was in three pieces. Doug said that the existing clutch that was in the car had not even been a very worn item. Apparently a customer had seen it lying in the garage and asked what car it was from.

"You should tell that owner he needs to modify his driving. He must be an absolute hooligan."

"Well, I can't really," said Doug. "He's in a race series."

The paddle clutch turned out to be fine in fact, nowhere near as sharp as I had feared. I'm not hard on clutches. Honest. But the MR2 was a fair bit heavier than a kit car. And I had been having to try hard...

Next outing for the absolute hooligan was Silverstone, just beyond Mrs R's range this time. I did a steady first three laps in the practice session, getting the feel and making sure of qualifying for the race. Time now to up the pace. Vroom, excellent. I saw smoke coming up from the bonnet ahead of me. Of course it's not an engine cover in the mid-engined MR2, but something was happening in there.

I saw a tarmac area on the right, with a gate that led off the track, and a Marshals' Post nearby, and immediately pulled over. This was getting really good now; I was chuffed that my quick-wittedness and pulling-over skills were so sharp.

Getting out and beckoning to the marshal, I spoke to her in a calm manner. The excellent pulling-over skills had bought a bit of time.

"Do you possibly have a fire extinguisher handy?"

Chris had fitted an electronic kill switch from a reputable supplier, for reliability. The common cable-operated ones, which pull a plastic flag-shaped lever which trips the switch, can suffer from corrosion after a while, making them hard to pull. Not a situation the scrutineers and marshals are fond of. The electronic one bypasses that eventuality, and kills the circuit by switching the earth return.

In this instance, something had shorted somewhere, and lots of little electrical atom thingummybobs were getting very hot and bothered trying to find their way out of their confinement via the electronic cut-out module, which was in the process of melting when we got the bonnet open.

Although a loose HT connection in the engine bay was found to be the originating fault, the incident left me less than keen to use an electronic kill switch from a reputable supplier, ever, ever, ever again. After returning home, I replaced it all with the simple crudity of a cable and flag switch.

That constituted the preparation for the trip to Pembrey in South Wales. I always enjoyed Pembrey, and the final meeting would be at Cadwell. With only one of the first four meetings I had attended having avoided the occurrence of some sort of mechanical disaster or horrible incident, if I did well at Pembrey and Cadwell I could turn the season into a moderate one of three good three bad.

And Pembrey went well, in spite of an understeer excursion at the tricky and fast Honda curve in practice, after which I pitted due to an unmistakable amount of wheel wobble. The issue was solved by taking one of the front wheels off and cleaning off the significant proportion of field that had stuck to the inner rim. Tractors are for fields, racing cars are for tarmac.

My mate Tony Gaunt was at the meeting. Now in the RGBs, he had developed his own car, starting with a Sylva R1OT chassis. He commented that the front-running cars looked rather more planted than mine coming through Dibeni corner, and the young hotshots were leaning on them a lot more. Probably lower on their springs, I thought. With Tony's bit of coaching in mind, I leaned on it a bit more through Dibeni in one of the races. Whoops. That'll be a nice roly-feeling pirouette then. At least I was trying.

The first race was notable for Wilkinson punting the back of another car so hard, somewhere in the scrum going into or out of the hairpin, that the radiator was clearly going to be wrecked. I came past him as the pack went by. Within a microsecond, he was off the grass and full in my mirrors. Carry on, mate, if you're that bothered. He managed to overtake about a third of the field before the second corner, which isn't that far away. Red mist is powerful stuff. Clearly, his race would be a short one, but he managed quite a bit more distance before coming to a steaming halt at the side of the circuit.

Even though I had finished nearly last, I felt I had done the best I could have, and still enjoyed the weekend, so my spirits were buoyed for Cadwell. Here, we would have a qualification race. I can't recall the intricacies except that I needed to finish not last and not second-to-last, to get into the final. It was rather an unfair system, which they modified the following year. Nina, in the only Mark 1 car, was the unlucky one at the back, leaving me needing to pass Mark Warren-Leighton to get through. Committing myself to a lunge in the braking area at the end of the back straight, he was fortunately alert to my presence, and away I went. Crumbs! An actual overtaking manoeuvre.

The races were reasonable, achieving a last and a penultimate. I will confess to a slight feeling of disappointment as I politely clapped the championship achievers, people I didn't really know, at the end of day gathering. Clearly my car needed a massive injection of red mist to get me anywhere even near the middle of the field. Or more specifically, a weight-saving programme (difficult), a blueprinted engine, modified springs and performance shock absorbers.

And ideally a driver about a third of my age who had prepared by doing a few years in karts.

Leaving aside the driver issue, the modification side of things would add up to quite a large financial effort.

I have come to the conclusion, from this experience and through observation, that formulas which purport to offer a level playing field, are something of a misnomer. In fact, in the real world, there are many participants who are only interested in winning; fair enough, it's racing. But they will do whatever is necessary to achieve it, through testing, development, use of a car provided by a professional team; anything to get that edge. And because the cars are specified to be 'equal', money will be spent on the ultimate modification allowed within the rules. So at the time of writing, for instance, people are said to be spending six grand on Crossflow engines for Locosts. Locost being something of an ironic term in this context.

Taking some consolation from the positive outings at Pembrey and Cadwell, which had raised the season to acceptably moderate, I came to some sort of accommodation with my modest but nevertheless un-effaceable ego. Even though I was not the sort of driving prodigy who could transcend even equal odds, never mind long ones, I was happy that I had given my best effort. Satisfied with this, I relaxed as the season drew to a close.

There had been a kit car race at Cadwell. Allowing for the presence of three SR and GT class cars bolstering the grid, a total turn-out of twenty-two still left nineteen kit cars, with two or three refugees from the defunct Tiger and Westfield championships coming out to play. Nigel Brown had been doing a good job in making them welcome.

Perhaps there was hope for the kit cars after all.

Hmmm…

15

Phoenix from the Flames

2012 was excellent, finishing fourth in the Zetec class despite only doing seven races. Nearly a prize! I pipped Spike Buckland, our old friend from the Guild event to Florence back in 2002, by one point. He had bought Clive Hudson's old Phoenix. Like mine, it was a survivor from the early 1990s. Old racing cars never die…

When I say nearly a prize, I mean only thirty-three points adrift of Adrian Cooper in third. Never mind.

We were often put together with the Sports Racing and GTs, to make up a decent grid. Kit cars were now known as Sport Specials, and though numbers were still hovering around the critical eighteen mark, there was still a chance the revival might gather a little momentum, after the recession-hit doldrums of 2009 and 2010. I found the greater variety of cars added some interest, and even at the slower end of the field, there was more chance to find an SR & GT straggler with which to have a bit of a ding dong.

Missing the first three races, I joined in at Cadwell in May. Sunshine, a race each day of the weekend, wife and family along, good craic, fabulous. You can't beat it. I arranged to buy some new tyres from Mr Polley, whose van was in attendance, and brought the spare set of wheels for them. Staying on the old set for Saturday's race, I changed the wheels at leisure, and was well psyched up for Sunday. I remembered going to Pembrey a few years earlier and seeing a big improvement, seconds, after fitting a new set of tyres. Today would be the same. Having posted a best lap of just under 1.53 the day before, this time I would be down in the forties, threatening to beat my best ever effort of 1.49.

I did improve. By three tenths of a second. Oh. Not quite what I had hoped for. In a flash of inspiration, I attributed the inexplicable similarity to an absolutely superb driving performance in the earlier race on the old tyres.

Next up was Donington. In my best ever start, I hooked everything up perfectly, overtaking Mark Bowd in his GT40 replica on the left, then Spike on the right, climbing two rows up the grid and about three places better off by the first corner. Stupendous. Although I didn't quite hang on to the placing during the race, I had attained legendary status, never to be forgotten, in my own mind.

Tony's wife, Heather, asked me at a later race meeting, if I could think of any tips for Tony, who was often qualifying well with the RGBs, but then losing ground at the start, and having to make up places just to get back to his original grid position. I was able to draw on this epic Donington effort in reciprocating his help at Pembrey the year before, and provide some carefully considered coaching advice.

The Phoenix's Zetec, although a relatively modern generation engine, had a carburettor intake system featuring twin Webers. Less predictable than a fuel injection system, it was important to avoid any fluffy moments and not to have the revs bogging down as the start lights went out.

"Tell Tony, that what I do whilst sitting there on the grid, is to pretend I am a teenager in a Vauxhall Corsa in Tesco's car park, looking across at my mates in another Vauxhall Corsa;

and just dance on the pedal, going RRRMMM RRRMMM RRRMMMMMMM. It works for me."

We went to Anglesey next, beginning a marital tradition of booking a campsite nearby for a couple of days after the meeting, and grabbing a couple of days extra holiday. A beautiful venue with friendly paddock staff who made up for any lack of gleaming newness in some of the facilities. It seemed the club was entering a phase of doing a Welsh round in Anglesey one year, Pembrey the next. If it had only ventured up to Knockhill in Scotland, we could have claimed the championship was truly an international series. It was a damp practice and I took advantage to get further up the grid than usual, fourteenth on the seventh row, with no less than 5 cars behind me. Chuffed.

With best lap times in the dry race of the order of twelve to thirteen seconds quicker, I was overhauled by some cars, but still managed to finish ahead of Mark in the GT40. In the second race I finished in a dizzying fifteenth place, but only by attrition, with my mirrors empty. Racing driver's euphemism for a specific finishing position relative to the rest of the competition.

In both of the races, I couldn't quite catch Charles Best in a well-driven Westfield Lotus 11 replica. We would have another couple of duels, with the same outcome, next time out, which was at Donington again. In the second of these, our best laps were within a hundredth of a second of each other, and we crossed the line, at the end, only half a second or so apart. He went astonishingly well in a car with only 1275cc.

I had entered a phase with the racing, where I pretty much turned up, got into the car, and went out and enjoyed the driving. I like reliability. OK, the car wasn't the fastest thing out there, but when you see people come to meetings, blow up or break down, and maybe struggle with issues on and off all year, it does make you glad it's not you. Then again, sometimes they solve the issues with midnight oil and sweep to multiple victories the following year.

One should never count chickens though. The season was to conclude at Mallory, and the meeting I think included a replacement race for an early season race at Donington which was snowed off. I remember booking a hotel and losing money on it one year, though it seems an odd fixture list that featured Donny *three* times. The precision of recollection is rendered irrelevant by my lack of participation…

We were in October by this time, with the predictable cold early morning as we got ready to join the queue for scrutineering. Weber carburettors are fitted with a choke facility, for cold starting, but it was common, even universal practice to just pump the throttle five or six times once the ignition was on, as this seemed the best way to coax them into life even under cold conditions. The car eventually started, but was as fluffy as an infant kid's bedroom full of bears, for quite some time. Teasing it up with some throttle, I got it running enough to try driving forward. It would clear itself eventually and the drive to scrutineering would help to warm it up, which in turn would finally result in a crisp throttle response.

As it turned out that day, a crisp throttle response would never happen. White smoke emanating from the bonnet in thickening wisps, would happen.

Remembering the similar time at Brands Hatch, I wasted less than a second thinking 'oh no not again' and even less time in outright denial that this was happening, even though I dearly wished I could linger in disbelief. Even though rules had changed so that a plumbed in fire extinguisher was mandatory (the hope being that it would give the driver time to get out, rather than necessarily save the car), I still kept an old style hand-held one in the cockpit. Climbing out and freeing it, I aimed it through the air intake, near where the carburettors lived. A few people spotted what I was doing, and somebody helped me carefully raise the bonnet a small amount to get at the source of the fire. With two people arriving with other extinguishers, we succeeded between us in putting it out.

I later asked for the club bulletin to put in a request for these people to get in touch; I could at least pay for an extinguisher replacement or refill. But nobody did. Like the Lone Ranger, they galloped off to the distance. Or maybe Leicester. But thanks anyway. I don't believe my single extinguisher would have been enough.

A flame spitting back had ignited one of the 'sock' style air filters that sat over the intake trumpets. Once that was on fire, burning quickly spread to the other three. And that was that. Although things could have been tidied up, and maybe the car run without filters, I didn't feel it was a wise move, so packed up and withdrew to fight another day.

At least there would be a car to bring out next year. The Phoenix had risen from the flames. Again. Perhaps racing cars shouldn't be named after incendiary birds.

During the winter there was just the one project: to rebuild the carburettors and redesign the air intake system. I found a backplate that fitted between the air trumpets and carburettor intake throats, and used it to draw up a basic design for an air box, from which a wide diameter tube ran directly forwards. At this end, a single large air filter could be mounted, well away from any intimate proximity to fire-spitting Webers. Then Patrick Shears, whom I had got to know when he built me a larger fuel tank during the phase of getting the Phoenix street legal, helped by welding the components together. All I then had to do was bash some aluminium into a half-tunnel shape and get it to mate up with the 'power bulge' aka engine cover in the middle of the bonnet. My work colleagues already thought that this resembled something wrought from 'bits of an old fridge' so I couldn't really inflict any more aesthetic pain upon the world. In fact, with it coming further forward and lower, I felt the new design to be a rather sleeker and more beautiful 'bit of old fridge'.

Most of this work took place in the car port at the side of Janet's house, where the small garage had never seen a car. But there had been room to transplant my bench from West Hull, and in amongst the wardrobes, garden equipment and freezer cabinet, I beavered, happy to behave in a seemly suburban manner.

With Peugeot, two MR2s and a van outside the house in various combinations, a fair bit of vehicle juggling took place between my new and old homes. Something had to succumb to logic, even for me. Red Donkey was the unfortunate candidate. With no tow bar capability and with less pose value than the black one... sorry, I meant to say, more saleability than the black one. Doug had taken the car in for a timing belt change over the Christmas period, and when a water pump bolt snapped, it turned into an engine out job. Dear Red was now the most expensive cheap MR2 in town, but I had to be ruthless.

So, the eBay button sealed his fate, which was a new life with Keith, a paint sprayer. Strangely, in a publicity exercise for Keith's business, his airbrush artist partner used Red as a blank mobile canvas and painted him to look like a barrel. Yes, a wooden whisky barrel. You couldn't make it up, but they did. The car was eventually bought by a woodworking business and Keith later did a couple of spray jobs for me. Old MR2s can be a surprising driver of the economy, the government should take notice.

The first race meeting of the year was not until late April, at Brands. Very civilized. Charles Best and I spent a fair bit of time poring over a very accurate Porsche 917 replica in the paddock. It was in fact coming out to race with us in the SR & GT class.

Its owner, Graham Turner, spent some time chatting to us; he was a mine of information on the 917's history. Thinking about drivers like Rodriguez lapping the old Spa circuit at record speeds in excess of 160mph was mind-boggling. And in that tiny cockpit... Did you know that Porsche used titanium bolts with the centre drilled out, to save weight?

Graham warned us that issues with his gearbox meant he would not be very fast, and so it proved. To add to that, there is an amusing photo on a website which shows me going past him at the apex of Druids, with him facing one way and me the other! Not the kind of car you want to drive into. What an attitude though, to have a car like that and come out and race it.

Two unspectacular drives brought fourth in class in both races. Guess how many Zetec-class cars were out there? Exactly. Enjoyable though, sharing the track with a great variety of interesting machinery. Both races were won by Rob Johnston, who had joined our championship back in 2004, with a Ford Pinto-powered Locost. His dad Alec almost always came along to help with the spannering. Rob was a fast driver whose early experience had been in stock cars on ovals, where the Pinto engine was more commonly used.

Now, he had moved to the Duratec class, with a self-built car called a Cyana MX500R. He had done a 'Cyana Mk2' for Anton as well. With Nigel in his Phoenix, and three of the rear-engined Eclipse make, designed by competitors Clive Hudson and Paul Boyd, out at this meeting, the Duratec class was growing and starting to sometimes outnumber the Zetec runners. With a 'Class C' to cater for 'everything else', the Sport Specials née Kit Cars seemed to have turned the corner and become a formula with a solid core of competitors. A praiseworthy job on Nigel's part.

Pembrey in mid-June was the usual fun. Spike had a different car, a yellow and red Sylva Striker inevitably christened Noddy. The Phoenix had gone to Marcus Roskill, fellow Guild veteran but new to our championship. Into the mix as well came Bridgette Smart, Spike's girlfriend, with a red Phoenix which had come from a successful sojourn with Dave Caldecourt, a talented mechanic and driver who had originally got the car from Tony Southgate, a famous designer of top-line racing cars who had enjoyed a bit of driving competition in the kit cars a few years earlier.

Bridgette, commonly known by her nickname Billy, was no slouch on track, and had finished ahead of me at Brands, but I got ahead of her in the first race, with Marcus and Spike further up the road. The second race was streaming wet, giving me the opportunity to execute actual overtaking manoeuvres on Spike and Nigel, which was enough of an ego boost to keep me on a high for months. Pity about the other sixteen cars in front... Rob ran away from everybody, particularly in the wet race, where he had had to start from the pit lane. Fantastic effort, meaning he had now won the first four races in the series.

At the end of June, we were due at Donington. The past year in particular had seen an increasing involvement with my mother's affairs, for myself and Janet, and my brother, who lived closer to her in the Manchester area. She had had a couple of brushes with pneumonia, but rallied after the worst had been feared. Janet and I had seen her in hospital a few days earlier, when, although she was quite chipper and lively on waking up, she had provided a black comedy moment as she grasped our hands, one at each side of the bed, and, wide eyed and urgent, had exclaimed.

"Janet!! David!! Have they sent for you?!! Have they sent for you?!!"

We laughingly reassured her that no such summons had been issued, or thought to be remotely necessary. A few days later she had spent all afternoon laughing and joking with her friend, before passing away in her sleep during the night.

My brother phoned on the Saturday morning with the

news. He urged me to go on with the race meeting; there was nothing that needed to be done there until the following week. Fortunately we had all day to get to Donington for the races on Sunday, so the feelings could be digested as we busied ourselves with the preparations.

The turn out for our race was quite low; perhaps people were on holiday. With no Marcus, or Spike and Billy, we just had Colin Benham, the Cooper brothers, and myself starting in Class B. Perhaps I could pick up some useful points. I had, for this year, booked to do all the races for once.

Adrian Cooper ran into some sort of trouble early in the first race. I saw his car at the side of the track. With Colin involved in a coming together with Lesley Wilson's Eclipse, that was him on the sidelines. I could not help thinking that I was, as a result, SECOND IN CLASS! Astonishingly, I then caught up with Paul Cooper, who slowed markedly, as if impeded by a celestial hand, on the straight leading to Melbourne Hairpin as I cruised by. Crikey! Could it be that I would win a triumph after a scintillating display of being the only one left? It was not to be. The celestial hand turned out to be sticking brakes, which benefitted from another bout of divine intervention in unsticking themselves, and Paul caught and passed me on the last lap. Bless him, he was almost apologetic about it afterwards!

In the second outing, Colin was back in the fray, but Adrian, potentially the fastest Class B runner, found himself out of luck again with a DNF. Paul's brakes, meanwhile, stuck good and proper, and he trailed in nearly two minutes behind me. Second in class again. Everybody was amused to see me presented with two trophies on the same day, and I took the opportunity to make a brief thank you speech about two sentences long. Theme – if you keep turning up, one day something might happen. On this one day, I had tripled my career total of racing trophies. Isn't mathematics wonderful?

Weirdly, I was also running second in the class placings for the series as we approached Rockingham for two races on the 13th and 14th of July. It was unlikely to last, but I was determined to hang on as long as I could. With Marcus back and going well, just behind Colin, the clawing of the gap had begun. But I had two good outings, my usual humiliation at the hands of Charles Best's bijou Lotus replica being reversed in the Sunday race when I caught up enough to enact a rather ungentlemanly lunge down the inside as we were about to turn in for the hairpin behind the pits. No harm done, thankfully.

We were at the Silverstone 'International' circuit towards the end of August. This is at the other end of the track from the 'National' circuit, and has nothing overlapping with it. I found it a much more enjoyable and involving layout. I tried to catch up with Lesley and Billy, but their cars were simply faster in the drag race down Hangar Straight. For once it's not an excuse but a fact. A bit frustrating in a way. Clearly my road legal, slightly heavy, not very peakily tuned car, was like a duck with its legs flapping madly below the waterline, compared to… well, almost everyone else really. Pesky swans.

We headed to Donington with Marcus having narrowed the points gap from twenty to two, so the coup de grâce for Class B runner-up would be delivered over the weekend. With the championship's final positions being based on the best twelve scores, persistence had its limits, with one's two lowest scores discounted if you did all fourteen races. I now had to watch out for Billy coming up on the rails. Hunt v Lauda 1976 paled into insignificance.

In the first race, I was held up behind a Ginetta G20 driven by an occasional entrant in SR & GT, Stuart Gibbons. He had been out at Brands earlier in the season, ahead of me, but I was 'on one' today, right on his tail. There was no profit to be gained from overtaking, I was well adrift of the other Class B cars, but this was a motor race, and we were fairly evenly matched. With his car fairly well positioned at the corners, and my car's lack of pace, I had to think of something else. Using a random selection of lines on the approaches, none of which had any chance of getting into the corner ahead of him, I was nevertheless giving, I thought, a reasonable impression of an absolute lunatic. Shortly before the end of the race, I was rewarded when his car twisted into a lurching spin out of the Esses before the pit straight, and I was through.

Not long afterwards, I discovered that I was 'Not-Classified', along with Stuart and another car, on the results sheet. Surely a mistake, as I had gone past the chequered flag. Perhaps the chequered flag guy had gone home by the time I arrived. Not normally a complainer, I had become a championship points junkie this year, and went to see Giles, the competitions secretary, in the office. The mistake was rectified and I picked up the seven points available. With my two lowliest results over the year being sixes at Silverstone, this was to have a significance later on. Squeaking home ahead of Stuart, and Martin Tyman in a Taydec, in the second race, I started the eager anticipation process for Cadwell in mid-October, where the actual chance of an award would be finally decided.

A chap by the name of Alan Robinson had been chatting to me in the paddock at one of the Donington races. I thought he was just an interested spectator, but I later realised he was one of the Guild crowd. And more significantly, that he was interested in buying the car. Crumbs. With my perception of the car being influenced by the perception of others from the 'bits of old fridge' school of description, I was astonished that anyone else would seriously want to own it. I viewed the car as being more backyard banger than Bauhaus, notwithstanding any affection I held for it. And it was the car I've had most of a soft spot for, something I rarely feel over a mechanical device.

Not only did Alan see the inner beauty beyond the much mauled bodywork of the sparkle-deficient Cinderella, but he also came bearing cash. He declared to me that he had an amount of money which, to my ears, sounded about fair. He also had his trailer with him, and we could do a deal after the meeting. Received wisdom in racing circles is that, when buying a racing car, you should always do the deal immediately after the last meeting. That meant that the vendor had no chance to get it home and take the best parts off it before collection. So Alan was being worldly wise here. Sadly, I didn't like to disillusion him, but there weren't really any particular 'best bits' on the car for me to be worldly wise about keeping. I said I'd have a think about it when the meeting was over.

There was another factor at play in this grand equation of fickle fate. Rob had mentioned to me that he was building a new car for the following season. That meant the current one, the 'MX500R' would be for sale. Would I be interested? I'm not sure if Rob expected any serious interest from me when he said this, or whether he was skilfully planting a seed of mechanical lust in the fertile ground represented by the owner of the apparent slowest car in the series.

I out-qualified Billy in the practice session. Times were very slow, so my vague recollection is backed up, in that it must have been pretty wet. The rain increased later in the day, to the extent that our race would be cancelled. We were due one race on the Saturday, one race on the Sunday. With the first race gone, surely this meant that I was home and dry, as Billy would be unable to complete twelve races, giving me a comfortable margin.

Janet stayed at home on the Saturday, but planned to come down in her car on the Sunday. With the heavy rain setting in for the night, I weighed up the options. Chewing the fat in the bar and then listening to the rain on the van roof all night, or commuting back home and coming back in the morning after a good night's sleep in a warm bed. Commuting won easily.

With a febrile mind in overdrive I motored towards the

Cadwell gates. Nobody might ever offer to buy the Phoenix for a fair price ever again. The money would go towards Rob's car. Which was potentially competitive. I would go for it! I would do it.

I was about 200 yards along the road to Louth when I had another thought.

I couldn't.

16

Onward and Sideways

Earlier in the year, I had been corresponding with *Practical Performance Car* magazine. This was as a result of them asking in the mag if any readers wanted to join them in forming a team to tackle the Birkett Relay. This is a famous race that takes place at the end of the season. Devised originally by Holland Birkett, one of the founding fathers of the 750 Motor Club, it gives competitors quite a lot of racing time and a chance of success in a mixed field of machinery, by virtue of an arcane and labyrinthine handicapping system that nobody except the handicappers understands. Teams of cars vary from four to six. I think it may be possible, though tiring, to operate a team of three, but I cannot swear to it.

With participation depending on ownership of a suitable racing car, plus overalls, helmet, etc., and possession of a valid race licence, the subset of magazine readers able to step forward with any hope of joining in was necessarily limited. PPC were looking for four volunteers to join the magazine's James Winstanley and Mark Hammersley in a team of six. I think I was one of the first to respond to the invitation in the magazine. Later they apparently issued the same request on social media and many more people came forward. Sign of the times. Not often a dinosaur beats more recently evolved forms of life to anything, but I had managed it on this occasion.

After emails flew to and fro for a while, we all met up to do a photo session at Blyton Park. I had the race car and trailer along, as next stop was the race meeting at Donington. The entry was in, and I would be joining James, Mark, Andrew Stacey, Ian Smythe and Geoff Wade in the team at Silverstone in late October. I could hardly back out now, after all the organisation they had done. Nor did I wish to.

Back at home after returning from Cadwell, wine was sunk, warmth was enjoyed, chat was conducted. We would set off in the van in the morning, not expecting too much. The extra Humber Bridge fees were a small price to pay for the home comforts. I would tell Alan that he would have to wait until I had done the Birkett, before doing the car deal.

We went along the more direct route to Cadwell, which featured all the B roads. In places we had to dodge substantial deep puddles, and the rain, though lighter, had still not completely stopped. It looked very unlikely that any racing would take place that day. I pondered on the situation, having had plenty of time to make calculations. I was on ninety-seven points, Billy on eighty-five. I would have to knock off one of my scores of six, but that still left me on ninety-one. With points for third in class and below differing by only one point at a time (10,9,8,7 etc.), it realistically only required me to stay on track and finish. But, I reckoned, whatever the permutations of possibilities that the cancelled race would cause, if I could stay ahead of her on track today, it would guarantee the result I wanted.

A convivial morning was spent in the Cadwell café whilst waiting for any verdict on whether racing would take place. By mid-morning the drenched track had still not dried out and we lingered over breakfast, talking business. Alan would be happy to wait for the Phoenix, and would repeat his 'arriving with cash and trailer' technique at Silverstone. I took a deposit on the understanding that it would be returnable should I prang the car at the Birkett. I then turned to Rob, who had joined us at the same table.

"Right. About the Cyana…"

As we talked, a practice session finally began. MR2s were going out behind a pace car; they would technically qualify for their race, but more importantly, the procession of cars would help to dry the track. Although we didn't have to practice, having done our qualification the day before, nerves began to twitch. With a bit of sun breaking through, it was time to think about getting overalls on.

Sure enough, racing was declared to be on, and we assembled for the last outing of the championship. It was the 13th October, 2013, race thirteen of the weekend on the programme, and it was the thirteenth race of our series.

Lights out and we were off. My position just ahead of Billy on the grid was lost as she accelerated away up the hill at Coppice. With her car being definitely faster, I had some work to do. Keeping in touch, we came round, up Coppice again, and as the second lap ended, she was two seconds ahead. But the run up Coppice rewards commitment, and I was able to keep momentum and gain ground going up the hill. With the throttle pinned, I held a good line through the double apex Charlies corner at the top of the rise and hurtled through as we dipped down the first half of the top straight. Avoiding any error at the end of the straight into Park Corner, I was on my way.

By the end of the lap I was one second ahead, by the end of the following lap, two and a half seconds. With Billy definitely slower up the Coppice/Charlies section, I had a comforting advantage. I did not reckon, though, on the fact that she could now see what I was doing through Charlies. She proved to be a very quick learner, and although our fifth lap saw me still two seconds to the good, the sixth was a different story, with a mere three tenths of a second between us across the start line.

A focused effort saw me hanging on, for the last lap. Nearly there! But now here comes Anton in the mirrors, squeezing through in Hall Bends, the most horrible bit of the track to be lapping others. He would, knowing me, expect that I would help him with the line. But the last thing I wanted was for Billy to tag onto his passing line and get through as well. On the other hand, to take a completely selfish line and hog the road brought a risk of misunderstanding and therefore collision. It's incredible how such detailed thoughts can be processed in less than a second as you brake for a corner and focus on the approach.

I managed to leave just enough room to avoid entanglement, taking the inside line for the tight right 'hairpin' at the end of Hall Bends, with the feeling that Billy was by now mere inches behind. One more corner to go. Barn corner. Not by any means un-cock-uppable. As early as I dared, I applied as much gas as I dared.

The back slid out. I corrected. Convinced that Billy would probably have instinctively backed off a touch to avoid this lunatic's possible imminent accident, I gunned it to the line as soon as it was straight. I finished just half a second ahead.

I would now forever be able to relate that I had clinched my coveted third in class by coming sideways out of the last corner of the last lap of the last race of the championship.

It was even, as far as I recall, enough to provoke the unseemly pumping of the fist cliché after we crossed the line. Call it letting off steam, to be charitable. Well, I might have done it. I can't actually remember. I could just as easily have been spending the rest of the drive down the straight heaving a massive sigh of relief.

There was a chance to find out some time later, when the

750 Club produced a video of the highlights. As luck would have it, the TV company had been filming that day, and there was quite a lot of footage of our race, leading up to the finale, as the cars crossed the line in sequence, accompanied by the voice-over commentary. I watched eagerly. Everyone else had been through, and Billy and I would emerge around the tree-shrouded corner at Barn any second…

And the credits rolled…

Behind a scrolled list of the leading lights of the championship, our epic battle would remain unmentioned, consigned to the cutting room floor or its digital equivalent.

No matter. I had done it. YEEEEESSSSSS!!!!!!!!!!

As it turned out, the one permutation I had not envisaged was brought into play. The organisers, in their wisdom, decreed that the best eleven out of the thirteen possible results would count. That meant that whoever had finished ahead at Cadwell, in the private race between Billy and me, would have pipped the other for third overall by one point. So it mattered. Gadzooks. Legendary.

And it had enabled me, for perhaps the one and only time in this whole book, to use the word 'hurtled'.

The end of October saw the journey down to Silverstone, arriving on a cold and rapidly darkening evening. I caught up with James for a chat, but most of the rest of our crew were spread around the paddock, hunkering down in support vehicles to await the morning. Nigel Brown was in attendance, as was John Moore, who had come along with his newly built self-designed Sport Special car on a trailer, even though he was not competing.

We convened in John's motorhome for a chinwag. Talk turned to cost and value. The way it worked was that the team was charged an entry fee, so a team of four, for example, would each have to find more individually than if the cost was spread in a team of six. Most people thought it good value, whatever the breakdown of cost, sharing a six-hour event on the Grand Prix full circuit. A lot of track time on a circuit configuration normally denied to the club racer.

PPC had some sort of arrangement going with the 750 Club, as Mark Hammersley was guest driving a Clio of a type that was to feature in a one-make championship which the club wanted to promote for 2014. So, because the magazine was running adverts and features which helped promote the club's racing, James informed me that the fees had been taken care of and I would not have to find a contribution. When I informed Nigel and John of this, their reaction was immediate and almost simultaneous.

"Professional driver."

"Professional driver."

"Well, no. I'm not being paid, it's just that I don't have to find the entry fee."

"Doesn't matter. Professional driver."

The following day dawned grey and rainy, so practice was rather wet. Each team had a number, the cars within it allocated a letter. So we were team 8 and I was car D. With sixty-nine or seventy teams in the mix, practice sessions were divided into six batches, and I sat snug in the open cockpit of the Sylva as I waited for session D to begin. In the drizzle. But what the heck. Once in a lifetime round the Grand Prix circuit.

Practice was interesting, mixing with all manner of machinery from hatchbacks to classic sports cars, huge Jaguars and a Camaro to Saker GTs which looked as if they belonged at Le Mans. And everything else you might think of even down to a team of Smart cars, and I'm not talking about the Smart roadster.

James had even recruited a team manager, Iain Jones, to organise the potential chaos. The plan for the race was for us to do forty-five minute sessions, and for Ian Smythe to take the first stint in his powerful rear-wheel-drive (!) Cosworth

Fiesta. This changed after the heavy rain in the latter part of practice, with Mark delegated to take the grid in his front wheel drive car with its more wet-friendly tyres. Ian was probably glad of the respite, having spent five hours the previous evening converting his clutch operation from hydraulic back to cable. The conversion to hydraulic a few weeks earlier being found to be unreliable. Rather him than me, but a Herculean effort nonetheless. As the years advance, I prefer to admire Herculean efforts rather than attempt them.

Mark made admirable progress, scything, by all accounts, through the field, but was then brought to a halt when some original Renault wiring came adrift. Andrew, in his MINI Cooper S, dived out into the fray, or should that be spray, and set about making up lost ground. He was followed by Geoff for the third stint, who had had to bring his spare racing car, a Puma-engined Fiesta, which he belatedly remembered buying one Shiraz-influenced evening on eBay. His intended chariot, a Honda Integra Type R, had developed an engine issue too close to the event for even Herculean efforts to be feasible. Digging the Fiesta out from the back of the garage, he drove it on to the trailer, thereby doubling its test mileage. He was reassured by the presence of a nice big speedo on the dashboard, which would be handy to help obey the strict pit lane limit. If it worked.

Geoff nearly managed the forty-five-minute target, with his lap times improving all the time, but had to pit five minutes early with impending drive shaft failure, so his place was taken by James in his BMW Compact. I would be next, sitting ready in the car in the garage. You can't wait until near the end of the predecessor's stint to get ready, in case he has an unexpected problem. I had selected the well-worn set of Yokohamas for the race, leaving the identically well-worn Yokohamas on the spare wheels in the van. But I had checked the wheel nuts as the early part of the race unfolded, so that people in the garage would think I knew what I was doing.

As regards tactics, I was inspired by a tale about Graham Hill, who, in the preparation and testing phase with the Rover BRM Turbine car prior to Le Mans in 1965, was given a lengthy and detailed explanation of how best to operate the vehicle, by a white-coated Rover boffin. After listening patiently to the in-depth technicalities, Graham then replied, saying, "The thing is, old boy, I'm not going to do any of that. I'm just going to get in and then go as fast as I can."

In fact the strategy, or lack of it, was compromised when James came in during a safety car period, but we soon got moving properly, and I overtook a 7-style car through Copse, then he wanted to get by me through the next wiggly bit which I think is Becketts. What did he think it was, a race? I was too busy trying to remember whether it went right-left-right-left, or left-right-left-right, to be too bothered. We then had another safety car period, and I found myself ahead of a pack of cars. Iain had given us a useful briefing earlier in the morning, to which I usefully listened. He said that the organisers, after a safety car period was called, would bring in the safety car and run a virtual safety car period using yellow flags and lights, until the track was cleared.

It looked like somebody had come to grief just after Stowe Corner (again). In any case, the yellows were out all around the track, and everyone else had closed up, so I was the 'virtual safety car'. Weird. Having no experience of this, I decided to go 'my quite quickly but safely' which is probably akin to a Radical's 'bloody slow get out of my way'. After what seemed far too long, we were given greens, which I had been told meant that next time past the start line, we were allowed to get racing again. This wasn't good enough for someone in a Saker just behind me, whose car was too expensive to spend time behind an upstart with unsightly bits of fridge on its bonnet. He blasted past on the straight leading to Luffield. If you're that bothered mate, crack on.

I picked it up a bit as we got round the complex and got on a safe line to give any other howling Neanderthals a chance, and then we were off. I passed, very satisfyingly, my counterpart runner from the Jota-prepared MX5 team who were sharing our garage, with their team of engineers, professional racing drivers, and high-tech equipment.

And then it was over, as the pit board came out to summon me in. Fifty minutes of extreme fun in the faithful little car's last outing with me. The end of an era.

Ian took over, scorching round the track on his slicks, with Andrew taking up the baton again after five hours to see us to the chequered flag. Except that he too now experienced drive shaft failure near the very end, and James, the emergency back-up, had to be hurriedly beckoned into action. The one full lap he was able to complete before the time curtain fell, so to speak, was the difference between finishing fortieth in the handicap standings and twenty-second, our final position out of seventy. And ninth out of twenty-six in our class.

Tom Bell, who will enter our story later, took the overall handicap award, with his team mates in four consistent and fast Saxos.

As James said, it would be nice just to sit around and enjoy the atmosphere for a while. Which I did. But not for too long, as the car had a rendezvous with Alan's trailer, and I would soon have an empty garage. Which is akin to having a vacuum waiting to be filled. And plans were already afoot to satisfy the gods of physics.

I'd reached a tentative agreement with Rob about buying his car as a rolling chassis. The Cyana had Phoenix-like qualities, derived from a period when Rob and his dad Alec had been doing some development work with a chap who bought the Phoenix Mark 1 project from Jeremy. So the shape was similar. The other Phoenix-like quality was its emergence in one slightly charred piece after surviving an oil fire which put Rob out of the last race of the year. The 750 Motor Club video shows him stuck on the wrong side of the track at Cadwell, desperately hoping for someone to get a fire extinguisher to him. Luckily they did… It was a disappointing end to a season which had started so auspiciously for him.

So it was a matter of arranging a date to go down to the Cyana workshop near Stoke-on-Trent and do a deal for a now slightly blackened chassis after Rob had taken the running gear off it to build his next car.

Mrs R had 'decreed' that one car must go to make way for any new arrival. Something to do with 'guests wanting to use the drive', a rather strange concept. Although the Cyana body/chassis was a straightforward replacement for the Phoenix, it still made sense to offload the remaining MR2, which was facing another winter of heaterless paralysis as we moved into November. It made its second rendezvous with eBay, and this year there was decent interest and the hammer fell, so to speak. Once more, an old MR2 would become a significant driver of the country's economy.

The chap buying it was a car dealer from the Oxford area, who wanted to start racing, and although he had contacts for vehicle transportation, arranging a rendezvous with any of them who weren't tied to a daytime visit (whilst I was at work) proved problematic. Eventually we worked out a compromise. There was to be a track day at Rockingham, where Rogue Motorsport were attending. If I could get the car there, they would give it the once over for him, and hopefully we could do a deal.

With my accommodating nature, I suggested a plan which would help me as well. I had a spare Phoenix bonnet which Marcus wanted for his car. With him being based in the south somewhere, a meeting at Rockingham would suit us both. Then, all being well, I would go on to Rob's where a deal for the Cyana could be done.

So, not too long after Alan collected the Phoenix following the Birkett Relay, a trip to Rockingham with the MR2 on the trailer ensued. My customer duly arrived, and we had a chat about the car. The price was a lot less than what had left my pocket in buying it, collecting the parts, and paying Chris. Typical racing car. Rogue's chief mechanic came over and had a look. I explained that the car was effectively a car to start racing with, unmodified under the skin except for the essential safety mods, cage, seat, belts, extinguishers etc., etc. Knowing this, and hearing the very reasonable price I was asking, he declared to my customer that the car was a bargain. So far so good. We sat in the van and I counted the folding money.

Now I had the dosh in my pocket, I was happy to unload the car. My customer sat in it, with a helmet on.

"I'm too tall for it. I can't see out properly."

I needed the empty trailer for the next leg of the trip.

"Oh. Are you sure? You're not much taller than me."

"Will the seat go down?"

I've got the cash in my pocket, I thought.

"Yes. But it's a spanner job."

"Hmm. I'm not sure. I'll have a word with Rogue."

I've got the cash in my pocket.

"You do that, while you're there I'll just sell this bonnet if you don't mind."

I went back to Marcus, who had arrived during our earlier deliberations, and we got the bonnet out of the van and he lashed it to his trailer.

Then back to Rogue's pit garage. I've got the cash in my pocket…

"What's the verdict?" I've got the cash in my pocket…

"They say they can sort it. I suppose it's OK." The guy's original intention to buy the car then join in the track day had evaporated somewhat. Good move. Buying the car was enough stress for one day.

For both of us.

Next stop Stoke.

We pored over the rather sorry looking, engineless chassis. The price had gone up somewhat from the rather vague suggestion in the Cadwell café. My own fault for not getting more specific. I don't think Rob had any ill intentions, we had always got on well. He had probably just thought it through a bit more.

"It's a race winning car, Dave."

We came to an agreement. The thickish wad from the MR2 and Marcus's smaller top-up vanished. Never has a bunch of readies burnt a hole in my pocket so quickly…

We then had to motor to Rob's house where the bodywork was stored in the garage. I was nonplussed to find that Alec had to take the mirrors off because they had come from his motorbike. Was Stoke a harder-boiled asteroid that had broken off the thrifty moon of Yorkshire eons ago? Although I was said to have the ability to peel an orange in my pocket, the frugality demonstrated by the dual purpose mirrors eclipsed any notions of careful housekeeping that I may have felt I possessed. We parted on good terms though, each of us looking forward with joviality to a winter in the workshop.

So after a rather long day on the Saturday, I was able to survey the new toy on Sunday, realising that the gleaming bonnet of a wet Saturday evening had turned into a rather heat-bubbled item as the spell wore off. But overall it was still a racing carriage rather than a pumpkin.

In fact, it was a whole week before I did the ritual sitting in it making engine noises thing, having spent a while clearing the decks in the garage first. There was a lot to do, including sourcing a fair few new bits to replace ones Rob needed for his next build, not least an engine. Plans were made soon afterwards to have a proper one built, for once in my life, but in the meantime I found a Mondeo with a suitable 2-litre Duratec, not too far away in Lincoln. With the engine from this, if it proved to be reasonable, I would get up and running with the race car, test out the cooling systems and so on.

Soon I was commuting in a Mondeo for a few weeks, but it wasn't going to be a complete car for long…

What was that about guests wanting to use the driveway, Mrs R?

17

Development Drive

The Mondeo was quite a nice driving car, but it had to be cannibalised all the same. It had taxi mileage, but then again taxis do most of their miles warmed up. At least, there were no nasty noises, so its entirely adequate performance in meeting the Ford engineers' design objectives ironically sealed its rather brutal fate.

The book says the subframe has to come out, but that's not the case if you are prepared to hack through the front of the car along with the driveshafts. The reciprocating saw, a gift from my thoughtful wife, proved invaluable, along with the angle grinder. I wouldn't like to do much on one of these if I had to reassemble it afterwards. The amount of sensors to be detached seemed infinite. I did study the manual as they all came off, confining my findings to my sieve-like memory rather than a notebook. Hmm… But things would be simpler in its new home.

The latter part of December was spent in a slow motion frenzy of expenditure, assembling various bits from such as Burton Power, Rally Design and a company I hadn't heard of before, RWD Motorsport. They provided a shiny new bellhousing suitable for cable clutch; it seems the offerings from other companies assume you are going to use a hydraulic set-up when mating the Duratec to the Type 9 gearbox. As the car had a cable set-up already, mechanical jiggery-pokery would have been required to change it, and Brands Hatch was not too far over the horizon. The whole plan was to spend a bit more where necessary if it resulted in a quicker solution, as for once in my life I had some reasonable funds for a project.

Whilst waiting for parts delivery, having to go in to work on several days of the Christmas period meant that I wouldn't have to sit idle on any garage days, even if it meant working on fitment of things like fire extinguishers and the battery, all of which had to be sorted at some point anyway. I did indulge in applying some blue paint to the roll bar, orange being my least favourite colour. There wasn't time to do the whole chassis though, so I had to risk giving the impression, to people who might look down into the car, that I had succumbed to the Gulf colour scheme race car cliché.

By mid-January I had dared hope that the engine and box might be installed. But I was still carefully filing the minimum off the clutch cover holes where they mated to the guide lugs to locate it to the lightweight flywheel. I hate having to do such things, especially if it involves a rotating mass, but the things would not have mated without that fettling. Two hours of messing, trying on, fettling, etc. But better than attacking it and having it loose. I figured the bolts rather than the lugs performed the main function of holding it, and they were only a 29 newton metre pressure. The flywheel bolts were a different kettle of fish, ARP ones with Locktite and a very strong torque setting. The makeshift L-shaped bracket I had used to hold the ring gear when undoing the Mondeo item wasn't up to this, and I eventually hit on the idea of turning against the bar on the front crank pulley bolt, wedged against the engine stand, which did the trick.

Speaking of things which didn't quite fit, the brackets for the Wilwood front calipers seemed to need drilling to accept bolts for the Cortina upright. Was this because there are two possible sizes of bolts on the Cortina upright? The front discs also needed a sliver machining off, to go over the hub. Never mind. I suffer from the quaint and old-fashioned delusion that parts you are paying substantial money for should fit first time, but what do I know?

What really put the brakes on progress for a little while was the clutch bearing. Firstly, the release arm would not accept the release bearing, being restricted in its sideways movement by the opening in the side of the bellhousing. Grumblings and mutterings ensued. Surely I would not have to modify the opening?! The logical first step was to drive to my old lock-up one Sunday morning, as despite a forced garage tidy-up, I could not find another arm lying about. The expedition yielded three release arms, two of them popped off spare gearboxes. My wife was very impressed with this unearthed treasure. Her 'bemused' expression is very similar though.

So I then had a total of four release arms. There are two slightly different shapes, one has a late taper, the other a more gradual one, and this latter was the one that fitted without fouling my bellhousing opening. So far so good, and the emotional rollercoaster was up. Now to fit the release bearing. It pushes and clips onto the lugs on the arm, basically with two very small wedges incorporated, which spring back after like the barb of a fishhook to hold the round release bearing onto the arm.

The original old design featured a sprung metal design, hard to make out on the one used example I had to hand, but with a reasonably shallow ramp to the clip, from what I recall dealing with Ford bits over the years. The replacement part I had, featured a steep ramp of plastic either side, which could only just be compressed enough to barely engage against the lugs on the arm. I had bought it from a trusted supplier locally for £10, rather than spend nearly £40 for the same part from the specialists. It had German writing on it. The chances of fitting it in situ seemed minimal.

I resorted to fitting it on the bench as an experiment, knowing, madly, that I would have to take it off to refit the arm on the input shaft. The experiment didn't work, evidenced by the mashed plastic wedge on one side when I finally thought it might push on to the arm which was held in the vice.

But the story had a happy ending. Rather than pay top dollar for an item which probably had the same German writing on it, and have to have all the hassle of sending it back had I preserved it, it had only cost me a mere tenner for the same thing, so I was thirty quid better off after the bearing ended up in two pieces on the concrete floor of the garage after I flung it.

Thank goodness for Yorkshire economics.

We took a weekend out to go to the 750 Motor Club awards dinner dance. My first time ever for this, and first time ever wearing proper dinner jacket and bow tie. My pupil at work said, did I feel like James Bond?

"Yes," I said, "but I'm deluded." This answer seemed to satisfy him.

I finally got the engine and gearbox in, after initially being stalled due to thinking I would somehow coincidentally have a propshaft that fitted first time. Doh. The one I tried did actually mate OK, but was too long. The local engineers came to the rescue and shortened and balanced it, changing one of the UJs as well.

The next job was the installation of the coilover dampers, which I had collected from Rob on the way back from the 'do', as he had decided to upgrade for his next build, and the ones originally on my car were now for sale. Obviously a ready fit, and somewhat more compliant than the four lengths of drilled angle iron which constituted the 'suspension' for transporting the chassis.

The front brake calipers needed the bolts which connect them to the brackets for the uprights, to be put in the freezer for a bit, as they were metric, and the American holes were imperial. How bizarre.

Which still left lots to do. The prompt arrival of an oil catch tank from a private eBay sale was another piece of the jigsaw, and I prepared to mooch the scrapyard for a Peugeot or maybe Vauxhall or maybe Volvo header tank. It needed to be a handy shape to hang on a bracket at the front of the engine, which is where the last one was, 'before the fire'.

Many years ago, I went to see a hot-rodded Austin A35. I remember it was described to me as having a Jag rear axle, some sort of tuned A-series engine I think, and the original A35 drum brakes. Hmmm… The car was in a lock-up somewhere, and the owner described how there had been a fire which had compromised its integrity somewhat. We sat in the owner's front room as he described all the mods and all the components belonging to the car. "And then the fire…"

Every feature was qualified by the above phrase. I still vaguely recall sitting in this cheerful chap's small sitting room in a small terraced house, counting the times he said, "and then the fire…". I never did get to see that hot-rodded A35….

I digress… picking things up, I had finally dared to make a job list, dangerously implying some vague conception of a finished car at some point in the future. This is when all the 'smaller' subsystems begin clamouring for attention, and you solve one problem whereupon another is noticed, so the list becomes a sort of Sisyphean[14] landscape, although the hill to push the rock up does vary in gradient. The trick to obtaining

14 Sisyphus was a figure in Greek mythology who was punished by the gods of the Underworld, by being set the task of rolling a huge stone to the summit of a hill, from where it would constantly roll down again.

the enjoyment of the build process, which my wife was insisting I experience, seemed to be to forget that the season opener, in weekend/evening car build time, was merely around the next corner.

Amazingly, after a week in the freezer, the bolts did worm their way through the calipers. It was a good idea to wind them with a spanner even though the aperture wasn't threaded. Then the nerve-wracking mounting onto the brackets, without that bit of slack which helps with feeling whether they are started nicely in the bracket threads. If they were to come off in the future, I figured it would be best to treat them as one unit, brackets included, like the set-up on a production car.

After this small triumph, I tried the thirteen-inch wheels which I already had, hoping I might save a bit of budget in this area. Fine on the front, but the Powerlite calipers I ordered for the back had a handbrake mechanism on. We didn't need it for the race series, but I thought the small compromise might help the car's saleability at some point in the distant future. Guess what bit was catching on the wheels... Luckily the small levers that were fouling the wheel turned out to be detachable.

Meantime, a rad and oil cooler were fitted, both obtained locally. I tried a rad for an MGF, which in fact proved a success, and being from a production car, would be easily replaceable.

With the addition of a purpose-designed water rail, the oil and water cooling systems were largely plumbed in; it just remained to make up an arrangement for a drive belt at the front of the engine. This involved a nifty bracket and adjustable pulley from Mountune at the top, and a welded bracket and L-shaped bracket scrounged at work, for the bottom. Thus the alternator, from a Rascal van or JCB, would live below the adjustable pulley on the intake side of the block. The pulley and alternator were mounted where the power steering and air con used to live on the Mondeo. You need the simple alternator as above, because I gather many original equipment ones are now controlled by the ECU in their production car applications.

I was now almost ready to arrange a date to take the car to Tom Bell at TBR Racing, to get the ECU and fuel systems fitted and then get the car on the rolling road. I had got to know Tom through the local engineering company, with whom he was working at that time. He had an excellent reputation as an engine builder, originally within the grass track community and lately supplying race-winning engines in the hatchback series in the 750MC. The long-term plan, if all went well, was to have him build a proper race spec Duratec engine for the car.

The advantages to employing Tom's expertise in getting the car running were several. First, he was an agent for Jenvey and Omex, second, he knew what he was doing, third, he was fairly near me in East Yorkshire, and finally, it would save me 'head scratching time' on bits I have never done before. I took the view all along, that money might have to be spent to save time if need be, and to maintain a vague chance of getting to the first meeting at Brands. Rather a long way to go for a test, but I saw little chance of the ideal scenario, that of doing a track day first, transpiring.

I meant to take a picture of the state of the garage after the car left, but the moment passed. A pity, as I regard these snapshots in time as something of unique artistic merit. Suffice to say, it took a couple of lengthy sessions to render the surroundings shipshape again. I recollect Robert Pirsig, in *Zen and the Art of Motorcycle Maintenance*[15], averring that there are two types of mechanic; those who have every tool neatly placed at all times, and those whose benches appear a picture of chaos. But both types, he confidently states, know exactly where everything is...

Nah...

15 *Zen and the Art of Motorcycle Maintenance: An Inquiry into Values*. Robert M. Pirsig. 1974. William Morrow & Co. (NYC).

16. More aerodynamic than a fridge. Cadwell paddock, 2013.
Photo: Janet Roberts

17. Into the last corner of the last, thirteenth, race. Cadwell, 13-10-13.
Photo: Steve Jones

18. Awards do. Maximum enjoyment. January 2014.
Photographer unrecalled

19. With Marcus and Colin.
Photo: Janet Roberts

20. "You look like Compo, Dave."
Photo: Janet Roberts

21. …but I have shiny power. The Cyana, 2014.
Photo: Janet Roberts

22. Ahead of Marcus, Colin and Billy. Anglesey, 2014.
Photo: Steve Jones

23. Start line at Donington, 2014.
Alan Robinson is in my old Phoenix, number 26.
Photo: Rick Roberts

24. My brother's mate Stuart helps with the staring.
Photo: Rick Roberts

25. Garfield assesses the damage after Croft.
Photo: Dave Roberts

26. “It’s lifting 6 inches!” Ready for take-off at Snetterton, 2015.
Photo: Richard Dawson

27. With Mel. Snetterton, 2016.
Photo: Richard Dawson

28. With brother Rick.
Photo: Janet Roberts

29. Team Cyana. With Rob and Anton. Croft, 2016.
Photo: Janet Roberts

30. And that's it… Snetterton 2017.
Photo: Janet Roberts

I was getting worse. The oil pressure sender which Rob had supplied me with, to match up to the TIM gauge on the car, was not near the oil light sender on the bench when the antediluvian layers of cluttered tools and components above it were excavated. That's where it should have been, and if I had taken it out to show someone the thread maybe, there was no way I was going to remember which pocket in which coat in which vehicle I just might've left it. So in other words, there was no plan B other than a phone call to Demon Tweeks for a Stack gauge, which, as is the norm, comes with its own sender. A good thing was that they had the M12/1.5 male to 1/8 NPT female adaptor, necessary for inserting the sender into the oil filter mounting that was supplied by Burton Power, enabling the filter to go on from the side rather than below, handy on a car with a flat floor just below the Raceline sump.

So to conclude, I present my own theory. There are two types of mechanic. Those who usually know where everything is, but every so often have to purchase something they already possess because they cannot spare the eons of time necessary to find it; and those who have everything neatly placed at all times. The latter being like a black swan. Theoretically possible, but I have never seen one.

Maybe it's the circles I move in…

The car was taken up to Tom's garage on my trailer, for the fuel system and ECU to be installed. A few days later, on a Friday, trailer behind the van just in case all had gone to plan, I called by.

I spotted Tom in the rolling road building, and asked him how things were going.

I like a succinct summary, on the basis that if a pill is bitter, why dwell on it? Tom's reply did not only save on syllables, but also minimised usage of surplus letters of the alphabet.

"Bad."

We had a slipping clutch, a misfire on idle, numerous oil and coolant leaks, and an alternator getting hot and tracking out.

"At least the exhaust is OK," I said, clutching at straws of optimism.

"We had to fix that too, it was blowing everywhere."

OK. That's only everything I've done then.

Tackling things logically, the clutch was the worst problem. I had been a bit uneasy about the feel of things when mating the engine and box, however it had lined up alright so I had hoped for the best, not necessarily a recommended engineering technique. Whatever, I had the number for RWD Motorsport on my mobile, so phoned Ian there, and ordered a release arm and bearing from them, on the basis that they were the only bits not supplied by them in the whole flywheel/clutch/bellhousing assembly.

Tom kindly undertook to pull the engine out and I went off to enjoy my enforced car-free weekend. We began emptying the pond in the garden, using the engine trolley with a tub on top of it. The bit of string I had tied to it for pulling proved to be the only triumphant vehicle modification I had accomplished in the recent past.

Hindsight is a great thing, once you plough through the setbacks of the present and get to the future where you can use it. So, jumping ahead, the release arm from RWD did the trick. It is modelled on the RS2000. At first glance it doesn't look much different to the one I had put in; however, putting it alongside mine on the workshop floor, a slight difference in the angle where it bends was apparent. Not much, but enough to avoid the pressure on the clutch that had caused all the problems with slippage. Glad about that, because there wasn't really a plan B.

The misfire turned out to be a dodgy injector, the various seepages mostly a consequence of my inculcated fear of stripped threads or simple limp-wristed efforts with jubilee clips. The question of whether to use PTFE tape on tapered threads anyway... answer is yes...

A silver lining was that, with time slipping by, Tom suggested that he could do the replacement of some of the flexi brake lines that I had planned. A major help, and well worth the extra day or two before getting the car back, saving me the problem amongst other logistics, of finding a helper slim enough and with brake pedal pressing experience, to aid with the bleeding of the system, not to mention the difficulties of specifying anything for a non-production vehicle.

Eventually I was able to collect the car, with just a list of odd jobs to finish, such as fire extinguisher pulls, tidying up coolant and oil cooler lines, fitting of transponder, etc., etc. I got a text saying how many horsepower it had, mind-boggling from a bog-standard engine when you think about it, and far in excess of anything in my previous racing cars. Once you have overcome the mental barrier of the cost of throttle bodies and ECU, it almost seems justifiable in everyday circles, and without doubt to anyone of a racing outlook on life. The emotional rollercoaster was UP!

One of the odd jobs was to fit the new seat belts, delivered some time earlier. They were far too long! Never mind, I would ring Demon Tweeks on the Monday and have a rant. I engaged Mrs R to help me measure them. She suggested altering the top arrangement where the belt slides through a sort of clasp thing, as it was just like a child's buggy belt.

Yes, that did solve it. I looked on the bright side, that I would save a phone call, save looking like an idiot, and that I had a very helpful wife who has obviously dealt with people with childlike knee-jerk responses, many times.

Brands still beckoned, for all of us with exciting toy cars...

The PPC magazine issue came out, featuring my build diary. I ventured to show it to a colleague or two at work.

"You look like Compo,[16] Dave."

I knew the glamour of racing would make an impression.

The car was collected, brake lines now renewed throughout and system bled. Tom said they weren't actually doing a lot till they bedded in.

The list to do was now quite short, matching the time available. A check of the lights found headlights and... that was it. Even the rain/fogs, working earlier in the build, weren't playing. So the Saturday of the Easter weekend was spent tracing and solving/bypassing various circuits, and by the end of the day just the brake lights remained to sort. This was easy to detect, as I remembered there was a pressure switch that lived in the transmission tunnel somewhere. Or it used to...

The new braided line that Tom's assistant had installed was wonderful. The deletion of the switch slightly less so. Not to worry though, because I finally found a box within a brake bits box, that said, 'Ford brake light switches,' on it. So by the end of Sunday morning I had rigged up one of these on a bracket behind the brake pedal. It worked great, as long as you didn't mind the brake lights staying on permanently, UNTIL you pressed the pedal, when they would go off.

The rest of Sunday and half of Monday saw the design of a Heath Robinson device hanging from the bracket, which was pushed away from the repositioned switch along a sort of primitive monorail against spring pressure from the only two suitable springs available out of about 200 in my various containers. A frequent theme, usually involving the suitability of washers or spacers, in my experience.

By about the fifth iteration of the design, I was reasonably happy that it was performing as intended, enough to justify the trip to Brands anyway.

At the meeting it was great to meet up with everyone again,

16 Character from the BBC comedy series *Last of the Summer Wine*.

including Alan with my old car, there for his first race. We had quite a healthy turnout, with a good few from the MEV exoskeletal school of design joining us, and some new faces in the more traditional type of kit cars, as well as John Moore with his own new rear-engined design.

Practice was abysmal. We were advised there was oil at Paddock, Druids and Graham Hill bends. To this you could add oil flags at Clearways when you got out there. So that's only virtually the whole track then. As it was wet too, there were many cars doing various pirouettes as you went past. I got caught out once, getting on the gas a bit early out of Graham Hill, swapping ends and backwards on the grass. I was quite pleased with my reversing skills prior to rejoining the track during a gap in the traffic.

The brakes were indeed doing next to nothing, despite some efforts to bed them in on some straight approaches. I had promised myself just to get used to the car and check the instruments a bit, so I wasn't disappointed to qualify last, as it would be one less thing to worry about when we started. It was clear the car had lots more power than the old one, so we would see what happened in the dry if conditions improved…

I spent some time looking at the brake light switch arrangement, modifying it to give more pedal travel. Aha! You never see the likes of Adrian Newey making such massive design strides at a stroke, do you?

The races were brilliant. The car was the first I have had that wasn't underpowered relative to most of the field. The day had become sunnier and I was able to work my way up the field and pass a few others. A couple of times I was puzzled as to how a slower car had somehow got past me. Then it dawned. I was LAPPING someone. Crikey.

In the first race I set off in fourth gear instead of the experimental second I had planned. I avoided this error in the second race, stalling it instead. None of it mattered, as I was able to drive past people using the power, a very novel feeling. Of course I didn't catch the front runners, being lapped myself by some, but getting round in the 56's when I had never done under 58 seconds there before, was promising. The tyre pressures had been left a bit high by the fitters, so I found time to lower them before the second race. The car felt distinctly better, but no faster on the best lap. So we now entered the arcane world of set-up, all the corner weights, etc. being complete guesswork at this point. Interesting.

We had a break after all this. Thank goodness all the work had been worth it, anyway. I was informed by Mrs R how much patience had been shown over the previous months. I think the translation of this involved gardening and shopping for furniture.

During our trip away, I was perusing *Motor Sport*.

"Look at this. Ayrton Senna's racing overalls coming up for sale. Estimate, £25,000 to £30,000."

"Dave Roberts' overalls that I had to prise off his back to wash them after he'd spent the past six months in the garage. Value. Two quid."

I knew she would be impressed by the glamour of racing.

The car went back to TBR racing after Brands, where they fitted a nifty brake light pressure switch from a motorbike. When we did a 'quick' check before loading the car, there were no rear lights whatsoever! I took the car anyway, rather than ask them to spend more time tracing a fault probably unrelated to their recent efforts.

By midday the following day I had tracked down the culprit. After Brands the exhaust can had been loose, and it was whilst fixing this on, stuck on the offside of the car swearing at the mountings, that I had noticed Garfield, our cat, carrying out a quality control inspection of the wiring on the nearside scuttle area.

Sure enough, he had pulled an earth wire off, homing in on the loose spade connector. Thank you, Garfield. He probably wasn't 100% happy with the lack of a working ignition warning light, the clutch cable secured in the release arm by tie-wraps, and the alternator HT cable being rather close to the engine block, either. To be fair, neither was I, but in the absence of a written report from Garfield, I left these jobs on the back burner whilst sorting stuff higher on the list.

The following Saturday we had a good trip down to Snetterton, though hardly able to see the river below the Humber Bridge in the torrential rain. After an excellent meal with friends in Bungay later that evening, we were ready for the racing on what turned out to be a much sunnier Sunday. The plan was to qualify further up the grid this time, and go from there.

Qualifying ended early for me when the clutch cable came adrift, resulting in a tow back to the paddock. Now I had to see Race Control over a mix-up about whether I had needed to attend a briefing, having raced here before on the '200' circuit but not the '300'. Easily sorted, but whilst up there I thought it best to enquire if I had done enough laps in qualifying. Two and a half didn't cut it, and I would have to do a third lap at lunchtime behind the course car. Plus attend a Sport Specials briefing about driving standards. Plus fix the car.

The clutch cable to release arm job was impossible to reach with two hands. It really needed an inspection panel letting in to the flat floor, a job I would only find time for later. Colin Benham helped with the adjustment of the cable, and pulled the pliers while I cut some sheathing away. Then I had to get a nut and bolt through the fat bit of the pear-shaped opening so that the cable couldn't get out again. After a lot of swearing, the nut and bolt magically transformed into a couple of new tie-wraps.

I then attended for my lap, finally relaxing sitting in the car, as I waited for the official in the course vehicle to show up. I was near the podium at the gate to the pit lane, whilst Motors

TV filmed the victors of the RGB race, just above me. This was undoubtedly the nearest I would be to a podium for the foreseeable future.

After scoffing a quick sandwich and putting some fuel in the car, it was time for race one. After a careful start, from the back naturally, I began to pass cars round the new twiddly 'short straights with corners' bit. Looking at the lap charts later, it seems I was about nine places better off at the end of the first lap! But coming round to the back straight it got away, and by the time I was facing the right way, there was quite a lot to do again. Jackie Stewart, if I recall, said he hardly ever spun off during his career, but that if you do, you should analyse why, or what's the point? My analysis was lacking at this time, but after later thought, I concluded that a dab of brake, with the car probably over-braked at the rear, was probably the culprit.

I passed a few cars. Again. Then went into 'Hamilton's' and spun off. Again. Analysis: stupid fast, understeer, grass lacking grip.

Regaining the track, I passed not quite so many cars. Again. Then the race ended.

They weighed us in the parc ferme. It wouldn't re-start. Temperature had looked high when I turned it off. Left it to cool off. Left owner/driver to cool off. Went to push it back, mostly downhill or flat, excellent news.

Bonnet off. Ribbed belt absent. Remains of it resembling a two-ribbed Mobius strip. Asked around paddock. Needed an 1163. Tried a 1250. No but thanks anyway, Anton. John Moore had a 1215 but he couldn't find it as it was at home. Ian Wilson, the Lotus Europa driver, came up with an 1150 spare from his dad's car.

I was beginning to resign myself by this time, but now everybody pitched in to help and so I felt obliged to join the frantic spanner wielding. We found some adjustment on the alternator bottom mount as well as the Mountune adjustable pulley at the top of the belt, and somehow it went on, with me pushing the car in gear and Ian and Nigel Brown persuading it over the final pulley.

Battery flat. Got in van to move it to do a jump-start. Mark Bowd, GT40 driver, produced a starter pack.

The alternator HT lead was now VERY close to the engine block and things got quite hot quite quickly. I hope your starter pack survived OK, Mark. Mark's helper somehow got a spanner on the inaccessible connection and we tweaked the HT lead out of harm's way. I got the van over as a last last last resort and the car finally started on the jump leads.

Helmet on, strap in, promise to be careful. Assembly area. Revs look weak. Revs look absent on the tacho. Revs despite a prod of throttle are now gone.

Somebody tried a push in response to my despairing hand, but the battery was so low it was never going to happen.

"Would you like a tow?"

"Yes please, that would be really helpful."

So that was it for the day.

But it wasn't too bad a weekend, with the craic and the helpful people.

Pity about the oil pressure not being quite as good as it used to be.

Pity about the shortcomings of preparation coming back to bite on every count.

Pity about Garfield being unable to insist on their rectification earlier, due to being a cat.

The day after we got back I made a job list to make me feel better. It included EVERYTHING I would like to do to the car, and was thus Chapmanesque[17] in its proportions, if not its engineering sophistication.

---

17 Lotus boss Colin Chapman was famed for the lengthy job lists he delegated to his mechanics in the lead up to races.

Mel's friend Dick had taken a fine collection of photos at the race meeting. Those from the latter part of the race revealed tell-tale wisps of blue smoke coming from the car. It had not survived the disappearing belt unscathed. Tom began looking for a base engine to do a proper build, whilst I busied myself with other distractions, such as removing the alternator and rearranging the dashboard wiring in order to relocate some switches more logically. The switches had probably evolved with the changes to the car in the past, going where there was a gap on the dash it seemed, particularly with the change to fuel injection. I worked on putting the switches for ignition, lift pump and high-pressure pump adjacent to each other. Not essential, but it would make me feel better.

Whilst rubbing the writing off under some dash switches, the thinner began to remove the orange paint fairly readily.

Now that really did cheer me up.

I also focused some attention on updating the fuse box and making a new splitter. The fuse box was modernised with a nifty little one from Autoelectric Supplies, which saves connecting several wires in a series across all the live feeds, or soldering one wire across them, which was also suggested. That would be fine, but the fuse box which allows a single live feed is neater and hardly breaks the bank. I also purchased three rolls of the latest thin wire in different colours, to have a bit more traceability under the bonnet. It does the same job with a multiplicity of thinner strands to achieve the same rating as the older spec of wire.

Autoelectric also supplied a new JCB/Rascal van alternator, and this time the wiring was carefully sorted to get the red ignition light operating properly. Progress.

After much trawling of 'net wisdom' involving people standing on the front of their modified cars etc., I decided on a nine-ply bit of wood as being the best compromise between strength and weight for a front splitter. The old one was thinner, but had seen much better days, and various impregnations of oil and insertion of air scoops had left it fairly flimsy. But it served as a good template for a quick manufacture of its replacement.

With Tom's help, the car was up and running before Rockingham. Now I had newness and even more power than before. Gulp. It turned out to be the first meeting of the year without some sort of major issue. Rob Johnston was able to attend this time, and helped with the spring heights and damper settings. Practice was a little bit damp, if I recall correctly, and I dialled out some rear brake, having come to the conclusion that the rear being over-braked was what had caught me out at Snetterton. Less twitchiness here bred some confidence, and the races were quite fun if not particularly spectacular, just trying to learn the car a bit more. The three hairpins highlighted the limitations of the fairly non-racy front pads, so that went on the list to do. The £5.50ish priced Chevette road pads had always seemed OK on the Phoenix… but now I was going a fair bit faster…

Anglesey followed, this time armed with 'Polymatrix A' front pads on the Wilwood calipers. Only about twenty times the price of the ones on my old car, but never mind. They work well from cold and are not unpredictable, in other words the modulation seems good. I spent the first three laps applying about 50% pressure, then upped it as practice went on. This was based on advice from AP Racing's website, rather than 'net wisdom'. At the end of qualifying I looked for my grid position on the printout, starting from the names at the back as usual. Quite a long read, and there I was at twelfth! By far my best qualifying result ever.

In race one I got a great start, and passed Paul Cooper going into Rocket corner as we braked. For a few laps I wasn't too far out of reach of the other two front-engine Duratec cars, then my performance tailed off a bit, perhaps paying too much mind to

Paul's presence in the mirrors, not that I could see much more than a bit of green noseband, such was their poor adjustment. Finally he got by at Rocket again, and then Colin Benham got down the inside at the long hairpin after the start, followed by a couple more class B cars.

All this earned me a severe telling off from Cyana management (Alec Johnston) for letting them by, so I resolved to try harder in race two the following day. I adjusted the mirrors better whilst promising to ignore them. The central one was set to look at the sky so that the slipstream would push it into adjustment this time… this idea from Tony Gaunt did actually work moderately well, thanks Tony!

But it was all a bit academic when, after another good start, I got the right-hand wheels slightly on the edge of the track going into the Corkscrew, resulting in a 180 spin. So the rest of the race was a bit lonely, although I did my best to keep on it, even with the fastest class B cars a bit too far down the road to catch, as it turned out.

Quite an auspicious meeting though. It seemed like the cupboard of racing driver excuses was finally bare, and I was left contemplating things like driving technique and even racecraft. How strange.

I didn't have a lot of spare time between Anglesey and the next meeting at Silverstone, but luckily there wasn't too much to do on the car.

The rear diffuser had come loose on one side, after my spin probably, and required dressing to get rid of the sharp edges caused by the subsequent erosion. I put an extra nut over the captive thread on the chassis where it was normally held, so hopefully the bolt wouldn't get jarred loose in future.

Most of the other stuff involved tidying and routine spanner checks, paving the way for the main project, designing some ducting to aid brake cooling at the front.

The head scratching to action ratio was about 60:40 in the end, but I came up with a design which held the ducting up just under the middle of the bonnet, at the cost of a kilo or so of aluminium angle and various intakes. It was short work to form a simple scoop to feed the two tubes of ducting near the front of the bonnet. The downside was some loss of aerodynamic efficiency, upside the lack of faffing and crawling to attach ends of ducts every time the bonnet was reattached. An unplanned bonus was the handiness of the scoop to act as a handle to lift the bonnet on and off if I was on my own.

I got the cylindrical flanged duct mountings from the front of the bonnet lower down, where they had previously lived. There were also another two round holes near each riveted flange, and I tidied up the surgery of removal by joining the two holes at each side, leaving an oval gap to let a bit more air in near the hubs, hopefully. Making the finishing surrounds for these took far longer than making the new scoop above.

In its previous life the ducting had been attached to the cylindrical inlets by hand; this was impossible now as I had added a rudimentary grille soon after acquiring the car. The reasoning here was that one errant stone into oil or water radiators could end the weekend's fun, and nothing to do with imagining that a bit of chicken wire makes it look a bit like a 1950's Aston Le Mans racer.

The new oval/pear-shaped inlets at the sides of the main grille aperture now had even more echoes of that classic Aston grille. In my mind… Quite worrying really.

Talking of things I should have been worrying about, I looked at the exhaust can the day before departure. Hmm… It had been a bit loose again after the last meeting. I tightened the clamp and made a mental note to add to the existing mental note, that it really needed sorting over the winter…

At last the day of the meeting dawned. Eagerly anticipated, but a bit disappointing in terms of building on the Anglesey qualifying, as I was further down the grid this time. Not quite sure why.

Nevertheless, the racing was fun, quite a bunch of the Sports Racing and GT cars were out with us. The first race featured a good duel with Paul Murphy in a Zetec-powered Cyana, and I was pleased with a couple of overtaking manoeuvres going into the fast Abbey corner. After slowing for some oil and yellow flags on Hangar Straight, I was repassed by a D-Type replica no less, and ended up in a gaggle of cars which hurtled into the sharp right to the Link like a high-speed traffic jam going round Hyde Park corner at 80mph. In fact someone alluded to the traffic at the Arc de Triumph in Paris, and I do believe our progress was nearly as fast and mad as a box of frogs, so to speak.

Surviving all this, I messed with the now even looser exhaust can, discovering that the one remaining inaccessible bobbin had also delaminated. Tightening up a nut on the fail-safe bracket I had added at the back of the pipe, I then made sure that the aluminium sill panel was securely fixed, so that whatever happened, the exhaust silencer could not escape onto the track. Here's where a full-bodied car with aluminium floor and sill forming the exhaust tunnel scores over a Seven-esque car. Planning ahead for something falling off by buying a particular configuration of vehicle is either professionalism of the highest degree or pre-emptive pessimistic preparation for presumed piss-poor planning. Take your pick.

The second race was rather more civilized, finally passing Mark Hextall going into Vale, and keeping up with a Cobra that had spun in front of us, although not quite close enough to instigate a safe passing manoeuvre. Then we ran out of laps before I could catch Paul Murphy again. A fun day's racing, and finishing in one piece, unlike two or three others on the day.

The long drive home that evening was followed by experiencing an extremely stiff and painful neck over the next three or four days. I used to think I had quite strong neck muscles, derived from hours of welding underneath various semi-corroded 'classics' and 'auction bargains' back in the eighties; but the fast Abbey and Stowe and the sharp turns which follow both shortly after, must take it out of you more than you expect.

And that was just two thirteen-minute plus one lap races. I didn't think the 1950s Aston at Le Mans fantasy was going to be fulfilled anytime soon…

After Silverstone, the car was tucked away for a while, as we had less than a week to go before a long awaited holiday in the USA. I made a note to deal with two major issues on our return: the wonky ribbed belt which had eroded two ribs, probably due to an alternator bracket issue, and the wonky exhaust, which would need at least a temporary modification.

And the ignition light wire had come off the alternator. I planned to make a short, tighter fitting one and join it to the existing wiring in a more accessible location, as the back of the alternator is somewhat buried away.

Back in the UK almost a month later after a fabulous trip, I ventured out to the garage on a Sunday with the shortlist. Just before the second Silverstone race, the ignition light had failed to come on in the assembly area, although the engine started and ran fine. Faced with a choice of my vow to investigate immediately in such circumstances, or join the revved up throng of cars heading for the track, red mist had won comprehensively. At the end of the race, the battery was totally unable to kick the car over, let alone start it again. However, discovering that the drive belt was still on, if slightly deranged, had given me a worry-free vacation.

All was explained now on undoing the alternator: the welded bracket had failed, hence the lack of alignment. Luckily I had left the 'pattern angle bracket' (pence from Wickes) on where the bolt went through, so the fail-safe instinct of belt and braces at least stopped the alternator coming completely adrift at the top bolt. The derangement had also caused the HT lead to snap at the join at the back of the alternator.

All this was sorted by making a new bracket from a piece of bent steel I found. I had rejected it on the original build because of the various drilled holes along it. Now it was the only correctly shaped option, and luckily the vital hole to mount it in the correct position on the block *just* squeezed in between two existing ones. With some spacing washers on the tensioner pulley, the new arrangement looked better than before the mishap. Two new LT wires from the back of the alternator to a better join with the existing ones completed the job.

The exhaust took longer, including swearing time. I found I had some BMC Mini exhaust bobbins, bought earlier, and used one of them, together with a rejigged fail-safe bracket to a U-clamp on the rear end. There was a facility for mounting the silencer can to the chassis with two bobbins, but it was just impossible to reach. So there would be a redesign on this over the winter.

Going back to work on the Monday, I found I had booked the Monday and Tuesday as leave. Never mind, I was able to work and save the leave time, as the jobs on the car had taken a lot of Sunday, but were done. Donington was to be two races on the upcoming Saturday; I encouraged Mrs R to make the trip down in the car on Saturday after I went down on Friday afternoon. Together with my brother and his pal coming along, it would make for a sociable day's racing.

I was in luck when I arrived. Thinking I was early, I nevertheless was let in before the prescribed 6.30 p.m. A massive bonus was being able to get signed on and scrutineered that evening, saving a horrendous 6.30 a.m. alarm the next day! Then I went out for tea, Mr Ecclestone's machinations a few years earlier having deprived us of the excellent Redgate Lodge hostelry that used to stand at the end of the paddock. It had been razed to the ground as part of the effort by an 'entrepreneur' to upgrade the track to accommodate the Formula 1 circus. Hubris and vandalism from a pawn in Ecclestone's perennial game of threatening Silverstone's hosting of the British Grand Prix.

The forecast rain arrived at 9.00 a.m. practice. A cautious first three laps were wise, ensuring qualification, but I seemed after that to be mired in carefulness, only starting to speed up properly just as the flag came out. So it would be a lowly grid position… The first race was also wet; I don't remember doing too terribly, but the main memory was of a misfire towards the end, engine dying out on the last lap, and being towed in.

Over lunch break, I missed the Sport Specials gathering to debate any future alterations to the rules. Never mind, it was more important to find the fault if possible. We'd had a lively e-mail debate already where I had put my pennyworth in, anyway.

Tom Bell was at the meeting, not competing after an accident at work. He brought the laptop over, thinking probably the coil. His assistant Rick managed to plug it in, volunteering to crawl upside down under the cockpit side cover with his mate ready to pull him back out by his feet if need be. Don't you just love modern technology?

I found a new replacement coil in a box, which I think Tom had produced at the time of the engine build. Together with a small alteration at the tensioner pulley, removing one of the spacing washers to cure a tendency for the belt to hop one rib over, I now had a smooth-running and smooth-looking engine for the last race of the season.

We had to wait ages on the Melbourne Straight assembly area, due to one or more incidents in the preceding Classic Stock Hatch race tying up the medical cover. But you do reflect at such times on the great job done by these medical staff and marshals, without whom we could not race.

When we got going, at least the sun was shining, and

I pressed on, overtaking quite a few. OK, they weren't the fastest in the field, but it was good experience, the car felt good, confidence and fun factor higher now. Towards the end I hauled in two battling MEVs, but the obvious passing place on the back straight was thwarted by yellow flags. And then it was over. A good finish to the season, and encouraging for the following year. I seemed to be back where I started at Brands Hatch those months ago, starting from behind and working my way forwards. But the car was a lot more sorted, and through all the ups and downs I hadn't missed any meetings, except for Cadwell while we were away. I needed to find a couple of seconds and get on a par with the other front engine Duratec cars. It should be there in the driver somewhere…

Shouldn't it?

18

A Genuine Wild Man

After Donington, the car was tucked up in the garage whilst other family conveyances fought for drive space. October came and went. And November. I helped with some garden work and watched the odd video from the season's racing. I wasn't entirely idle, devoting my spare minutes to daydreaming about improvements to the car. Daydreams turned into phone calls and I did some research about possible ways forward.

The serious research led to serious spending. By the time March came around the twenty-five quid second-hand Sierra gearbox had been to Kent and back and was now a heavy-duty close-ratio item from BGH Geartech. The exhaust system had been improved, with a stainless steel silencer and connecting pipe, by Pipetech of Hunmanby, not too far away near the Yorkshire coast. Messing about with the cockpit cover resulted in having an arrangement where the 'passenger side' bit could be removed independently of the screen – that, at least, only cost my time. I rejected the temptation of new bodywork from Rob to replace the tired and toasted original, on grounds of reeling bank account, inability of gleamingness to improve lap times, and irrational fear that the law of sod might come into play and prang it first time out.

After driving the car one yard back and one yard forward, it was time for the theoretical good idea of doing some sort of shakedown with the car. So I did the well-organised thing of booking with Javelin for their track day at Blyton Park in mid-March. I sometimes think that when I do well-organised things it is a massive temptation for the fickle finger of fate, and that I should stick to the tried and tested strategy of last-minute panic, as it has often worked reasonably well in the past.

In this case, the fickle finger of fate inserted itself within the tightly crammed bonnet innards of my Transit, and began to rummage, not in a good way. I usually asked Doug to look at the van stuff for me, as I rarely had time or facilities, let alone the inclination, to get too involved. It had just had a yearly service and MOT, and coincidentally the Dual Mass Flywheel/clutch arrangement was overdue for sorting, so much so that they couldn't get it running reliably enough to do the emissions testing on the first MOT visit. I got a Valeo solid flywheel/clutch conversion kit, very reasonably priced, and Doug fitted it, sorting the troublesome EGR valve also while access was… moderate. The normal access condition being near impossible on the RWD Transit.

Result! Running fine, torquey, quiet, no rattles. The plan was to use it for a few days, then take it back to the garage to re-bleed the clutch. Then it wouldn't start after work on the third day… I got a lift home, without the mental strength to summon the RAC till the following day. The RAC guy got it going with Easy Start, pointing to a fuel issue. It was OK once it got going, just being a bit down on fuel pressure when cranking. So I was able to drive it to the garage, where it sat whilst I stewed and phoned Javelin to cancel the track day. There were no fault codes, so it pointed to something physical, so to speak. There was no reason to think the problem couldn't be solved eventually, but the problem was now in my head, in that it owed me, and had failed in its loyalty. Instead of calmly reviewing logical possibilities, I found myself daydreaming of cutting a branch, with which to thrash it.

The van was a 2006 model, 2.4 Duratorc turbo diesel. The newest tow vehicle I had ever had, and so far the only one to let me down on the way to a race meeting. After that, it did build up some credit for quite a while. But…

It disgraced itself with a weep of oil from the sump, which was… the sump becoming rusty enough to become porous… when did that used to happen in simpler days??

Immediately after getting that done, I found a noise to be… the crankshaft pulley loose due to becoming delaminated… when did that used to happen in simpler days??

And more recently of course, the DMF disintegrating, which we knew was on the cards at some point… when did that used to happen in simpler days??

When you go on Internet forums to look at people's experiences with these faults and the starting issue, it seems Transits (the straightforward, traditional rear-wheel-drive layout) are cans of worms powered by hornets' nests within an enigma wrapped in a conundrum surpassing most people's ability to have the faintest idea how to solve any issues. The funniest comment I remember was the sardonic assertion that we now have to view flywheels as routine service items…

Whilst awaiting developments, I typed in 'what van is the most reliable' on Google. I was going to type in 'what van breaks down the most' but it threw up the former search, so I checked it out. Staggeringly, the Transit has in recent years topped the poll of reliable vans by fleet and hire operators. What that says about the rest, goodness only knows.

My conclusion is that fleet and hire operators get rid of these vehicles before they are five years old, and then the general working guy bears the brunt of the cynically designed complexity and lack of standardisation which is now built in to modern vehicles. Nothing gets scrapped for age-related corrosion any more; it doesn't last long enough before some 'module', which never existed until recently, fails, or appears to fail through lack of knowledgeable diagnosis, either way the vehicle becomes an immobile money pit putting some hapless tradesman back on the dole.

So if you can't afford a new one, you're a pleb and must suffer accordingly.

As a pleb, I typed in 'Tow Bar' to eBay. Hoping that if there was one attached to some sort of cheapish and mechanically predictable vehicle within a reasonable radius of Hull, I thought I might stand a chance of getting to the racing season…

Thankfully it didn't come to that. Doug found 100,000 miles worth of eroded high-pressure pump minuscule fragments in the fuel rail, enough to prevent the right pressure building up on cranking. The pump itself seems to last reasonably well on these models, however the reliance on diesel fuel for the lubrication where a triangular central cam bears on the small pistons that generate the required colossal pressure, would appear to be the Achilles heel of these common rail systems. The pressure they develop precludes the inclusion of a filter between pump and rail…

So, having saved a random amount of money through not finding a desperate eBay impulse purchase with a tow bar fitted, I was a bit more relaxed going down to Donington for the first meeting, in the familiar Devil I Know (Transit). The mood was further improved when early arrivals were able to get their cars scrutineered on Friday evening, saving a hideously early scramble in the morning.

Practice went well until the clutch pedal went to the floor just before the pit straight, at least convenient for coasting in. The nut and bolt through the clutch release arm end had gone missing from the wide part of the pear-shaped aperture where they were installed to prevent the cable end escaping.

Again. Through the wide part of the pear-shaped aperture presumably…

At least for this year I had installed a small trapdoor affair in the flat floor for just this eventuality, so after jacking the car up, I had vaguely acceptable hand access to install a better bolt arrangement, instead of the virtually impossible scream-inducing swear-fest of trying to reach it from above. Then people started walking past reminding me about a drivers' briefing, which I had heard nothing about. I did find an updated set of instructions from the club after I got home from the meeting, but que sera…

So it ended up with a rush to get out after dutifully listening to this year's strictures on staying on the grey bit, not the green bit. And I thought the clutch cable adjustment would do, at least for the first race…

It was OK for the start, but not for getting second gear. By the time I somehow got the gear selected, I was last away. On the bright side, this removed any immediate worry about whether the new mirror arrangements on the car were adequate. I managed to pass a few cars and was just coming up to pass Alan in my old car, into the chicane, when the crunchiness trying to find third lost me all momentum. We went through side by side, Alan congratulating himself on the tactical acumen of securing the inside line on exit, me fishing for second whilst steering through on to the straight. Multi-tasking never works well for a bloke, according to my wife.

I eventually got up through the gears, catching up with Alan again and then, once in fourth, resolving to leave it there for the rest of the race. It wasn't a bad result considering, some fairly consistent lap times and a position of eleventh, but nevertheless frustrating, as the new third ratio had been quite handy in parts of the track.

I hadn't joined in the pre-season frenzy to acquire the Avon wet tyres we were now allowed. I was frankly a bit weary of all the expenditure, exhaust, gearbox, and lately the van. I would have preferred the other option on the table, a gradual transition to Toyo 888's, thus saving carrying two sets of wheels to meetings, but more participants must have voted for the Yokohama plus Avon Wets option. I had a secret master plan though. Hope, strongly, that it wouldn't rain on Sunday for our second race of the weekend.

The Strong Hope plan was a failure. I had spent the dry late afternoon of Saturday getting the clutch cable adjustment sorted. This was good, for the forecast rain did indeed make Sunday morning a misery, and at least I wasn't working on the car. In the race, I found second gear fine, and the wheelspin with it. So last away again, and this time I just could not find the traction to get past the MEV ahead of me. Eventually I spun coming out of Redgate. Keeping it running going backwards, I flicked it round as nothing was coming for a while, then remembered that if I went backwards as far as the gravel, I would likely be stuck broadside to the track. So I waited patiently, broadside on the smooth grey bit, till Mark Hextall, who had been delayed by a problem, came round Redgate and slowed and didn't drive into me. Thank you, Mark, I knew my plan of your actions would work.

Then on to the finish. A somewhat mixed weekend, but some signs of promise among it all. We were on holiday during the next round, Silverstone National, not my favourite track anyway.

So my attention turned to Croft, where we were due to race in late May. I had bought a Mark 2 Mazda MX5 some months earlier, as a toy to have a more entertaining ride to work. In this I journeyed north, and I met my brother up there for one of Javelin's track days on Good Friday. Despite it being damp at best, all day, we enjoyed it greatly amidst the red flags where people got caught out. The legal but well-worn Pirellis on the front of the car caused comical understeer on Hawthorn and

Tower especially, but it was nevertheless a good way to learn the best way round, in addition to a few laps with Helen the instructor, near the start of the day.

And in a flush of enthusiasm, I even booked the 750MC test day before our race weekend, a first for me. I had done a pre-season day with the MR2, but never joined the serious fraternity on a pre-race test day before. I would be able to practise what I had learned, at race speeds. And if the clutch cable would stay put, I might emerge into the rarefied air where there are no excuses left.

Somewhere I have a tape cassette from the last century, circa 1979. It features Frank Zappa recorded from a Radio 1 programme where he was the guest DJ. On it he features a track from the more than slightly deranged Wild Man Fischer, for whom he produced an album. By way of preamble, Frank relates a story to illustrate the point that Larry Fischer was 'a genuine wild man', describing how Fischer broke his own brother's breastbone in an attack with a hammer. "One day," he says in his inimitable drawl, "they found themselves walking towards each other on the UCLA campus. Larry had the ballpein hammer, and his brother had the bad luck…"

After the weekend at Croft, I felt a little like Fischer's brother, or at least my car did. It all started quite innocuously, up there in good time on Thursday for the test day on the Friday, meal in the pub, chat with a couple of the Sport Specials lads, turn in reasonably early ready for a fairly civilised first session start of 9.30.

The car had been slightly high on noise at Donington, to the extent I had had the silencer box off just to check, the weekend before. Nothing amiss with the wadding, and giving a consistent 100db on my driveway near to the house, so it couldn't be improved upon anyway. Making sure it was warmed up properly in my garage (I had parted with an extra thirty quid in a fit of plutocracy and rented a pit garage) I drove out to the pit lane, where it passed the noise test without comment.

Then we were out. Working my way up to some sort of race pace, I wasn't being caught by any of the Sport Specials lads as far as I knew, and even seemed to be hauling in Tony Gaunt in his RGB car up ahead, till he finished fiddling with whatever switch enabled his bravery pill to take effect and shot off into the distance. A few laps later, he and one or two other of the RGBs had gone past me, and I was aware of another one of them somewhere behind as we tackled the Clark Esses. This section leads into Barcroft, a shallow right hander which is 'pretty simple', according to Mark Hales in his CCC (*Cars and Car Conversions*) analysis a few years ago.

I took an outside line, figuring this would leave plenty of room for the RGB car to go through on the inside onto the straight stretch before 'Sunny In', the tight right-hander. It turned out he didn't want to take this route, instead appearing suddenly in my blind-spot area. What happened next took place in a fraction of a second and was a matter of instinct as much as reasoning. It seemed he wanted the same piece of road that I was heading for, and given that there was no road remaining on my left, my last recollection of him was of the RGB car heading away from me on that outside line, before my consciousness was filled with the green green grass of what the hell next.

Some of us walked the track later that evening, and the grass area where my wheel tracks were was about fifty feet wide. Just now, with my perceptions in overdrive, it looked about a hundred feet wide. Still a massive problem though. The first job was to ease it off a collision course with the Marshals' Post and tyre wall, which I managed. The second was to stay as long as possible on the grass, which I didn't. Gradually the car slewed, ignoring the judicious bit of corrective lock, and quite soon I was a victim heading almost broadside towards the track, hoping what traffic there was, would miss me.

It didn't. The other victim was a green RGB car heading straight on into Sunny. I had about a car length of travel to go whilst anticipating the inevitable sickening crunch. We both ended up on the infield, fortunately uninjured, corners of cars in tatters.

With a helpful recovery crew, the car was returned to the garage I had rented for the day. Ironically, Rob was on his way up fairly early to do the final set-up of his new car. But he didn't carry spare wishbones, so that was game over for the weekend, and there was no desperate rush to remove torn splitter, patch wrecked bonnet, find a radiator, and remount the engine which had moved forward tearing all its mountings. That included the gearbox tailshaft mount, which had sheared.

Various people passed the garage offering sympathy, and an occasional opinion. Most of the opinions from anybody in the RGB fraternity involved variations on the 'Him… Oh yes, we know all about him' theme. He was probably psychologically incapable of conceptualising that he had caused all the carnage just before Sunny corner, if he came by during the red flag period.

I spent the rest of the day taking some damaged bits off the car and getting it eventually on to the trailer, with the help of Alan Robinson's generator trolley. I stayed over and enjoyed some good yarns with the Sport Specials competitors, then it was back home on the Saturday to fill our old pond in, a job originally earmarked for the Monday and Tuesday, which were now devoted to car unloading and stripping.

The trouble with going out on a test day with other classes, is that you are not familiar with their driving standards, and may not recognise the odd wild man bringing the bad luck.

A plan was formulated, to create a chance of getting out

for Cadwell. The episode was character-building, as they say, although I couldn't help but feel that after over forty years of adult trial and error, I had already built it and shouldn't have had to dip into the 'cheerful resilience' reserves yet again.

The first task in getting the Cyana into some sort of shape was to extract the engine and box, as the rear gearbox mount would have to be welded back together where it had sheared off. I found a very helpful chap in Tony of AJ's Motorcycles, who had been recommended to me by a colleague who had had a Lambretta engine casing reclaimed by him. He did a great job on this small plinth which incorporates the threads for the locating bolt at the back end of the type 9 gearbox, boxing in the sides for extra strength whilst he was at it.

Rob Johnston kindly agreed to mould a new bonnet and remake the bent wishbones, but couldn't start until the week before Cadwell. In the meantime I had plenty to do, finding a replacement radiator, and engine mounting bobbins. Not to mention replacing the gearbox on the bellhousing and thence onto the engine.

After another weekend's work replacing the engine and box, I was ready to trek to Rob's workshop in the Stoke area, where on the following Saturday Rob and Alec produced my bright RAL 5017 'Traffic Blue' bonnet. The shade matched the paint I had used on some parts of the car, so was a bit more predictable than something chosen from a small oblong on a colour chart. Black was never going to be an option this time. Surprisingly, despite my desire to show up clearly on other competitors' YouTube videos, I managed to resist the Fuchsia Pink route, Mrs R feeling that the anti-theft pink race trailer had already put enough strain on the household's machismo reserves. (After three out of the four trailers I had owned since starting racing had been stolen, enough was enough. I knew I was on the right lines when the bullet-headed Chopper Harris lookalike in the paint suppliers was horrified by the choice – what self-respecting thief would be seen with it?)

I left the car with Rob overnight and returned on the Sunday afternoon, by which time he had remanufactured the offside wishbones and got the car on four wheels again, using some loaned shocker units. The right-hand damper had also bent in the crash, and I had to send the original pair to Protech, to see if they could refurbish the damaged one to the original spec. All Rob's work was greatly appreciated, as he and father Alec gave up a good part of the weekend to help get me going again.

It then remained to attach the new radiator, sort out various ancillaries, and mount the new bonnet. All this, together with the gradual enlargement of the air filter aperture, which must be a tight fit to the filters to comply with the regulations, took all of Monday, Tuesday, then the Wednesday, Thursday and Friday evenings after work. Amazingly the bonnet fitted near enough first time on Thursday, my measurements having worked as far as the small fixings at top and sides were concerned. A relief to say the least, as there was no time for any rectification or redesign had it been needed.

Finally I started the car up and sat in to try the clutch, at about 7 p.m. on the Friday evening. The straightened operating rod to the new rod end spherical bearing which screws into the chassis, and the new cable, a cut down Ford item, didn't want to play ball, and the car just kept creeping forward. Just before fish and chips were put on the table at 8.15, I tried detaching the stop bolt at the bottom of the pedal, believing this to be the source of the slight clunk I could hear at the end of the travel, rather than the release arm coming into contact with the outer bellhousing due to some unfathomable stupidity during reassembly.

This was the last resort really. Only utter despair beckoned otherwise. It worked!

We travelled to Cadwell on the Saturday morning, taking advantage of a late scrutineering session for once. Practice was a bit tentative, and my eventual speeding up didn't quite materialise when we were red-flagged after only four laps. But I was back out there, and the car felt pretty good considering no set-up work had been done on it whatsoever.

An enjoyable weekend's racing ensued, bringing it back in one piece. I had obtained some Honda CBR 600 mirrors from Tony at the motorcycle place, which I fitted during the course of the meeting. After adjustment before the Sunday race, I was much happier than I had been with the old arrangement. These mirrors were standard for the car, according to Rob!

The only thing which caused me some concern was the degree of underbonnet pressure evident on the faster parts of the track. It was obvious that some sort of venting towards the back of the bonnet would help. The mountings at the front were pretty strong, but any hint whatsoever of a large blue fibreglass shell taking to the sky above Cadwell Park was somewhat inhibiting to flat-out speed, and some caution prevailed.

There had been no time for even thoughts of a replacement splitter, let alone any action. Anton Landon remarked that I had dispensed with the splitter, but I said that it was the oncoming car that had done that! At least I could drive it onto the trailer at this meeting rather than messing with extra ramps. And I had taken the rear spoiler off to balance things out a bit. Very scientific.

2015 turned into an extended experiment on the effectiveness of underside aerodynamics. An empirical investigation as opposed to an academic perusal of theory. Why follow the wisdom of well-qualified experts when you can make it up as you go along?

In fact, the piecemeal rebuilding of the front-end bodywork

was dictated by time constraints rather than the desire to compare various configurations of GRP and aluminium. Nevertheless the effects were interesting if hardly about to change Adrian Newey's[18] world.

After the rebuildathon following the prang, Cadwell was tackled with the new bonnet attached by wing nuts onto threaded studs at the front, where the underbonnet valance is mounted to the spaceframe extension. Plus the usual spring clips at the side and vertical pins with latches near the bulkhead.

I like to include vents at the back of the bonnet on this type of car, especially this Cyana where the flat floor closes off the area where air might normally readily escape under the propshaft tunnel. But there had been no time at all for such a refinement; just getting the bonnet to fit on the day before the race had been an achievement. And remaking an air dam and splitter to replace the shattered plywood one was a complete non-starter at this stage.

Watching the top of the bonnet flexing upwards on Cadwell's back straight confirmed my fears, and three large air outlets were made later. I was able to get to a track day at Blyton before our next race at Snetterton, and the experience was much more enjoyable, no sign now of the flexing. So I thought Snett could be tackled with more peace of mind, without rushing to sort out a splitter etc. But you didn't really get out of third gear in this car at Blyton…

So the question to be answered was… if you have a flat floor, is it worth running without an air dam and splitter; might the reduction in drag from the air dam be a worthwhile advantage in terms of top speed down the straight?

No.

---

18 Adrian Newey, highly successful race car designer with Williams, McLaren and Red Bull in particular.

Or rather, I don't know. Because I didn't quite dare to go flat out due to the amount of front-end lift on the whole car, never mind the bonnet. I had left the rear spoiler off, which had it remained, would have presumably made the issue even worse. As it was, Colin Benham, watching on the pit wall, was vociferous.

"It's lifting six inches!!"

An adjustment of ride height helped a bit before the second race, but it was clearly time to get my finger out and organise the splitter.

I took the opportunity to do it in aluminium, 16-gauge. Patrick Shears did a fantastic job welding the air dam part to the flat splitter part.

I used 3mm rubber sheet from Industrial Supplies in Hull to seal the gap between bonnet valence and air dam. The bonnet simply rested against it, with the rubber obviously flexing, but having enough firmness to maintain its 'verticality'. The air pressure does the rest.

Together with a redesigned bracket to hold the top lip of the bonnet to the mounting holes on the lower valance, addressing the issue of lift on the front surface of the bonnet behind the air intake, the combination made its debut at Castle Combe, in the aerodynamic equivalent of re-inventing the wheel.

Much better. On a track I had never seen before, I was happy with modest placings. I think that's a euphemism for 'last' actually, but I enjoyed the outings.

So to Mallory, the last meeting and the last chance to find my lost driving mojo. Misfiring issues in qualifying were tackled by a swap of coil pack, however this didn't prove to be the answer. Prompted by Colin, I overcame my deep-seated fear of deep-seated spark plugs and swapped them for a new set.

Eureka. I was finally up to some sort of speed, the sort of

pace I should have been at before Croft, and much faster than I had ever been round Mallory before.

So, after an uphill climb, finally arriving at square one with body and car intact was a welcome relief.

But it had been the last race of the season.

So, nevertheless, doh!

19

2016. A Season of Unequivocal and Unparalleled Success Using an Innovative Tactic which Nobody Else had Contemplated

We'd had a whale of a time at the 2014 awards do when I went for my 2013 trophy. So we thought we'd go to the dinner dance again in January 2016, just for a jaunt this time. It would be a treat before the new season.

It was fine until after the meal, when the band unfortunately thought that extreme volume might be a substitute for confidence and skill. Well, they may have had some skill, but you couldn't discern whether or not this was the case, such was the sonic attack. We braved the bludgeoning soundwaves for a couple of dances, but then took our bleeding ears out of range, to the more civilized environs of the lobby.

Here it was possible to hear people speak, and it was no great surprise to find that the year's new rules were the main topic amongst many. There had been an evolution the previous year, with the variety of cars that were coming out to play. We still had Duratec (A) and Zetec (B), but Class C, for everything else, had been a non-championship class before 2015, when it became more formalised by introducing a power to weight limit, which enabled people to compete for championship points.

Now there was talk of upping the power to weight ratio figure. (340bhp per tonne including driver if you're fascinated.) People were getting excited. Racing drivers always get excited by more power. Even though all the other racing drivers get excited by more power. So you just end up in the same place, only faster.

It had all rather passed me by, but with just five regular competitors in the standard spec Duratec class at the end of the year, it seemed the class wasn't appealing to new entrants in the way the Zetec class used to do some years earlier. And Nigel and Anton had a gleam in their eyes. As probably did Rob, always interested in outright wins.

What did I think? Tempting?

That's what everybody else thought.

I just saw more expense.

The only expense I had planned was for a more cosmetic project. The car was still half black and half blue. Which was OK for Inter Milan or a Rolling Stones album title, but a trifle unsubtle on my car, which currently arrived as blue but still departed as black. So I asked Rob to do a rear-end-cum-cockpit surround in my favoured RAL 5017, Traffic Blue.

Without being outrageous, it was pleasantly bright; enough to stand out when looking for myself on others' YouTube video recordings. There weren't any other bright blue cars on the grid usually either. All I had to do was go a bit faster to get in front of someone like Colin Benham, whose son Richard had produced some involving race films from the on-board camera. It was a plan that wasn't entirely foolproof. Nevertheless, a video camera was on the list of things I didn't want to afford, along with uprated engine and racing trolley jack lower than an ironed snake doing a limbo dance.

I was grateful to Stephen Ward for letting me borrow his racing trolley jack lower than an ironed snake doing a limbo dance, when we got to Oulton Park for the first race of the year. Conditions were horrible, the change to wet tyres essential. So getting the front end off the ground with one lift was appreciated.

Leaving the heroics to people like Rob, Clive and Adrian at the front, I was happy to survive the drenched first race. I caught up with Billy but felt a kamikaze dive to pass wouldn't be worth the risk. The second race was a lot more fun; you could even see where you were going, which I prefer. I worked my way past Alan, Colin Childs, and finally Billy, but then threw it all away exiting Lodge Corner. A rear wheel on the wooden washboardy bit that protected the grass didn't worry me, such was my exuberance.

It should have worried me, because the lack of grip resulted in a spin that took me over to the inside of the track before it finished. Luckily Billy, whom I had just passed, didn't collide with me, and I resumed and reached the finish. I was still upbeat; at least I was trying, albeit nearer the Brambilla than the Stewart end of the tidiness spectrum. My brother had come along to watch, along with his mate Mark, who was tickled to inform me that the commentator had said I was 'having a bit of a ding dong' with the cars around me. Can't be bad.

Even better, there was a bizarre development at the end of the day. Nigel and Anton had indeed breathed on their engines and decamped to the Class C. As had Rob. And Clive. And Paul Boyd. Leaving only me and John Moore in Class A. Which would be an interesting challenge, on the evidence of John being third fastest in qualifying and me being twenty-second fastest.

But John hadn't finished the second race for some reason. Which left me taking home a trophy for first in Class A. Weird-o-rama.

Next time out, at Brands Hatch, would be tougher on the trophy hunting front. John had brought a second car for an 'arrive and drive' competitor to sample. Young Paul was fast, too. But with a mechanical issue on the second car, John had to hurriedly re-jig the seating in his own car for Paul to get out racing. And then, for some reason, Paul didn't complete the second race. Which left me coming away with, strangely, a trophy for second, and another for first in class. Bonkers.

Phil and his wife came along to watch, and I passed Alan going in to Paddock Hill on the inside, which would be a move I could bore people with in the telling, for years to come, should I wish. Alan managed to cover my line all through the second race though, and I never got by, so I wouldn't be relating the story of that particular race quite so often.

Croft was the third meeting, where I discovered that John had moved his two cars into Class C. Which left me as the only Class A competitor for the rest of the year. Which left the top of the chest of drawers in our lounge hosting a forest of trophies at the end of the year. Which needed polishing. Which I was constantly being reminded about. Drat.

Croft was a lot of fun, relaxed, quite fine weather, cheerful paddock. But my wife thought I was rather inhibited round the Barcroft/Sunny area. Which was disappointing. Now I had to be my own sports psychologist as well as my own engineer. Well, I do have a psychology degree…

Snetterton 300 was next up. Quite fun if damp. I left the wets on for race two, which was an error really, as the track had dried too much. I was by now operating a strategy of staying with whatever tyre choice had been made half an hour before the off. I just didn't want the ball-ache of swapping them in any sort of hurry. Which left me hoping for a shower that never came.

So the car was a bit slidey, but I didn't really mind that. I minded the slowness a bit but it didn't spoil the day. Perhaps that's the secret; winners have more spoilt days if they don't do well.

Receiving the customary two trophies for finishing, I was pleased to present Mel with one of them, as chief mechanic. He had helped with spanner wielding as I rectified the customary alternator derangement.

Cadwell followed, behind Alan both times. He had made a lot of improvements to my old car, and had got his hand in as a driver, but I didn't find either thought offered much compensation. I was still outside that old 1.49 Phoenix time as well. Thank goodness my engineer didn't have much to do this year, because my psychologist was struggling. Bloody degree…

Rockingham. Qualified quite well in the wetness. With the race being wet too, I beat Alan, Billy and Colin Childs fair and square. Reasonably pleased. Mark Hextall caught and passed me as I used a defensive line at Tarzan Hairpin – which gave him a quicker line out. Never mind, you live and learn. Wasn't it getting a bit late for that? Maybe I hadn't had enough experience of holding off following rivals over the years. Being at the back already…

Credit to Mark for catching up. Getting in range gives you a target. And the target might start looking in his mirrors too much. Which is psychologically damaging on the racetrack if not in the driving school environment. Thanks for that one, Mister Psychologist.

The second Rockingham race was on the following day. Facilities at Rockingham consist of garages. And quite a few other garages. We spent the evening in said garages talking about next year's formula. Over beers, naturally. For next year, my Class A would be no more, my hegemony over a vacuum no longer tolerated. Hardly surprising. The trophy budget was probably strained.

There would be two power to weight classes only. All that remained was to vote on a maximum engine size for the Class

B/270bhp per tonne runners. Clearly 1800cc would be fairest, as the 1800cc version of the Zetec had been specified hitherto. Why should they end up spending money in a new power race if it was upped to 2000cc? My wife took the piss out of me for arguing against my own interests 'for the sake of the formula.'

As a member of the outside world, I guess she didn't see such heroic altruism as something that would seriously dent the genetic theories of the likes of Haldane and Dawkins.

In the race on Sunday, my start wasn't too impressive, but what was worse was the failure to reel in the Class B runners ahead of me, in dry conditions. The pendulum swung towards a keen sense of disappointment.

I had become obsessed with the throttle linkage around this period, fearing I wasn't getting full travel. A twin cable system from Jenvey looked like a sensible upgrade. The previous single cable had always worked, but the pedal box area had provision for two cables. Yet after changing it, it seemed impossible to adjust for full opening at the butterfly. The system relied on a threaded rod coming up from a lever near the bottom of the pedal, which was kinked in an S-shape to go through a spherical bearing attached to the bulkhead. In this way it was restrained from flopping about and contacting any pedals.

The psychologist had abdicated responsibility to the engineer, who toiled for hours over all possible adjustments. In the end I delegated the job to the local engineering shop after Cadwell. Just solve it.

Tom was still working with them at the time, but I assume the job was done by a junior guy. They had drilled another hole, I was told. Fine.

When I looked closely after getting the car back, I didn't find a new hole somewhere in the quadrant near the throttle bodies where I had assumed it would be. No, somebody had used a bit of lateral thinking. It was so lateral that I would never have thought of it. The spherical bearing had previously been mounted through a small steel plate welded to the chassis. Which prevented the necessary travel downwards, of the small plate near the top of the threaded rod, which pulled the cables. Now the spherical bearing was mounted lower, through the aluminium part of the bulkhead. Err, what?

It worked, but only because there was now a degree of flex where it came through the aluminium. It would be wise to check the tightness where the bolt coming through the bulkhead joined the spherical bearing, before each meeting. Subject to this, I felt OK to go out in it. Of course, a year or so down the line as I write, the flexing has started to enlarge the drilling in the aluminium bulkhead where the bolt and bearing come through. Predictable.

So much for abdicating responsibility from the psychologist to the engineer to the lateral-thinking bodger...

We finished off at Donington. People had been amused to comment that I might walk away with the overall championship, the way things were going up to Cadwell. Thankfully, that wouldn't quite be possible, since if starters in a class are fewer than five, the points are limited, so you get nine instead of fifteen for winning the class. The bare-faced front to accept a class trophy had been easy to muster, but the overall championship might have tested the thickest skin.

The heavens opened just before our race, resulting in a wait on the grid getting wetter and wetter whilst lengthy deliberations took place. Eventually I climbed out and joined most of the others in the garages, leaving the car on the grid, knowing the seat would now no longer be the only dry bit on the car. Alan, being a yachtsman, stuck it out much longer. It all became academic when racing was abandoned for the day.

The second race was on the Sunday, so we had to stay over. We drove to a pub a few miles away, to have an evening meal. Thanks again, Mr Ecclestone.

I enjoyed the race for the season finale, finishing ahead of

Alan, Marcus and Paul Cooper, but I think they all had a spin at some point. But, to finish sixteenth, first you have to finish…

In fact, it was a good year for finishing, I'd done every race with no DNFs at all. And I could have had '5' on the car for the following year, because I finished fifth overall. But I preferred 27 even though I'm no Villeneuve. Some years back a journalist went round the 750MC paddock interviewing every competitor who was running with the number 27. He told me that most of them had never thought about the connection with Villeneuve. Incredible.

That'll be even more the case, now. We went to view a Croft Nostalgia race meeting not long ago, where a couple of young hot-shoes were interviewed by the commentator after caning some historic Formula 3 cars to a close finish. What type of engine is in the car, one was asked. He didn't have the slightest idea.

My dad, by way of contrast, was so keen on treating machinery with respect, that he threw a complete wobbler on witnessing Roger Daltrey twirling his microphone around on *Top of the Pops*…

There is one thing to be said for digging one's heels in and stubbornly refusing to follow the herd into the future…

It can bring a class championship.

But only if the moon is in the seventh house and Jupiter aligns with Mars.

And one racing driver isn't bothered about more power, which happens about once a century.

20

The Blue Dragon

There is an odd little tale by Kurt Vonnegut, which Denise pointed out to me a few years ago, as it concerned a sports car. Vonnegut was best known for the novel *Slaughterhouse-Five*[19], in which he tries to exorcise some of his thoughts concerning his experience of the firebombing of Dresden in WW2, as a prisoner of war sheltering in a meat locker in the abattoir which served as an internment camp. Those were different days, when Air Chief Marshal Arthur Harris, the RAF's head of Bomber Command, was stopped one night for speeding in his Bentley. The policeman made his point.

"You could kill somebody, driving like that."

"I kill hundreds every night."

Different days. Or so we say. The earth seems always overburdened with lunatics who are prepared to initiate such conflagrations.

We take refuge in the everyday, the mundane. And Vonnegut was no exception. He had to earn a living, writing short pieces for magazines and so on, before his magnum opus catapulted him to the bestseller list.

---

19 *Slaughterhouse-Five, or the Children's Crusade: A Duty-Dance with Death.* Kurt Vonnegut. 1969. Delacorte.

The story, *The Powder Blue Dragon*, first published in Cosmopolitan in 1954, involves a youth living in a resort town in the USA. He works all hours in several unremarkable jobs, bothering no one, exciting no one. He patiently saves his money for four years, and one day walks across the road to the car dealership where he helps out during the summer season. He shocks his boss by placing an order for a rare electric blue Italian sports car. Nobody of his social background would dream of owning such an exotic and delicate beauty of an automobile. Yet he buys it, with all the money he has so patiently saved up.

When it arrives from the dealership in New York, he is given the keys, as a crowd watches in wonderment. The dealer warns him to protect the precision components in the engine, which he describes as being like jewels, by gradually breaking it in, limiting his speed for the first few thousand miles.

He drives away. Encountering a beautiful girl driving a Cadillac on the highway, he follows her to an exclusive watering hole, where he attempts to engage her in conversation. After a while her boyfriend shows up in his British sports car. Humiliated by the way the bartender and the boyfriend have treated him, he follows the couple after they leave in the British roadster, which looks like a 'black pig' next to his exquisite Italian beauty.

Overtaking them, he engages in something of a race. Drives faster and faster until the black car is left far behind. The engine becomes hotter and hotter, the oil gauge at zero and the temperature gauge off the scale by the time he pulls up outside the showroom where he started. The dealer is heartbroken when he sees what the lad has done to the jewel-like engine components, which have melted and fused and collapsed into a worthless mess. The protagonist walks away, feeling that he has slain a dragon, and the story ends.

No car enthusiast would be able to understand this story. I

still don't. Yet after a track day at Cadwell Park in the middle of the 2017 season, I was to recall it.

I had booked the day to test the car whilst running with slightly hotter rated plugs. Tom, the engine builder, had recommended NGK '9' plugs (each manufacturer has a different numbering system, very helpful) at the start of the year. The 9s are so called 'cold' plugs, less likely to melt in the environment of a highly-tuned engine. Your road car might use NGK 6, for example. The logic is to start with cold ones, moving to hotter until you get reliability – plugs are cheaper than pistons.

But the 9s had been found to be extremely sooty at the end of a race, so here I was testing 8s. It seemed a good idea at the time.

After following the track day course-car around on the obligatory sighting laps, I relaxed with a sausage sandwich while the early hotheads got out on track. Preparing at my leisure to go out, I got changed, sat in the car, pressed the starter. Nothing. Oh please, not the starter motor again.

The battery, hitherto a reliable servant, had picked this day to sigh its last. Fortunately, it was a reasonably accessible component, in the left passenger space rather than the original rather bizarre location behind the left rear wheel where Rob had it. You can carry weight-distribution tweaking rather too far at times.

I had a spare battery in the van, and with tools and boxes scattered everywhere after digging for it, I was eventually ready. Again.

I think I did one exploratory session before changing the plugs. Memory seems to have been obliterated by the trauma which came next. I think the lunch break intervened before I went out with the fresh set of plugs.

Get up to speed. Yes, these are better. I think. Accelerate up Coppice Hill. Oh no. They're not better. Misfire.

Was it a subconscious desire to slay the Blue Dragon? A deep and unexplored subterranean labyrinth of my mind into which I ventured, with my shield of scientific knowledge and sword of truth, seeking the lair of the terrifying demon within.

No.

It was pure stupidity.

These spark plugs are no better.

It's not running right.

I can smell oil.

The top bend is a bit slippy. (It will be if you've got oil on your wheels.)

Maybe I am going faster, because it's difficult to slow at the end of the straight. (It will be if you've got oil on your wheels.)

It's definitely running badly.

Much worse. (It will be if the oil is on your wheels instead of in your engine.)

Don't want to go bouncing over the grass, this low splitter will get wrecked. (A much cheaper item than the engine, although it was probably too late by now to save the latter.)

Got to get back to the paddock.

Turn engine off. (Before it turned itself off.)

Got to look underneath.

Got to mop up oil.

Got to admit crass stupidity to organisers.

Got to spend the best part of an hour mopping up oil.

Got to accept I had cost people half an hour's driving by leaving oil over half the track.

Got to thank helpful young people next to me in their Clio, or was it a Saxo, for helping me mop.

Got to drive home knowing that things have gone from bad, to much, much worse.

Got to text Tom.

Got to see if he's got time to rebuild engine.
Got to make sizeable incursion into bank balance.
Got to miss Brands Hatch.

Tom did rebuild the engine, which was a bigger mess than if I had stopped on smelling the oil. Looking at the oil gauge might have been a good idea as well, but that was all history now.

The issue had been caused by an oil pipe coming adrift, which is ultimately my responsibility. The one silver lining, if you can call it that, is that it would have otherwise happened at Brands Hatch. So a rueful drive home after a Cadwell track day, of fifty miles, was better than the 200-mile drive of shame and despair that would have ensued after Brands, if I had not done the Cadwell outing.

I think that bit of speculation is just about on the acceptable side of considering alternative universes. One existence is really enough these days, which is why almost any sci-fi which flirts with time-travel storylines is just a device to deprive you of an hour or two of your life without any tangible benefit in either learning or enjoyment. Time travel – you have moved forward an hour or two in your life, and don't know where it went.

The only reasonable time-travel opus is an obscure Czechoslovakian film from 1977, entitled *Tomorrow I'll Wake Up and Scald Myself with Tea*. It was shown only once on British TV. One report says it took the place of a cancelled World Cup football qualifier, but I can't testify to that. I can only testify to its inventiveness and wit making it one of the funniest films I have ever seen. The plot, involving surviving Nazis, spry from anti-ageing pills, travelling back in time from 1999 (!) to 1943 to give Hitler an A bomb with which to change the course of history, is far too convoluted to dwell on here; suffice to say that the time-travel spaceship pilot (who has replaced his twin brother on the day, as you do) comes out on top and resolves all, or at least most, of the paradoxes created by the dabbling with time.

At one point, the Nazi henchman chases the hero, finding himself back in Prague in the present. But as he has come from the past, he finds himself walking along a bridge, towards his present-time self. Throwing his perplexed current (or was that past?) self over the parapet to his doom, he explains his reasoning.

"It was just getting too complicated."

I felt somewhat the same way. If I had known at the beginning of the season…

It had all started so well. The usual glow of optimism, the usual mild boasting about how good it would be. Should be. I never like to tempt fate by issuing proclamations.

The decision to have the engine 'breathed on' rather than merely 'refreshed' seemed logical at the time. To be able to compete a bit rather than pottering around at the back with the Class B cars. A last fling.

The first price quoted had been rather a shock. Tom had teamed up with the local company 'Race Engineered', and the price their MD gave me was really more than I wanted to entertain at the time. Of course, with the oil pipe debacle, I'd now spent much more than that, but que sera…

The MD's assistant had later worked out a price for me, based on starting with my maximum budget, and the quote entered the realms of 'go for it' rather than 'gulp'. The previous Class A, Duratec with standard spec camshafts, had naturally died out for 2017, since I finished 2016 as its only competitor, so now the old Class C, 340bhp per tonne, was designated as Class A for the upcoming season.

So although nothing said I *had* to, I gave the green light (and the cheque) for Tom to uprate the spec and achieve 225bhp, instead of the previous 200. Being a pure race car, the option of the higher power route would make the car more saleable at the end of the year.

All I had to do was show the car's mettle in the best light and challenge the front runners. Easy…

21

Inner Turmoil

The first meeting with the 'Not-underpowered Car for the First, or maybe Second or Third Time in my Life' of the new year was at Donington in late March. Mrs R came along but only because I'd booked a hotel near the airport. She doesn't do cold van beds in March. Neither did I these days come to think of it. The booking of the hotel turned out to be the best strategic move of the weekend.

All was fine in qualifying. Then the bugbear of intermediate weather raised its head, and we were all changing wheels before going out. Colin Benham pitched in with his cordless wheel wrench to help me finish mine, because although around my age, he is energetic and spry. Spryness exists for me now as a memory only.

So far so good, and I had a reasonable amount of time to change before we were summoned for the race. I leaned down in the van to tie my race boot… AAARGH! I wouldn't classify the feeling as agony, but I had never felt pain and incapacitation to that particular degree in my previously pummelled back. Summoning Mrs R to help me to my feet, I eventually got the race boots sorted and slowly, very slowly, inserted myself into the car. She looked down at me. I have seen a lot of expressions on her face, but I had never, ever seen this one before. It was essentially questioning my sanity. She routinely questions my sanity on a daily basis, but this was different. It said 'I won't stop you but you shouldn't be doing this.'

I got to the assembly area and thought, I shouldn't be doing this. I could feel every little bump in the old seat where Rob's back was a different shape from mine. I had just decided to see sense and drive back to the van, when the whistle went. Thank goodness the wait was over; it was easy now to follow the Pavlovian response and drive to the grid. We'll see how it goes.

And off we went. For the first lap I wasn't even last. But by the end of the second, I was. It had been pretty stupid to even try this, and I pulled back in through the pit lane. I just wasn't comfortable enough to be competitive and therefore relatively safe. Eventually the leaders would come round and catch me, which introduces a risk, however small. And for what gain?

Luckily my wife, with her background working in the NHS, carries a veritable pharmacy in her bag, and we survived the night in the hotel thanks to painkillers and a pizza delivery. I was a bit better on the Sunday but not enough to race so we just watched. Clive and Paul in the Eclipses left all the others miles behind. It was clear even at that point, that the purpose-designed rear-engine cars would now dominate the formula.

I had a week off work, avoiding driving. Then we entertained ourselves by making a seat by the ritual method of sitting in a plastic bag whilst expanding foam within it moulds to the svelte contours of the racing driver's body. Very professional. We did it in two stages, first the arse, then the back. So there's a tip for you. Better than trying to get it all in one mix, panicking to get comfortable before it sets.

Thus armed, and on a high after retiring from work the day before, we arrived at Silverstone in late April. I'd tried to retire on a Sunday to get a couple of days extra pay, but my employers didn't see that as a legitimate option.

I had to sort a misfire after the practice. Ironically, in view of later developments, this time it was just the plug leads. Modern automotive spares seem to have a fraction of the longevity of old, for, in many cases, several times the price. I started from the back and was overtaking several cars including people I'd never caught before. I was heading for a result ahead of a lad that I'd never beaten, who had expressed an interest in maybe buying the car. A good advert for the car's capabilities until I lost it on the penultimate corner of the penultimate lap and spun off. Finished the meeting without the alternator belt and with starter motor issues but at least there was some promise.

We went to Croft in May, a very bumpy circuit especially if you take the high part of the kerbs, which I don't. We had people with wishbones and even a chassis being welded. My problems were merely the loss of starter motor bolt, alternator nut and bolt, and possibly the seed of later disaster on an oil pipe union. On Saturday, the black cloud formed above, just minutes before our race. There was no way I had time to change the dry tyres, and sat in the assembly area as the downpour started. I will freely admit that my bravery pill dissolved at that very moment. In the past I have said to myself, yes, rain, an equaliser for an underpowered car, it's down to the driver now. But those were the days when everyone was on the same 'not very good in the wet' specified tyres. Colin arrived moments before the whistle went, on his wets, with his spryness, and I watched as he and all the others gradually disappeared up the road.

Sunday was fine and jolly after a convivial evening with pizza and beer in Spike and Bridgette's motorhome swapping life stories. The performance on track, though, was less than jolly, as I watched the others disappear up the road ahead of me again. I'd changed to the last set of spare plugs before the drenched race, and of course they'd fouled up as I did my

Driving Miss Daisy routine at the back. I was going to say, drove like a granny, but not only is this sexist and ageist, but many grandmothers I have seen, do go quicker than me even on the public road these days.

On to Cadwell and the loss of the oil pipe from the oil cooler, the loss of self esteem and the loss of funds. I figured I had three choices.

Give up and write my memoirs. At least I had nothing.

Get the engine rebuilt to the old spec. If only the car had been road legal or easily converted to be, this might have made some sense regarding resale.

Get the engine rebuilt as it was. Back to square one.

So back to square one it was, after missing the meeting at Brands Hatch.

Next time out was Anglesey, which brought a difficult practice, the front left brake doing nothing. Clearly, despite a clean-up, the oil had impregnated the pads far more thoroughly than I'd thought possible. It was sorted with some different pads and the race wasn't too bad. Held up just behind Sylvia in the MEV, I used the time to check gauges and be diligent, making sure all was well with the rebuilt engine. Then, on the Sunday, I was behind Sylvia again. But not held up this time. No. If you're gradually getting left behind, you can't really claim to be held up, can you?

Was it the plugs, now grade 7? With Tom convinced 6-grade would risk the engine, I was down to the last option. Was it me? The glass ceiling of what speed you're comfortable with having descended a little in the last couple of years? I had to go and see the clerk over something, apparently someone perhaps passing me under a yellow flag. I gave my version, which was a bit vague. I knew there'd been a yellow, but only by deduction, having seen the green at the end of the sector, Rocket corner. I stood on the balcony, cooling off as best I could, in my overalls in the hot sun, whilst they interviewed another driver. The nub of it was, I should have been going fast enough not to be lapped, not spending time in the mirrors. At least I didn't have to mingle with the rest of the crowd. On a high after a good race, comparing notes. Enjoying themselves…

22

Thruxton

So here I was.

Thruxton, the flat-out blast around the perimeter of an ancient airfield, ghosts of P47 Thunderbolt fighter planes invisibly brooding, stocky powerful thugs of the uncompromising wartime skies.

A track without the smoothness and the straightness of Silverstone. Daunting probably the most apt word.

But I had invested some time and money two and a half weeks earlier, had come all the way down to Hampshire and done some laps in a Porsche with an instructor who knew the place. Beats trying to learn an unfamiliar track in a mixed test session, in my opinion. OK, there are other cars on the track having an 'experience', but it's not like being out with a bunch of potential nutters from other, faster classes, whose habits you are unfamiliar with.

What it achieved was the removal of the fear factor. Not entirely, but enough to approach the long-anticipated day of the meeting in good heart. The weather smiled, and I arrived in good time, pulling up in a spacious paddock next to Ian, an RGB driver who used to compete in our kit car category. The RGBs, as we have seen earlier, are high revving, flappypaddle-gearchange projectiles which look rather like a Le Mans prototype car (the ones prior to the stubby-nosed ugly hybrid things which attracted hardly any motor manufacturers to spend their millions on development).

Ian and I chatted before I trotted off to get my bearings. The RGB entry was a mere fourteen cars, one or two of which seemed to have eliminated themselves during the test day. Some of the competitors were 'disgruntled'. The category had moved to such a level of expenditure that midfield runners such as Ian and my old pal Tony were finding it impossible to approach the level of the small factories with their trucks and mobile workshops and clientele with deep pockets. I smiled.

"RGBs, disgruntled. Never..."

I found the garage area, where our lot were allocated our space. Exclusively. Ironically, the weekend was sunny and the luxury of a roof was superfluous. Nevertheless, we had the expansive area of tarmac behind the ribbon of garage doors all to ourselves, a complete contrast to the cramped paddock squeeze of the picturesque Ty Croes circuit in Anglesey a few weeks earlier.

This year the club scrutineers had again been offering their time on the evening before the race, a worthwhile advantage for the competitor who can get there the day before, cutting out the scramble for the early morning queue of cars on race day. So, after signing on, I lined up the car earlier than ever before. Relaxed. Relatively happy.

Early scrutineering, of course, gives them more chance to say, "Could you just fix that before the race?" (and come back and show us before getting your ticket), as opposed to "You're OK for today but could you fix that before the next meeting please?" So it's swings and roundabouts as to which scrutineering timing is best if you've got something that's a bit marginal. Of course, they won't wave something through if it's out and out dangerous or illegal. But some of them are a bit more pernickety than others, shall we say.

On this occasion, they were paying particular attention to helmets and Hans Devices. The Hans Device (Head And Neck Something-or-other) is a sort of cradle round the neck and shoulder area, held down by the seat belts, with tethers that attach the helmet to prevent the neck snapping forward in an accident with potentially fatal consequences, where the forces involved can cause a basilar skull fracture. So they are a good idea.

On this occasion, the kit which I had been using for the last six and a half years was deemed to be illegal. Oh… A memo had been served from on high. 2010 Standard helmets had to have 2010 Standard tethers on the Hans, not 2002 Standard tethers like mine. Which had been legal when I bought the stuff.

My Hans Device was politely impounded and I was sent to trawl the paddock seeking to beg or borrow a compatible Hans Device. Of course most people possess just the one of each component, which they need themselves, so it's not an easily fruitful type of search. Eventually I had to settle for the promise of people arriving later on, who might have spare kit. So somebody cracked some bottles of beer and a few of us settled down, sitting on trailers and chewing the general, and the Hans Device, fat.

In the end, Giles, our competitions secretary, was able to confirm that Trevor, who would be helping him on the race day without competing, would bring his own Hans Device, which I could borrow. Thank you, Trevor. In the final end, Nigel Brown, our formula official, discovered some paragraphs of small print that *hadn't* been in the memo to the 750MC scrutineers. The paragraphs deemed my particular 2002 tethers to be legal after all. Thank you, Nigel. Thank you sarcastically, Motor Sports Association.

So I wouldn't even have to buy new tethers before the next

meeting. At the end of the day's racing, when I went to reclaim my Hans Device, Bob, the chief scrutineer, apologised to me, having investigated and confirmed Nigel's findings. I said that it wasn't his fault and that an apology was not needed, but thank you anyway. Maintaining an affable relationship is like saving a few shekels in the Bank of Scrute, in my book.

I had remained strangely calm throughout the episode. After all, there was little I could do except talk to people and hope that a compatible Hans Device would turn up, which it did. Mrs R, when I returned home and related the details in full, confirmed the feeling of outrage which had stirred within her when she had read my brief text about it the night before.

"It's outrageous that you weren't told..."

"Never mind. No harm was done. I got out to race."

"It's outrageous..."

I watched the steam coming out of her ears for a while.

Mrs R hadn't made the long trip to Thruxton with me.

Bob didn't know how lucky he was.

The qualifying was a little tricky. Somebody was off on lap two or three, and we were red-flagged back into the pit lane for a while. But I got round, trying to find a bit of a rhythm. My dreams about prior experience of the track enabling me to surprise people a bit, were in fact dreams. And the consolation, that the tranquil waters at the back of the grid might provide a less hazardous start, was denied me by the fact that two or three of the faster runners had not completed their minimum three laps of qualifying. So they would most likely be starting just behind me, subject to the approval of the clerk of the course.

So nervous had the car felt in qualifying, that I contemplated asking Mr Polley, the Yokohama tyre man, if he had any new ones my size. Scrub the invisible waxy coating off in the first laps of the first race, and then go for it more in the second, would have been the plan. But the tyre van was unmanned; he must have fulfilled his pre-orders on the test day yesterday, and gone for a well-earned rest.

So I settled down with Phil, my endurance rally mate, over a coffee. He had arrived in his Caterham 7, in which we were to venture to Spain in a few weeks for a Guild of Motor Endurance event. There would be, he said, discussing luggage capacity, room in the tiny car for me to bring a toothbrush and a spare pair of underpants...

In race one, I got into a little bit of a stride, not quite needing the spare pair of underpants. I do hate that terminology but it's forced its way into the narrative here. Despite me feeling moderately fast, the others were faster and I had to watch them motor away as I focused on my own race. A lonely position but there was plenty to keep me occupied, and I was not too unhappy with it.

We then had a civilised gap between races, which included the lunch break. Phil moseyed off to a barbeque given by the Caterham team for which he does some lorry driving. Leaving the car in the cool of the garage, I treated it to a new set of spark plugs. The ones that came out weren't too bad, but the new ones looked nicer. Pristine.

They were now '7' grade, having ruled out the use of the 8s and 9s. Even the 7s after Anglesey had seemed a bit 'fuelly' and I wondered if that had anything to do with my poor showing in the second race there. Maybe I was just not caning the engine enough to burn off the deposits. Given that Tom seemed to think 6s carried a risk of burning a hole in a piston, changing the 7s quite frequently was the only option at the last-chance saloon.

I fell into a conversation with John Moore, regarding my intention to retire, performances, the way the car felt. He rightly said that one can only drive to the way the car feels, and that this track was not the place to come unstuck. I'd never had the time and budget to do worthwhile testing, in the sense of developing the car. Not to mention the necessity of taking along at least a willing timekeeper, preferably one with mechanical skills.

A few years earlier, I walked into the office where I worked, texting on my phone as I went through the door. A bored crew were awaiting the starting gun. Somebody piped up.

"Who are you texting, Dave, who are you texting?"

"Well, what it is, is that I'm texting T-Mobile for my balance. In a minute they'll text back, and it sounds as though I've got a mate."

John, who has a mate, was someone who did do testing and development. He said that on a race day, he'll only do *small* adjustments, a strategy I can run with. I had in fact been thinking of softening the back end for the second race, and after all there was little to lose. John thought the car might cope with the bumps better. Maybe, but a bigger benefit would be an element of user friendliness, less looseness.

And this proved to be the case. The car felt perkier with the new plugs, and handling wise, I felt more comfortable and hit more of a groove, finally getting somewhat to grips with the place. At the end my best lap proved to be seven seconds better than the one in the first race. Sounds huge, but I was starting from quite a low baseline.

Confidence is a funny thing. Maybe I've never been quite at ease with that car. Maybe I've sworn at it in the garage once too often. There's no real reason I should be wary of it, but planting your foot through Church corner…? I knew I wasn't doing that. There's a lot of talk about 'flat' around the racing scene. But has everybody got their foot literally to the boards? I don't know, but these days the others' feet seemed a little more willing than mine, to push.

At least I got through, and with six DNFs, sixteenth out of twenty-two starters didn't seem so bad. I would have been perfectly content with that when I first started.

And in fact, I was content, up to a point. Unlike Anglesey,

there had been an improvement, a progression, something to build on. If I'd been coming back next season.

There's always more you want to do, adjustments to make, engines to pay for, speed to find. But it would soon be over. I began to look forward to Snetterton, the last meeting. Leave the tyres, the brake improvements, leave the dampers as they were now. Just go out and have some fun. Treat it like a car someone else has let you have a go in.

The day after the long trip home was beautiful. Bathed in sunshine and positivity and a sense of some achievement. Mowing an English suburban lawn on a glowing, late summer day. This is the nearest to paradise.

I relaxed after lunch, watching some of the Belgian GP until I dozed off, handily regaining consciousness a couple of laps from the end, in time to watch Hamilton and Vettel on the podium. One for whom an engine failure every few years is 'unacceptable', the other who finds it easier to present an affable demeanour, until things go wrong and the spoilt child persona comes to the fore.

And then there was Verstappen, whose car had failed, given the chance by the interviewer, rising to the bait of the loaded question and declaring that he may have to consider his options. The implication being that the one of three teams in the world that can win, that gave him his opportunity and riches, might have its hand bitten.

These young men seemed to know nothing of the wider world. Trapped in a bubble of preternatural talent, growing up glued to a kart on a track, forever focused. Round and round, but not necessarily well-rounded.

The thought that I could save several hours later in my life, by never reading their biographies, was soothing. My mind drifted back to memories formed as a fourteen-year-old boy, devouring any motor racing book which appeared in our local library, especially those featuring the photography of Louis

Stanley. He may have cut an incongruous figure as a Formula 1 principal in the later, declining years of the BRM company, but the images he captured were supremely evocative. Gritty men in grassy paddocks. Grubby overalls and grimy fingernails. Cars like cigar tubes, stripped to a raw and sometimes deadly beauty.

It is wrong to even hint of glamorising the dark side of this bygone era. Yet the bewinged behemoths of today only fascinate me with their overblown dimensions. The overblown technology, and the literally overblown aerodynamic capabilities, are about as interesting to me as the study of a washing machine manual.

As my mind wandered, no summons to help with any gardening came. I switched the TV off and basked in the aftermath of my weekend's efforts. Catlike in my supreme laziness if not my reflexes, I blissfully re-dozed.

23

Fight, Fight

I lie awake. Some of the old doubts resurface. Should I change the brakes before Snett after all? Changing the pads means changing the discs. I don't want to give more money to Rally Design at this stage. The brakes work, albeit with an embarrassing squeal. Horrible.

More to the point, I don't want the bother of doing the work. To maybe find out it doesn't improve the times much anyway. For one race meeting. I hear you say, fight, fight, for every tiny scrap of advantage. Why? Like the people who say, follow your dreams, you can succeed by hard work and become what you want to be. The great con trick of the modern world. Leaving aside the spiritual life, the attainment of untold riches as an entertainment star will simply not happen for most who wish for it. Believe it or not.

Motor Sport arrives on the doormat, with an updated format. Keeping up with the times. The times of electric cars and multi-million pound campaigns which leave me cold. A limited edition Aston Martin is shown; orders were 'naturally' sold out. It cost an obscene amount of money and was based on one of their race cars. I find it hard to conceptualise that 150 people in the world have that kind of money to throw at a *car*. Why would you want to fold yourself into a capsule based on a metal-caged sweat-bath that demands freakish levels of fitness to drive it at a competitive pace for more than a few miles? Countless machines of this ilk vie for the Arab dollar or the banker's bonus. Meanwhile we see footage of subsistence farmers in India, flooded, losing what very little they ever had. Hell on earth, while I watch from heaven on earth, leafy suburbia, one of the lucky small percentage, an accident of birth.

A cardinal's death is announced. He had 'theological acumen', whatever that is. Is it a business man's brain trapped in a medieval belief system? A game of souls? My grandfather was a Methodist minister. Theological acumen, in his time, was an escape route from the mines of South Wales, a framework leading to the wider world. Unless you became a doctor, a teacher or a minister, all that beckoned was the pit. And no doubt he provided comfort to members of the human herd in times of birth, marriage and death. Provided a framework.

The cardinal was said to have helped Tony Blair with his conversion to Catholicism in 2007. Catholicism is bad enough, without converting to it. A Greek tragedy of a man who converted the Ministry of Defence into the Ministry of Attack. I can't see how Catholicism would offer much succour.

Maybe I have too much time to ponder. The supreme irony is that I now have plenty of time, since retiring from employment. And yet I don't have time at all, just sands rushing through the venturi in the hourglass of racing days as they draw to a close.

The car is for sale. I texted Tom to ask for a résumé of the engine work, that I could put on my 'For Sale' board at Snett. Everything's done by text these days. The act, though, was another staple fired into the proclamation of intent, by the horrible gun of logic. The act of saying the car was for sale.

Not that I'm sentimental about it. In fact, the reverse almost applies. The clutch mechanism is fairly horrible, the throttle pedal connection is crude although it performs, the brakes are as previously discussed. That accounts for the foot department. I should have addressed these things when the car was stripped to the bones, but such a long moment has never quite arisen in between races or dealing in the off-season with some of the more major accessible issues.

The flat floor is a pain, leading to the need for an air dam and splitter, leading to the impracticality of arranging a bonnet hinge, leading to having to nab passers-by at track days to help lift the bonnet off the car. The system also necessitates something called a diffuser at the rear of the car, to complete the venturi effect as air is squeezed underneath and expands into a wider, controlled channel. The rush of air through the middle of the underside before it slows in the diffuser should create a suction effect. I'm not sure if I've ever gone fast enough to notice any difference if I'm honest.

As with many of these issues, if I had only pedalled the thing as fast as the original builder of the car used to, I'd be more entitled to moan about its shortcomings. But I will still have the moan.

You will see these 'diffuser' shapes at the back of modern Mondeos, SUVs and the like. Below the back bumper, basically. The main suction effect they have is probably on the purchaser's wallet.

Mine was originally riveted on, to the crossmember at the back of the floor, in front of the rear axle. Joining the power to weight class this last year meant modifying it to make it more easily detachable, by means of a riveted flange on the crossmember and the use of Dzus style clips. Reason? The club possesses a rolling road, in order to check compliance, i.e. check that the power of the car is as stated on one's entry for the season.

My car won't go onto a rolling road without the diffuser fouling the floor or the rollers. So it has to be detachable at the track. So that's another fair and equitable idea that in practice is potentially an absolute ball-ache.

Like wet tyres. We used to have one specified type of tyre, same for everybody. Rubbish in the wet, but the same for everybody. Then competitors were given the chance to vote, and more wanted the option of a wet tyre. So if you want to keep up on a wet day, you have to have purchased another set of wheels and tyres. The worst thing is the 50-50 day, which might necessitate scrabbling around to change wheels just prior to your outing. And my car doesn't have very easily located jacking points. Because of the lowness and the flat floor and the relatively fragile front splitter. And the dog-tiredness of the owner.

I should get an Austin 7 Special without aerodynamics. And a tiny engine with spaghetti-strength internals designed originally to propel a small 1930s' family, wearing smart hats, to a giddying 40 mph with a following wind. And 1930s' mechanicals of which I have no experience, and no burning desire to learn. So maybe not, though I admire those who pilot them.

We are creatures of our time, and I felt the ebb of that time. Wanting to make a list, to tinker and improve things, maybe to strip it all down and start again. But having pulled the string to drop the curtain on it all.

Does the decision itself make you slower? Less committed? Or could it be turned around, the decision leading to an abandonment, a willingness to wring its neck, thrash it to pay for all the tribulations it had visited upon me?

We would see. Either way, it wouldn't be tormenting me much longer. If nobody comes forward to part with the requisite cash, with the requisite rose-tinted spectacles to embrace this provider of multifarious degrees of joy and despair, then I will reduce it to the sum of its parts.

With use of spanners and remaining sanity.

24

Back to the Beginning

The long-awaited day rolled around. Relaxed preparation, plenty of time, an organised van. No brake changes, no tyre changes, no adjustments. Fluids and any dodgy linkages all on best behaviour. And even the sun was to smile.

The only fly in the ointment, my good pal Mel being unable to get along on the day, due to illness.

We even got plenty of room in the paddock. More tarmac had been added over the awkward grassy knoll bit of yore, and because we were only a one-day meeting, following the HSCC's outing on the Saturday, there weren't too many 750MC classes attending.

A decent meal in the bar on the Saturday night, chat and banter with some of our fellow drivers, including reflections on Guild of Motor Endurance events of the past, and the forthcoming one in the Pyrenees, soon to come just a week or so after the race meeting. Some of the Sport Special drivers are fellow GOME-ists, and reminiscences of the madness were shared.

Blue skies, then, all of Sunday. I aimed for one of the less picky scrutineers in the morning, and we were away. Practice brought a red ignition light, worrying but intermittent, which at least showed that the belt was still attached. I tightened it a bit on returning, but it didn't seem really loose anyway. The slight concern had infiltrated my right foot enough to ensure a safe start from the back of the grid.

We then had a long morning, before two races quite close together in the afternoon. I had some good nattering sessions with racing friends around the paddock. Subjects being, mostly, racing, treadmill of expenditure, racing, treadmill of expenditure, chasing the tail of a moving target, treadmill of expenditure. That sort of thing. But with a smile.

I was able to help a lad who had parked next to us, turning up in a road legal Caterham 7 with nothing much except a few tools, a petrol can, and a bagful of optimism. He had a French surname and a French accent, but had come from Cambridge that morning. Arriving from France might have been pushing it a bit, given that you hardly ever see anyone driving their road car to a race these days. It should be compulsory!

Fair play to Charles, he was pretty well organised for his first ever race. Later I was able to point out that he needed to tape his scrutineering ticket to the car; I think he expected to hand it to the marshals before going out. It's good to be able to guide someone, even slightly, as there is a lot to remember the first time you go out there. He did well in the first race too, as I didn't see much of him ahead of me. Before the second race an electrical issue prevented him getting to the start, but at least he sorted it later before his drive home. Welcome to motor racing! What was that about driving there in the race car?

I went out for the first race having checked all possible connections, but with the ignition light still refusing to go out. In a brainwave, I decided to blame oil contamination in the alternator, but then recalled that I had bought a new one and delivered it to Tom to fit when the engine was re-installed. So that was good. I had been organised and done the wise thing. But the light was still showing and the mystery remained. All I could do was go out and hope to get round, at worst, on battery power. If it stopped, it stopped.

On the grid, the revs rose. The red light went out. And stayed out. And it all became fun again.

I pursued Martin Hayward, who had got round me in the scrum coming up to the first hairpin. But after two or three laps he spun coming out of Hamilton corner (been there, done that) and I was away. Out of touch race wise, but focused and enjoying the drive.

At the finish, we were held in parc ferme for a while. Why do they do that when they don't want to check the cars? Eventually we were released. Predictably, the starter showed no sign of useful life and I ended up pushing the car back down the paddock. Martin helped me get it to the slightly downhill bit and then a nice lad who was helping John Moore lent his weight to the roll bar for the rest of the way.

As we rolled up to our spot in the paddock, human powered, Mrs R was waiting. An expression says a thousand words, or, in this case, six. They were, "Oh God, what's up this time?"

Luckily, after a pause for refreshment, swapping to the spare battery was enough to get me out on the grid again. Just as before, I would go until it stopped, so there was no point in worrying about anything. In fact it behaved OK, the second battery being fresh from my organised pre-race charging two days earlier. This time I got away from Martin early on, but gradually lost the others. Nevertheless, pressing on and refusing to get disheartened produced the dividend of very nearly getting to the end without being lapped. Clive and Paul got past coming out of the last corner, and then it was all over. Saluting the marshals, remaining in one piece, success.

Charles was next to us in the paddock, sorting his wiring issue. "Welcome to racing," I said, the irony escaping him as he shook my hand and thanked me for my earlier help.

The day concluded with a lot of chat at the prizegiving.

"You'll be back." It was nice that they didn't seem to want to see my departure, but of course one must decide for oneself.

I managed to perplex Rob Johnston and Clive Hudson by suggesting that I would be happy to dismantle the car rather than sell it for a knockdown amount. We'll see.

The trip home worked OK, using the adrenaline to press on, holding station behind a moderately quick lorry after King's Lynn, preserving the concentration muscles for a while. Then selecting the Allman Brothers at high blast from Lincoln north, and over the bridge and home.

A good feeling. I had beaten my previous best around the Snetterton 300 circuit, which was set in 2014. Only by two-thirds of a second, but it proved that on the right day I could at least access my younger pace from three and a half years earlier. Enough justification to carry on, changing tyres, brakes, car set-up?

No. It was over now. That two-thirds of a second had cost me a lot this year, but it meant a lot. It meant that I had been able to finish on a high, bookending nearly 140 motor races, at the very place I had first turned up for my culture shock in 2002.

Well north of three grand to get out again and do better by two-thirds of a second? It meant everything.

Mad? Of course.